Street, Beach & Sky

Street, Beach & Sky: A Cookbook

ISBN 978-1-989647-51-6

© 2024 Andrew West
A Byrd Press Publication
Toronto
www.byrdpress.com
publisher@byrdpress.com

Street, Beach & Sky

A Cookbook

Dedicated to Marie-Antoine Carême (1784-1833) and Grimod de la Reynière (1758-1837)

-Marie-Antoine Carême, the architect of flavor, whose meticulous artistry and dedication to quality ingredients continue to inspire chefs and elevate the art of fine dining.

Carême's legacy lies in his meticulous approach to cooking, his emphasis on high-quality ingredients, and his role in codifying classical French cuisine. These principles continue to be foundational for many chefs today, even if adapted to modern sensibilities. His detailed recipes and techniques serve as a historical record and a valuable resource for culinary professionals.

And,

- Grimod de la Reynière, the original gourmand, whose sharp wit and critical eye laid the groundwork for modern food criticism and our appreciation for the culinary experience.

Grimod's influence lies in his pioneering role as a food critic. His witty and often scathing reviews helped to shape public perception of restaurants and elevate the status of food as a topic of conversation and critique. His work provides a fascinating glimpse into the Parisian culinary scene of the early 19th century and continues to inspire contemporary food writers and reviewers.

"New dishes are but old ones disguised." - Grimod de la Reynière (French gastronome, 1808)

STREET

Bangkok, Thailand 14
- Gai Yang (Grilled Chicken)
- Moo Ping (Grilled Pork Skewers)
- Satay
- Grilled Green Curry Asparagus & Fish Satay
- Fiery Pork Skewers - Kor Moo Yang Style
- Kai Yang Pad Thai
- Od Mun Kung (Shrimp Cakes) + Enoki
- One-Pan Savory Khanom Buang (Crispy Coconut Crepes)
- Spicy Som Tam (Green Papaya Salad)
- Sticky Rice
- Cucumber Kimchi
- Homemade Thai Chili Oil
- Thai Green Beans
- Thai Peanut Dipping Sauce
- Spicy Thai Rice Crackers
- Spicy Thai Fritters

Penang, Malaysia 26
- Penang Satay
- Asam Laksa (Spicy Sour Noodle Soup)
- Murtabak (Stuffed Flatbread - Penang Hawker Stall Style)
- Roti Canai (Layered Flatbread)
- Penang Har Mee (Prawn Broth Soup)
- Otak-Otak (Leaf-wrapped Fish Cakes)
- Pegaga Masak Lemak (Watercress with Coconut & Kaffir Lime)
- Nasi Impit (Compressed Rice)
- Acar Rempah Pelbagai Sayur (Penang Pickled Medley)
- Cicah Kari Masam Manis Kelapa (Spicy Sweet Coconut Dipping Sauce)

Osaka, Japan 38
- Sweet Onion, Chili & Garlic Negiyaki Sauce with Sesame
- Ribeye Kushikatsu
- Offal Kushikatsu
- Okonomiyaki Pork Belly, Choy Sum and Endive Tower
- Clam & Seaweed Takoyaki
- Spicy Sausage Kimchi Takoyaki
- Shrimp & Sweet Heat Takoyaki
- Yuzu Watermelon Gazpacho with Pickled Ginger Mignonette
- Sunomono Salad with Radish, Pickled Tomatoes & Sesame Crunch
- Roasted Edamame with Pistachio and Balsamic Glaze
- Japanese-Style Pear and Sesame Crackers
- Kewpie Potato Salad (Japanese Style)
- Spicy Pickled Walnuts, Garlic, Ginger & Kombu Tsukemono
- Tempura Shiitake with Wasabi Vinaigrette, Toasted Pine Nuts & Citrus Symphony
- Miso-Glazed Eggplant with Shichimi Togarashi

Mexico City 52
- Pineapple Pork Carnitas Tacos
- One Burner Cast Iron Elote
- Tlacoyos
- Red Mole Boston Butt Tortillas
- Burrito with Guajillo-Braised Turkey, Caramelized Plantains, and Chorizo Crema
- Mexican-Style Chili Corn Pudding with Roasted Pepitas
- Rustic Arborio Rice with Black Beans and Caramelized Plantains
- Yucatan-inspired Chorizo and Cheese Stuffed Peppers
- Citrus-Pickled Red Onions with Jicama & Green Tomato

Marrakech, Morocco 62
- Moroccan-Inspired Skewers with Chermoula Drizzle
- Grilled Eggplant Salad (Zaalouk) with Charred Peppers and Toasted Spices
- Moroccan Flatbread
- Tomatillo Harira with Crispy Duck and Herb Gremolata
- Preserved Lemons
- Moroccan Honey Glazed Sweet Potato Rounds
- Khobz dyal Zraa (Barley Bread)
- Harissa-Spiked Carrot & Cannellini Bean Dip with Toasted Pine Nuts

STREET

CONTENTS

Lima, Peru 70
- Ají de Gallina
- Lomo Saltado
- Anticuchos de Pescado
- Cau Cau
- Arroz Chaufa
- Papas a la Huancaína
- Ají de Pallares
- Torrejas de Choclo

Hanoi, Vietnam 78
- Bún Chả with Pickled Peppers and Chiles
- Beef and Oyster Banh Mi with Deep Roasted Garlic & Chili Paste Sauce
- Our A+ Bánh Goi (Crispy Fried Wontons)
- Our A+ Bò Nướng Xả (Grilled Lemongrass Beef)
- Canh Chua Hanoi-Style
- Hanoi-Inspired Đồ Chua Arancini with a Kick
- Sweet, Sour, & Spicy Vietnamese Salad with Peanuts

Ho Chi Minh City Vietnam 86
- Our A+ Mi Quang (Turmeric Noodle Soup) - Ho Chi Minh City Style
- Goi Cuon (Spring Rolls) with Spicy Peanut Dipping Sauce - Ho Chi Minh City Style
- Canh Thi (Winter Melon Soup) with variations for all seasons
- Bánh Xèo (Crispy Coconut Crepes)
- Cơm Lam (Bamboo Rice)

Los Angeles, California 94
- Hokkaido-Inspired Tempura & Roe with Pear Fusion Tortillas
- Burmese Bowl with Duck
- Ethiopian Chicken & Berbere Fusion Burrito
- The Krimson Karenderia: A California Filipino Fusion Burrito
- Joojeh, Stone Fruit & Grilled Serrano Skewers with Dual Dips
- Yuzu Kosho Brussels Sprouts
- Kimchi Gazpacho

BEACH

Oahu, Hawaii 104
- Hawaiian Poke
- Huli Huli Chicken with Grilled Spicy Pineapple Skewers and Tropical Slaw
- Our A+ Hawaiian Spiced Pork Skewers with Spicy Pickled Pineapple, Plums & Hearts of Palm
- Hawaiian-Inspired Chicken & Shrimp Bowl with Lilikoi Vinaigrette
- A Simple & A Complex (double chicken broth) Saimin
- Lau Lau (Hawaiian Steamed Parcels)
- Fire-Kissed Hawaiian Steak with Mango Salsa and Macadamia Butter
- Our A+ Kulolo (A Cherished Hawaiian Dessert)
- Hawaiian Sweet Rolls
- Spicy Pineapple Boat
- Cucumber Salad with Sesame Ginger

San Sebastian, Spain 116
- Atun Ahumado con Tomate Fresco
- Patatas Bravas
- Gambas al Ajillo
- Tortilla Española
- Paella Negra
- Blistered Olives with White Bean & White Anchovy Crema with Toasted Pecorino Crust and Crushed Pistachios
- White Bean Nachos with Chorizo, Anchovies & Caramelized Onions
- *Almejas a la Marinera Andaluza con Hinojo y Estragón*
- Roasted Butternut Squash with Crispy Prosciutto
- Pisto Manchego
- Rustic Txakoli & Quince Biscotti with Rosemary, Smoked Paprika, and Guindilla Pepper
- Piquillo Pepper and Manchego Gougères

Playa del Carmen, Mexico 128
- Papadzules (Egg and Pumpkin Seed Envelopes with Tomatillo)
- Yucatan-Inspired Tacos with Charred Corn, Queso Fresco, Flank Steak, and Crispy Poblanos
- Pescado Tikin Xic (Grilled Fish with Achiote)
- Fiery Fiesta Dip with Charred Peppers and Pickled Anaheim Chili
- Meso-American Harvest Salad with Green Mole Drizzle
- Quick Mini Nopalitos Tamales
- Cocoa-Rubbed Roasted Cauliflower with Gouda and Jalapeño Dipping Sauce
- Mango Yucatan Spiced Beef Jerky

Cottesloe Beach, Perth, Australia 136
- Aussie Fusion Cornbread with Vegemite, Macadamia, & Feta
- Pan-Seared Beef and Prawn Patties on Toasted Buns
- Our A+ Smoked Paprika and Olive Damper
- One-Pan Thyme and Zest Flatfish with Plum Sauce and Hazelnut Crumble
- Our A+ Lamington: An Aussie Classic Elevated
- Roasted Sweet Potato and Wattleseed Salad with Bush Tomato Vinaigrette
- Grilled Pineapple with Chilli Lime & Mango Salsa

BEACH

Bali, Indonesia 144
Spicy Duck & Rye Bread Open-Faced Sandwiches with Poached Egg
Pepes Ikan in Banana Leaves (Steamed Marinated Fish)
Balinese Lawar with Minced Chicken
Mie Goreng (Indonesian Fried Noodles)
Nasi Goreng (Indonesian Stir-Fried Rice)
Gado-Gado Salad with Peanut Sauce
Coconut Curry Glass Noodles

Phuket, Thailand 152
- Simple Green Curry
- Pad See Ew
- Tom Yum Goong
- Phuket-Style Yum Pla Duk Foo
- Phuket-Style Rad Na with Mussaman Curry Beef
- Khao Pad Krapow
- Gang Khua Gai
- Khao Pad Sapparot
- Tom Yum Soup with Shrimp
- Yum Nua Sai
- Khanom Jeen Sot Curry Variante

SKY

CHETTINAD, INDIA 164
- Spicy Yogurt Marinated Fried Chicken
- Hetty Chicken 65
- Spicy Chettinad Shrimp Skewers
- Chettinad Eggplant Roast
- Our A+ Meen Kuzhambu (Tangy Fish Curry)
- Our A+ Appalam (Crispy Lentil Crackers)
- Our A+ Coconut Rice Crackers
- Chettinad Cauliflower Popcorn
- Chettinad Pineapple Raita

MONTREAL, CANADA 174
- Lobster Blinis with Maple Drizzle
- Blueberry Maple Flank Steak with Pine Nut Crunch
- Montreal Portobello Steak with Fig-Infused Red Wine Vinaigrette and Black Pepper Roasted Walnut
- Spicy Montreal Bagel Panzanella Salad
- Elevated Tourtière with Pork & Wild Mushroom Ragout and Oka Mash
- Montreal Hazelnut Tartlets with Genmaicha Custard

CALGARY, CANADA 182
- Alberta Rib-Eye Chili
- Alberta Sizzlin' Hash
- Alberta Wild Mushroom Tartlets with Goat Cheese
- Spiced Peach and Apricot Cobbler

NEW ORLEANS, LOUISIANA 188
- Smoked Ricotta & Cajun Deviled Eggs on Pecan Parmesan Crisps
- Cherrystone Clam Seafood Gumbo
- Sweet Corn Pudding with Peas & Pecans
- Dirty Rice
- Sweet or Savory Vanilla Shrimp Croquettes

INTRODUCTION

Welcome to "Street, Beach & Sky: A Cookbook," where every recipe is a journey, and every dish tells a story. I'm Andrew West, Author of "The Instant Chef: American Classics" and "The Savoury Chocolate Cookbook" and I invite you to join me on a culinary adventure that spans the globe—from the bustling street markets of Bangkok to the serene beaches of Bali, and up to the vibrant destination cities like Montreal. This book is a celebration of the world's diverse food cultures, brought to life through a collection of recipes that range from the traditional to the innovative, all crafted with the home cook in mind.

As a passionate explorer of the world's culinary landscapes, I've always been fascinated by the way food connects us to a place and its people. "Street, Beach & Sky" is more than just a cookbook; it's a passport to experiencing the flavors of the world without leaving your kitchen. Each recipe has been carefully selected and tested to ensure that you can recreate authentic and adventurous dishes wherever you are.

The journey begins on the streets, where food is not just sustenance but a way of life. Street food is immediate and intimate, offering a direct line to the heart of a culture. Here, you'll find dishes like Gai Yang, a marinated grilled chicken that sings with the flavors of Thailand, and Tacos al Pastor, a Mexican classic that's a riot of color and taste.

From there, we move to the beaches—a place to relax and recharge, where food is about freshness and simplicity. Imagine yourself in Lima, preparing a vibrant Ají de Gallina by the ocean, or in Perth, savoring a Smoked Paprika and Olive Damper as the sun sets over the water.

Finally, our journey takes us to the cities, those great melting pots of culture and cuisine. This is where tradition meets innovation, where chefs and home cooks alike push the boundaries of what food can be. Experience the sophisticated fusion of a Montreal Genmaicha Hazelnut Tartlet or the bold flavors of a New Orleans Cherrystone Clam Seafood Gumbo.

Throughout this book, you'll also find "Showstopper" recipes—dishes designed to impress and delight, perfect for special occasions or when you simply want to celebrate the everyday. These recipes are marked by their uniqueness, flavor impact, and visual appeal, ensuring they'll be remembered long after the meal is over.

"Street, Beach & Sky" is not just about following recipes—it's about embracing the spirit of discovery and innovation that drives the world's culinary traditions. It's about the flavours and techniques behind the dishes, the taste of cultures, and places that inspire. So, whether you're a seasoned chef or a curious cook, I hope this book inspires you to explore new flavors, experiment with different techniques, and celebrate the rich tapestry of global cuisine.

Let's cook, learn, and enjoy together. Welcome to the table—the world awaits.

SHOWSTOPPERS

re: 'Showstoppers' found in this Book.

A "Showstopper" recipe in a cookbook typically possesses several key characteristics that set it apart from other dishes:

1. Uniqueness: It should have a unique twist, either a new flavor combination, an unexpected ingredient, or an innovative presentation that sets it apart from the ordinary.

2. Flavor Impact: The dish should deliver a memorable flavor experience. This could be through bold spices, rich textures, a surprising combination of sweet and savory, or a unique blend of culinary influences.

3. Visual Appeal: Showstoppers often have a visually striking presentation that makes them stand out on a table or buffet. This could involve vibrant colors, interesting textures, or an artistic plating style.

4. Storytelling: A Showstopper dish often has a story behind it, whether it's rooted in cultural traditions, inspired by personal experiences, or a result of culinary experimentation.

5. Versatility: While not essential, a Showstopper dish that can be adapted for different dietary preferences or occasions (e.g., vegetarian, vegan, gluten-free) adds to its appeal.

6. Wow Factor: Above all, a Showstopper dish should evoke a sense of excitement, wonder, and admiration. It should be a dish that guests remember and talk about long after the meal is over.

Remember, a Showstopper can be a classic dish elevated with a creative twist or a completely new creation that pushes culinary boundaries. Ultimately, it's about creating a memorable and enjoyable dining experience that goes beyond the ordinary.

GRILLED CHEESE EXPERIENC

KODAK PORTRA 400

BOROUGH MARKET

STREET

Street food, in its purest form, is a window into the soul of a city. It's a reflection of the people, their history, and the symphony of flavors that define their culinary heritage. In this section, we embark on a gastronomic journey through the vibrant streets of eight iconic cities, each with its unique culinary language.

From the bustling markets of Bangkok and Penang to the lively stalls of Osaka and Mexico City, we'll savor the smoky aromas of sizzling grills and the intricate dance of chopsticks and tortillas. We'll delve into the fragrant spice markets of Marrakech and Lima, where centuries-old traditions mingle with modern culinary creativity. And we'll explore the hidden alleyways of Hanoi and Ho Chi Minh City, where steaming bowls of pho and delicate rice paper rolls reveal the essence of Vietnamese cuisine.

Rather than an exhaustive encyclopedia, we aim to offer you a taste – a curated glimpse – into the heart of each city's street food scene. These recipes, both traditional and innovative, are an ode to the bustling culinary cultures we encountered. We've taken beloved classics, honed over generations, and given them a fresh perspective through the lens of our test kitchen. Alongside these familiar favorites, you'll find entirely new creations, inspired by the vibrant pantries and local foodways of each city. These dishes aren't just a collection of ingredients; they're a culinary passport, inviting you to experience a snapshot of the world through its street food.

So, roll up your sleeves, awaken your senses, and prepare to embark on a culinary adventure that will transport you to the heart of these extraordinary cities. It's time to discover the true meaning of street food, one bite at a time.

Bangkok, Thailand

Bangkok, a city where culinary history intertwines with modern-day innovation, beckons food enthusiasts to explore its vibrant and ever-evolving food scene. From the bustling street food stalls of Chinatown to the Michelin-starred restaurants helmed by world-renowned chefs, Bangkok offers a kaleidoscope of flavors that reflect the city's rich cultural heritage and its embrace of culinary experimentation.

The roots of Thai cuisine run deep, drawing inspiration from ancient traditions and the diverse influences of neighboring countries like China, India, and Malaysia. Over centuries, Thai cooks have mastered the art of balancing sweet, sour, salty, and spicy flavors, creating a cuisine that is both complex and harmonious.

Today, Bangkok's culinary scene is a dynamic blend of tradition and innovation. Street food vendors continue to serve up beloved classics like pad Thai, green curry, and satay, using time-honored techniques and fresh, local ingredients. Meanwhile, a new generation of chefs is pushing boundaries, incorporating modern culinary techniques and global flavors to create exciting new dishes that challenge the traditional palate.

This collection of recipes celebrates the vibrant and ever-evolving nature of Thai cuisine. You'll find new classics, like our innovative take on *Gai Yang* (grilled chicken) and *Moo Ping* (grilled pork skewers), alongside original creations that showcase the bold flavors and culinary ingenuity of Bangkok's food scene. Whether you're a seasoned Thai food enthusiast or a curious newcomer, this chapter offers a glimpse into the heart of Bangkok's culinary soul, where tradition and innovation meet to create a truly unforgettable dining experience.

Gai Yang (Grilled Chicken): A classic Thai street food featuring marinated, grilled chicken bursting with lemongrass and fish sauce flavors.

Moo Ping (Grilled Pork Skewers): Sweet and savory Thai grilled pork skewers, perfect as a snack or appetizer.

Satay: Southeast Asian grilled meat skewers infused with turmeric, peanuts, and a vibrant dipping sauce.

Grilled Green Curry Asparagus & Fish Satay: A modern twist on satay, featuring fish marinated in green curry and grilled with crisp asparagus. (Showstopper)

Fiery Pork Skewers - *Kor Moo Yang* Style: Inspired by Thai grilled pork neck, these re-worked skewers deliver sweet, savory, and intensely spicy flavors. (Showstopper)

Kai Yang Pad Thai : A fusion dish combining the tangy flavors of *pad thai* with the smoky goodness of grilled Thai chicken. (Showstopper)

Od Mun Kung (Shrimp Cakes) + Enoki: Traditional Thai shrimp cakes elevated with the delicate texture of enoki mushrooms.

One-Pan Savory *Khanom Buang* (Crispy Coconut Crepes): A reimagined take on the crispy Thai street snack, now with a savory filling perfect for a light meal. (Showstopper)

Spicy *Som Tam* (Green Papaya Salad): The quintessential Thai salad delivering a punch of sweet, sour, salty, and spicy flavors.

Sticky Rice: The essential accompaniment to many Thai dishes, with a fluffy and subtly sweet glutinous rice.

Cucumber Kimchi: A Korean-inspired side dish offering a refreshing, tangy, and lightly spicy counterpoint to Thai flavors.

Homemade Thai Chili Oil: A customizable condiment adding depth and fiery heat to any Thai dish.

Thai Green Beans: A simple Thai-style stir-fry highlighting the crispness of green beans and savory sauces.

Thai Peanut Dipping Sauce: A versatile and creamy sauce enhancing the flavors of any grilled or fried Thai dish.

Spicy Thai Rice Crackers: A crunchy snack delivering a burst of savory and spicy flavors.

Spicy Thai Fritters: Crispy savory fritters infused with Thai flavors and a fiery kick.

THAI MAIN DISHES- STREET

Gai Yang (Grilled Chicken)

Prep time: 10 minutes (marinating time not included)
Cooking time: 10-14 minutes
Servings: 4

- 1 pound boneless, skinless chicken breasts or thighs
- ¼ cup soy sauce
- 2 tablespoons fish sauce
- 1 tablespoon chopped lemongrass (or 1 teaspoon lemongrass paste)
- 1 clove garlic, minced
- 1 shallot, minced
- 1 tablespoon brown sugar
- 1 teaspoon ground coriander
- ½ teaspoon freshly ground black pepper

Marinate the Chicken:
In a large bowl, combine soy sauce, fish sauce, lemongrass (or paste), garlic, shallot, brown sugar, coriander, and black pepper. Whisk well to create a marinade. Add the chicken pieces and toss to coat them evenly. Cover and refrigerate for at least 30 minutes, or up to overnight for deeper flavor.

Preheat your grill to medium-high heat. Remove the chicken from the marinade, letting any excess drip off. Grill for 5-7 minutes per side, or until the chicken is cooked through and nicely charred.

Moo Ping (Grilled Pork Skewers)

Prep Time: 15 minutes (marinating time not included)
Cooking Time: 10-14 minutes
Servings: 4-6

- ½ pound ground pork
- 2 tablespoons soy sauce
- 1 tablespoon oyster sauce
- 1 tablespoon honey
- 1 tablespoon light brown sugar
- 1 teaspoon white pepper
- 1 clove garlic, minced
- 1 shallot, minced
- Metal Skewers

For the Peanut Sauce (Optional):

- ¼ cup creamy peanut butter
- 2 tablespoons soy sauce
- 1 tablespoon brown sugar
- 1 tablespoon rice vinegar
- 1 tablespoon water
- Thai Chili Oil, to taste

Marinate the Pork:
In a large bowl, combine ground pork, soy sauce, oyster sauce, honey, brown sugar, white pepper, garlic, and shallot. Mix well and knead until everything is well incorporated. Cover and refrigerate for at least 30 minutes, or up to overnight for deeper flavor.

Wet your hands to prevent sticking. Form the marinated pork mixture into small meatballs. Thread the meatballs onto the soaked wooden skewers.

Preheat your grill to medium-high heat. Grill the pork skewers for 5-7 minutes per side, or until cooked through and slightly charred.

Peanut Sauce (Optional):
In a small bowl, whisk together creamy peanut butter, soy sauce, brown sugar, rice vinegar, water, and Thai Chili Oil (to taste) until smooth and creamy.

THAI MAIN DISHES- STREET

Satay

Prep Time: 15 minutes (marinating time not included)
Cooking Time: 6-8 minutes
Servings: 4

- ½ pound chicken breast or pork tenderloin, cut into thin strips
- ¼ cup soy sauce
- 2 tablespoons brown sugar
- 1 tablespoon vegetable oil
- 1 tablespoon lime juice
- 1 clove garlic, minced
- 1 shallot, minced
- ½ teaspoon ground coriander
- ½ teaspoon ground cumin
- Pinch of red chili flakes (optional (continued)

Marinate the Meat:
In a large bowl, combine soy sauce, brown sugar, vegetable oil, lime juice, garlic, shallot, coriander, cumin, and red chili flakes (if using). Whisk well to create a marinade. Add the chicken or pork strips and toss to coat them evenly. Cover and refrigerate for at least 30 minutes, or up to overnight for deeper flavor.

Wet your hands to prevent sticking. Thread the marinated meat strips onto soaked wooden skewers (soaked for at least 30 minutes to prevent burning).

Preheat your grill to medium-high heat. Grill the satay skewers for 3-4 minutes per side, or until cooked through and slightly charred.

Serving Suggestions:
Serve your Gai Yang hot with a side of sticky rice or your favorite dipping sauce, like a simple lime and chili sauce.

Grilled Green Curry Asparagus & Fish Satay

Prep Time: 15 minutes (marinating time not included)
Cooking Time: 10-12 minutes
Servings: 4

For the Green Curry Marinade:
- 1/2 cup green curry paste
- 1/4 cup coconut milk (full-fat)
- 1 tablespoon soy sauce
- 1 tablespoon lime juice
- 1 tablespoon brown sugar
- 1 clove garlic, minced
- 1/2 inch ginger, grated
- 1 teaspoon vegetable oil

For the Skewers:
- 1 pound firm white fish (cod, halibut, or mahi-mahi work well), cut into 1-inch cubes
- 1 pound white asparagus spears, trimmed and cut in half
- 1 red bell pepper, cut into 1-inch squares
- 1 red onion, cut into wedges
- Vegetable oil (for brushing)

In a bowl, whisk together green curry paste, coconut milk, soy sauce, lime juice, brown sugar, garlic, ginger, and vegetable oil. This is your flavor bomb marinade!

Add the fish cubes, asparagus spears, bell pepper squares, and red onion wedges to the marinade. Toss to coat everything evenly. Cover and refrigerate for at least 30 minutes, or up to overnight for deeper flavor.

Preheat your grill to medium-high heat. Once preheated, thread the marinated fish cubes, asparagus spears, bell pepper squares, and red onion wedges onto the skewers, alternating ingredients for a colorful presentation.

Brush the skewers lightly with vegetable oil. Place them on the preheated grill and cook for 5-6 minutes per side, or until the fish is opaque and cooked through, and the vegetables are tender-crisp.

These unexpected satay skewers are delicious on their own, but you can also serve them with a drizzle of leftover marinade for an extra green curry kick, or a simple dipping sauce like peanut sauce or sweet chili sauce.

Fiery Pork Skewers - Kor Moo Yang Style

Prep Time: 20 minutes
(marinating time not included)
Cooking Time: 7-10 minutes
Servings: 4-6

- ½ pound boneless pork shoulder, thinly sliced (around ¼ inch thick) – Ask your butcher to "shave" it for easy prep.
- ½ pound pork belly, thinly sliced (around ¼ inch thick)

The Marinade:
- 3 tablespoons light soy sauce
- 2 tablespoons fish sauce
- 2 tablespoons oyster sauce
- 2 tablespoons palm sugar (or brown sugar)
- 4 cloves garlic, minced
- 2 stalks lemongrass, white part only, finely chopped
- 1 tablespoon galangal, minced (or substitute with ginger in a pinch)
- 2 kaffir lime leaves, finely chopped
- 1 red chili, deseeded and finely chopped
- 1 teaspoon ground coriander
- 1 teaspoon ground white pepper
- 2 tablespoons vegetable oil

The Dip
- Juice of 1 lime
- 2 tablespoons fish sauce
- 1 red chili, deseeded and finely chopped
- 1 tablespoon chopped fresh cilantro (optional)
- 1 teaspoon palm sugar (or brown sugar)

Marinade the pork:
In a large bowl, combine all the marinade ingredients – soy sauce, fish sauce, oyster sauce, palm sugar, garlic, lemongrass, galangal (or ginger), kaffir lime leaves, chili, coriander, white pepper, and oil. Whisk it all together until the sugar dissolves.

Place the sliced pork shoulder and belly in a shallow dish. Pour that delicious marinade over the meat, making sure every piece gets a good coating. Now, the key part – marinate for at least 2 hours, or even better, overnight. The longer the marinate, the deeper the flavor.

Take a slice of pork shoulder or belly and fold it in half lengthwise.

Thread the folded piece onto the skewer, with the open side facing outwards. This creates a more "open" structure for better heat penetration and prevents bunching.

Repeat with other slices, alternating between pork shoulder and belly for a delightful textural experience. Don't crowd the skewers.

Turn your gas stove to high heat Get a cast iron grill pan nice and hot. Carefully place the skewers on the hot grill. Resist the urge to fidget – let them sear for a good minute or two to get those beautiful grill marks. Then, give them a good flip and repeat on the other side. We want them cooked through but still juicy, not dry and overdone!

Once cooked through, take those beauties off the heat and let them rest for a few minutes on a platter. This allows the juices to redistribute, resulting in a more tender and flavorful skewer.

For the Dip

While the skewers rest, whip up your dipping sauce. Combine lime juice, fish sauce, chopped chili, chopped cilantro (if using), and palm sugar in a small bowl. Mix it all up and taste! Adjust the seasonings to your preference. Want it sweeter? Add a touch more palm sugar. Craving more heat? Throw in some extra chili flakes.

Kai Yang Pad Thai

Prep Time: 30 minutes (marinating time not included)
Cooking Time: 20-25 minutes
Servings: 2

Chicken

- 1 boneless, skinless chicken breast – pounded thin for even cooking
- 1 tablespoon soy sauce
- 1 tablespoon brown sugar
- 1 teaspoon minced garlic
- ½ teaspoon ground ginger

Homemade Chili Sauce

- 2-3 red chilies (depending on spice preference), deseeded and roughly chopped
- 2 cloves garlic, minced
- 1 shallot, thinly sliced
- 1 tablespoon chopped fresh ginger
- 1 tablespoon palm sugar (or brown sugar)
- 2 tablespoons fish sauce
- 1 tablespoon lime juice
- ¼ cup water

Assembly

- ½ pound dried rice noodles (pad thai noodles or thin rice vermicelli work well)
- 2 tablespoons tamarind paste (or substitute with 1 tablespoon lime juice and 1 teaspoon brown sugar)
- 3 tablespoons fish sauce
- 2 tablespoons soy sauce (light soy sauce preferred)
- 1 tablespoon palm sugar (or brown sugar)
- 2 eggs, beaten
- 2 cloves garlic, minced
- 1 shallot, thinly sliced
- ½ cup chopped roasted peanuts
- 2 tablespoons chopped fresh cilantro
- 1 lime, cut into wedges
- Vegetable oil for cooking

Make the Homemade Chili Sauce:
In a mortar and pestle (or a food processor if you don't have one), grind together the chilies, garlic, shallot, and ginger until you get a coarse paste.

Transfer the paste to a small saucepan. Add the palm sugar, fish sauce, lime juice, and water. Bring to a simmer over medium heat and cook for 5-7 minutes, or until the sauce thickens slightly. Taste and adjust the seasonings as needed.

Remove the sauce from the heat and let it cool slightly.

-

Marinate the Chicken:
In a shallow dish, combine soy sauce, brown sugar, garlic, ginger, and a teaspoon (or more to taste) of the homemade chili sauce. Add the chicken breast and toss to coat well. Marinate for at least 30 minutes, or up to overnight for deeper flavor.

-

Soak the Noodles:
Place the dried rice noodles in a large bowl and cover them with hot water. Let them soak for 10-15 minutes, or until softened but still *al dente* (with a slight bite). Drain the noodles well.

-

Make the Pad Thai Sauce:
In a small bowl, whisk together the tamarind paste (or lime juice and brown sugar), fish sauce, soy sauce, and palm sugar. Set aside.

-

Grill the Chicken:
Heat a grill pan or cast iron skillet over medium heat on your single burner. Add a tablespoon of oil. Once hot, remove the chicken from the marinade and cook for 3-4 minutes per side, or until cooked through. Set aside to rest and slice.

-

Scramble the Eggs:
Add another tablespoon of oil to the pan. Swirl to coat the pan. Pour in the beaten eggs and cook, stirring constantly, until just set. Remove the eggs from the pan and set aside.

-

Stir-Fry the Aromatics:
Add another tablespoon of oil to the pan. Once hot, add the garlic and shallots. Stir-fry for 30 seconds, or until fragrant.

-

Incorporate the Sauce and Noodles:
Push the stir-fried ingredients to one side of the pan. Add the drained rice noodles to the empty space in the pan. Pour the Pad Thai sauce over the noodles and toss well to combine.

-

Add the Rest:
Once the sauce is well distributed, add the cooked and sliced chicken, and the cooked eggs back to the pan. Toss everything together to combine.

-

Finishing Touches:
Add the chopped roasted peanuts and most of the chopped cilantro. Stir-fry for another minute or two, until the noodles are heated through and the sauce is well incorporated.

Od Mun Kung (Shrimp Cakes) + Enoki

Prep Time: 20 minutes
Cooking Time: 15 minutes
Servings: 4

- ½ pound fresh shrimp, peeled and deveined (you can chop them yourself or ask your butcher to do it for you)
- ¼ cup chopped green beans
- 2 tablespoons chopped fresh cilantro
- ½ cup enoki mushrooms, trimmed and roughly chopped (separate the enoki clusters)

The Base:
- 1 tablespoon red curry paste (adjust for spice preference)
- 1 tablespoon fish sauce
- 1 egg, beaten
- 2 tablespoons panko breadcrumbs (or crushed rice crackers for a more traditional touch)
- 1 tablespoon chopped green onion
- 1 clove garlic, minced
- ½ teaspoon grated ginger
- Salt and freshly ground black pepper to taste

For Serving:
- Vegetable oil for cooking
- Sweet chili sauce for dipping (see recipe below)
- Lime wedges for squeezing

Prep the Shrimp and Enoki:
In a food processor or with a mortar and pestle, pulse the shrimp a few times until coarsely chopped. Roughly chop the enoki mushrooms, separating the clusters.

Combine the Base:
In a large bowl, combine the chopped shrimp, green beans, chopped cilantro, chopped enoki mushrooms, red curry paste, fish sauce, beaten egg, panko breadcrumbs (or crushed rice crackers), green onion, garlic, ginger, salt, and pepper. Mix well to ensure everything is evenly distributed.

Form the Fritters:
Lightly grease your hands with oil. Scoop out about 2 tablespoons of the shrimp mixture and gently shape it into a flat patty. Repeat with the remaining mixture, forming as many patties as you can (depending on the size of your pan).

Get your outdoor griddle or cast iron pan nice and hot over medium heat. Add a thin layer of vegetable oil to coat the cooking surface.

Carefully place the formed shrimp cakes onto the hot griddle. Don't overcrowd the pan – cook them in batches if necessary. Cook for 2-3 minutes per side, or until golden brown and crispy on the outside, and cooked through on the inside.

Transfer the cooked *Od Mun Kung* to a plate lined with paper towels to drain any excess oil. Serve them immediately while hot, with a side of sweet chili sauce for dipping. A squeeze of fresh lime adds a refreshing touch!

Sweet Chili Sauce (Optional - for a homemade touch):

- ¼ cup red bell pepper, finely chopped
- 2 tablespoons white vinegar
- 2 tablespoons sugar
- 1 tablespoon water
- 1 clove garlic, minced
- ½ teaspoon cornstarch mixed with 1 tablespoon water (to thicken)
- Pinch of red chili flakes (adjust for spice preference)

Simply combine all ingredients in a small saucepan and bring to a simmer over medium heat. Cook for 5-7 minutes, or until the sauce thickens slightly. Remove from heat and let cool slightly before serving.

Prep Time: 20 minutes
Cooking Time: 20-25 minutes
Servings: 4-6

One-Pan Savory Khanom Buang (Crispy Coconut Crepes)

The Savory Filling:
- ½ pound ground chicken or pork (or a combination)
- 1 tablespoon soy sauce
- 1 tablespoon fish sauce
- 1 teaspoon oyster sauce (optional, for extra umami)
- ½ teaspoon grated ginger
- 1 clove garlic, minced
- 1 shallot, thinly sliced
- ¼ cup chopped carrots
- ¼ cup chopped green onions
- 1 tablespoon chopped fresh cilantro
- 1 red chili pepper, deseeded and finely chopped (adjust for spice preference)
- 1 egg, beaten
- 1 tablespoon vegetable oil

The Crepe Batter (One-Pan Version):
- ¼ cup rice flour
- 1 tablespoon tapioca flour (or cornstarch)
- ½ cup coconut milk
- 1 tablespoon sugar
- ¼ cup water
- pinch of salt

Notes
While a griddle pan might be ideal for achieving the classic thin and crispy *Khanom Buang* texture, this one-pan method offers a convenient and portable alternative. It's perfect for camping trips, picnics, or anytime you have a single burner available. The slight difference in thickness doesn't take away from the deliciousness of the savory filling and the unique flavor of the coconut crepes.

Prepare the Filling:
In a medium bowl, combine the ground meat, soy sauce, fish sauce, oyster sauce (if using), ginger, and garlic. Mix well and marinate for at least 30 minutes, or up to overnight for deeper flavor.

-

Cook the Filling:
Heat the vegetable oil in a small pan on your single burner over medium heat. Add the shallots and cook for 30 seconds, or until softened. Add the carrots and cook for another minute.

-

Push the vegetables to one side of the pan and add the marinated ground meat. Break it up with a spoon as it cooks. Cook until the meat is browned and almost cooked through.

-

Add the chopped green onions, red chili pepper (adjust amount for spice preference), and chopped fresh cilantro to the pan. Stir-fry for another minute until fragrant.

-

Stir in the beaten egg and cook until it sets and is incorporated with the filling mixture. Remove from heat and set aside.

Making the Crepes:
Heat a single burner to medium heat. Lightly grease the bottom of a small, lidded, non-stick pot with oil.

-

In a separate bowl, whisk together the rice flour, tapioca flour (or cornstarch), coconut milk, sugar, water, and salt until smooth. The batter should be thin and pourable.

-

Pour a small amount of batter (about 2-3 tablespoons) into the hot pot, swirling to coat the bottom. Immediately cover the pan with the lid. This will trap steam and help cook the crepe through, creating a slightly thicker texture compared to the griddle version.

-

Cook for about 1 minute, or until the edges of the crepe begin to set. Carefully peek under the lid and check the bottom of the crepe. If golden brown, it's ready.

-

Uncover the pan and quickly add a spoonful of the pre-cooked savory filling to the center of the crepe. Since using a single pan makes folding a bit trickier, here's a one-handed folding method: Use a spoon to gently fold one edge over the filling, then fold the opposite edge over that to create a small, enclosed pocket.

-

Carefully slide the filled crepe onto a plate. Repeat steps 3-6 with the remaining batter and filling.

Spicy Som Tam (Green Papaya Salad)

Prep time: 10 minutes
Cooking time: n/a
Servings: 2-3

- 1 unripe green papaya, peeled and julienned (matchstick-thin)
- 1 carrot, julienned
- 1/2 cup green beans, snapped in half
- 2 tablespoons fish sauce
- 2 tablespoons fresh lime juice
- 1-2 Thai bird's eye chilies (or red chilies), finely chopped (adjust for spice preference)
- 1/4 cup roasted peanuts, roughly crushed
- Fresh cilantro, chopped
- Lime wedge, for garnish (optional)

Prep the Vegetables:
Shred the papaya, julienne the carrot, and snap the green beans in half. Remember, Ramsay wants them thin and even-sized for even cooking and flavor distribution.

Make the Dressing: In a bowl, whisk together fish sauce and lime juice.

Add the chopped chilies to the dressing. Start with less and adjust for your desired spice level.

Combine and Season: In a large bowl, toss together the papaya, carrot, green beans, and the prepared dressing. Season with crushed peanuts and chopped cilantro.

Mortar and Pestle (Optional): For a more traditional and textured *Som Tam*, use a mortar and pestle to lightly pound the salad ingredients together. Don't overdo it, you want some bite left!

Taste and Adjust: Take a bite and adjust the seasoning as needed with more fish sauce, lime juice, or chilies. It should be a balance of salty, sour, spicy, and refreshing.

Plate the *Som Tam* and garnish with a lime wedge for a refreshing touch.

Sticky Rice

Prep Time: 5 minutes
Cooking Time: 25 minutes
Servings: 2-3

- 1 cup rinsed jasmine rice
- 1 ½ cups full-fat coconut milk
- 1 cup water
- ¼ cup sugar (palm preferred, white works)
- ½ tsp salt
- Pandan leaf (optional, for aroma)

Rinse Rice:
Get rid of starch. Rinse jasmine rice in cold water until clear.

Combine & Heat: In a pot, mix rice, coconut milk, water, sugar, and salt. Bring to a boil.

Throw in a pandan leaf for a touch of vanilla-like aroma, if you have it.

Reduce heat to low, cover tightly, and simmer 15 minutes. Don't lift the lid.

After 15 minutes, turn off heat and let rice steam for another 10 minutes, covered.

Once steamed, fluff rice with a fork, separating grains without crushing.

Serve hot with your favorite Thai curries or stir-fries. Fluff it up for a restaurant-worthy look.

Cucumber Kimchi

Prep time: 10 minutes
Cooking time: n/a
Servings: 2-3

- 1 large cucumber, thinly sliced
- 1 tablespoon fish sauce
- 1 tablespoon Thai Chii Oil (see recipe, below)
- 1 clove garlic, minced
- 1/2 teaspoon grated ginger
- 1 tablespoon rice vinegar
- 1 teaspoon sesame oil
- Pinch of salt

Slice it Thin:
Grab your sharpest knife and thinly slice that cucumber. You want them paper-thin for maximum flavor absorption.

In a bowl, whisk together fish sauce, Thai Chili Oil (start with less, adjust for heat later!), garlic, ginger, rice vinegar, sesame oil, and salt.

Toss the sliced cucumbers in the marinade, making sure they're well coated.

Cover the bowl and let it sit for at least 30 minutes, but an hour is even better for maximum flavor and crunch. The longer they marinate, the spicier and more tangy they'll get.

This Spicy Quick Kimchi is perfect alongside noodles, rice bowls, or anything needing a spicy and refreshing kick.

Homemade Thai Chili Oil

Prep Time: 5 minutes
Cooking Time: 4 minutes
Servings: 1 Cup

- 1 cup neutral oil (avocado, canola, or vegetable)
- 2-3 guajillo peppers, stemmed & seeded (optional)
- 4-5 dried red chilies (adjust for spice)
- 4 cloves garlic, thinly sliced
- 1/2 inch ginger, julienned
- 1 lemongrass stalk, white part only, bruised
- Pinch of salt

Toast *Guajillo*:
Heat a dry pan, toast Guajillo peppers 1 minute per side (skip if not using).

Heat Oil & Aromatics: In a saucepan, heat oil over medium heat. Add Guajillo (if using), chilies, lemongrass (if using), and ginger (if using). Sizzle for 1 minute.

Add garlic, saute 30 seconds (watch not to burn).

Steep & Strain: Remove pan from heat, steep for 30 minutes (or overnight) in oil. Strain oil into a jar, discard solids. Season with salt.

Store: In a cool, dark place for up to several weeks

Thai Green Beans

Prep time: 5 minutes
Cooking time: 5 minutes
Servings: 2-3

- 1 lb green beans, trimmed & cut bite-sized
- 2 tbsp vegetable oil
- 4 cloves garlic, thinly sliced
- 1-2 Thai chilies, seeded & sliced (adjust for spice)
- 1 tbsp oyster sauce
- 1 tbsp fish sauce
- 1 tsp sugar
- Black pepper and White Pepper (to taste)

Heat oil, sear garlic & chilies (30 seconds).

Add beans, stir-fry 2-3 minutes (tender-crisp).

Stir in oyster sauce, fish sauce, sugar & pepper.

Serve hot! Garnish with cilantro (optional).

Thai Peanut Dipping Sauce

Prep Time: 5 minutes
Cooking Time: n/a
Servings: 1 cup

- 1/4 cup creamy peanut butter
- 1/4 cup coconut milk (full-fat)
- 1 tablespoon each: soy sauce, lime juice, fish sauce, brown sugar
- 1 red chili, seeded & chopped (adjust for spice)
- 1 clove garlic, minced
- 1 inch ginger, grated
- Pinch of red pepper flakes (optional)
- Water (to thin)

Whisk it all together:
Peanut butter, coconut milk, soy sauce, lime juice, fish sauce, brown sugar, chili, garlic, ginger, and red pepper flakes (optional) in a bowl.

The sauce should be dippable, so add water 1 tablespoon at a time if it's too thick.

Add more lime juice for tang, or a touch of fish sauce for extra savory punch.

Use with grilled meats, skewers, veggies, or anything that needs a flavor boost. Drizzle it on a plate or serve in a bowl for easy dipping.

Spicy Thai Rice Crackers

Prep time: 5 minutes
Cooking time: 10 minutes
Servings: 20 crackers

- 1 cup cooked jasmine rice (cold, leftover is perfect!)
- 1 tablespoon Thai red curry paste (adjust for spice!)
- 1 tablespoon fish sauce
- 1/2 teaspoon sesame oil
- Pinch of salt
- Water (1-2 tablespoons, to adjust consistency)

Mash the cold cooked rice with a fork until it mostly breaks down, but still has some texture.

Add the red curry paste, fish sauce, sesame oil, and salt. Mix well to combine.

The mixture should be moldable but not sticky. Add water, 1 tablespoon at a time, until it holds its shape when pressed.

Lightly flour a surface and roll out the rice mixture to a thin sheet (about 1/8 inch thick).

Use a knife or cookie cutter to cut the rice mixture into desired shapes (squares, triangles, etc.).

Heat a non-stick pan or griddle over medium heat. Add a thin layer of oil and carefully place the rice crackers in the pan.

Cook for 2-3 minutes per side, or until golden brown and crispy.

Enjoy these hot and crispy Thai rice crackers on their own or alongside your favorite curries or dips.

Spicy Thai Fritters

Prep Time: 5 minutes
Cooking Time: 10 minutes per batch (makes about 20 fritters)
Servings: 4

- 1 cup chopped chicken (shredded leftover is perfect, or use tofu for a veggie option)
- 1/2 cup chopped red bell pepper
- 1/4 cup chopped green onion
- 1 stalk lemongrass, white part only, finely chopped
- 1 red chili, seeded and finely chopped (adjust for spice!)
- 1 clove garlic, minced
- 1/2 cup panko breadcrumbs
- 1/4 cup chopped fresh cilantro
- 1 tablespoon fish sauce
- 1 egg, beaten
- Vegetable oil (for frying)
- Lime wedges, for garnish (optional)

If using leftover chicken, shred or pulse it in a food processor a few times for a finer texture.

In a bowl, combine chicken (or tofu), bell pepper, green onion, lemongrass, chili, garlic, breadcrumbs, cilantro, and fish sauce.

Crack in the egg and mix well to combine. The mixture should hold its shape when pressed.

4. Heat Oil: Heat enough vegetable oil in a large pan or wok over medium heat (oil should be about 1/2 inch deep).

Using your hands, form the mixture into small, flattened patties (about 2 tablespoons each). Carefully add a few fritters at a time to the hot oil.

Fry for 2-3 minutes per side, or until golden brown and crispy. Drain on paper towels to remove excess oil.

Plate the fritters and garnish with lime wedges for a refreshing touch (optional). Serve hot alongside your favorite Thai curries, noodles, or stir-fries. These fritters are the perfect flavor bomb for any Asian-inspired meal.

Penang, Malaysia

In the heart of Penang, Malaysia, a symphony of sizzling woks, fragrant spices, and the rhythmic clang of utensils beckon you into a world of culinary wonder. This vibrant island, a melting pot of Malay, Chinese, and Indian cultures, boasts a street food scene that tantalizes the senses and nourishes the soul.

Penang's culinary tapestry is woven with threads of tradition and innovation. It's a place where age-old recipes, passed down through generations, intermingle with bold new creations, where the smoky aroma of char kway teow dances alongside the fragrant steam of nasi lemak.

In this collection, we celebrate Penang's rich culinary heritage, offering a curated selection of both classic and contemporary dishes. From the fiery embrace of asam laksa to the comforting warmth of roti canai, each recipe captures the essence of Penang's vibrant foodways. We've taken beloved classics and elevated them with a modern twist, ensuring a harmonious balance of flavors that will delight your taste buds. And we've crafted original recipes, inspired by the island's unique pantry and culinary traditions, showcasing the boundless creativity of Penang's street food scene.

Whether you're a seasoned foodie or a curious novice, this collection invites you to experience the diverse flavors and textures that make Penang a street food paradise. So, step into the bustling markets, embrace the tantalizing aromas, and let your culinary adventure begin.

Penang Satay: These grilled skewers, infused with aromatic spices and served with a rich peanut sauce, embody the harmonious blend of Malay, Chinese, and Indian flavors that define Penang's street food scene.

Asam Laksa (Spicy Sour Noodle Soup): A fiery, flavorful fish broth brimming with noodles, herbs, and tamarind tang, this dish reflects Penang's multicultural heritage and its love for bold, complex tastes.

Murtabak (Stuffed Flatbread - Penang Hawker Stall Style): A savory, flaky flatbread filled with spiced meat and vegetables, showcasing the Indian-Muslim influence on Penang's culinary traditions.

Roti Canai (Layered Flatbread): This buttery, flaky flatbread, often served with curry or dhal, exemplifies the Indian heritage deeply rooted in Penang's food culture.

Penang Har Mee (Prawn Broth Soup): A rich and fragrant prawn broth with noodles and toppings, reflecting Penang's coastal location and abundance of fresh seafood.

Otak-Otak (Leaf-wrapped Fish Cakes): These flavorful fish cakes, steamed in banana leaves, showcase the resourcefulness of Penang's cuisine and its use of local ingredients.

Pegaga Masak Lemak (Watercress with Coconut & Kaffir Lime): A creamy, aromatic curry featuring watercress, coconut milk, and kaffir lime leaves, highlighting Penang's love for fresh greens and vibrant flavors.

Kuih Kapit Ikan Bilis Mas (Golden Pinched Anchovy Snacks): These original crispy, savory snacks made with anchovies and spices represent the island's rich culinary heritage and its creative use of seafood. (Showstopper)

Nasi Lemak Loaf (Savory Coconut Rice Loaf): A modern twist on the classic coconut rice dish, reflecting Penang's openness to culinary innovation while paying homage to its traditional flavors. (Showstopper)

Tamarind Shrimp Rice Balls: These tangy, flavorful rice balls, made with shrimp and tamarind paste, showcase Penang's coastal cuisine and its love for bold, punchy flavors. (Showstopper)

Chilled Buttermilk Cucumber Raita Soup: Our unique, refreshing, cooling soup inspired by Indian raita, featuring buttermilk, cucumber, and spices, offering a welcome respite from Penang's tropical heat. (Showstopper)

Nasi Impit (Compressed Rice): These compact rice cakes, often served with curries or satay, highlight the practical and ingenious nature of Penang's street food.

Acar Rempah Pelbagai Sayur (Penang Pickled Medley): A colorful assortment of pickled vegetables, reflecting Penang's diverse culinary influences and its penchant for preserving fresh produce.

Cicah Kari Masam Manis Kelapa (Spicy Sweet Coconut Dipping Sauce): This complex and flavorful sauce, with its balance of sweet, sour, and spicy notes, embodies the essence of Penang's cuisine and its love for bold, harmonious flavors.

Penang Satay

Prep Time: 30 minutes
Cooking Time: 25 minutes
Servings: 4-6

The *Rempah* (Spice Paste):

- 1 inch fresh galangal, chopped
- 1 inch fresh turmeric, chopped
- 2 stalks lemongrass, white bulb only, chopped
- 3 shallots, chopped
- 4-6 red chilies (depending on spice preference), chopped
- ½ cup roasted cashews
- 1 tablespoon shrimp paste (optional)
- 4-5 kaffir lime leaves, torn

The Marinade:

- ½ pound chicken breast, mutton, or prawns (peeled and deveined)
- ¼ cup coconut cream
- 2 tablespoons *kecap manis* (Indonesian sweet soy sauce)
- 1 tablespoon light soy sauce
- 1 tablespoon palm sugar (or brown sugar)
- 1 tablespoon vegetable oil

For Serving:

- Peanut Sauce (see recipe below)
- Chopped fresh cilantro (optional)

The A+ Peanut Sauce:

- ½ cup roasted peanuts, no skins
- ¼ cup coconut milk
- 2 tablespoons kecap manis
- 1 tablespoon lime juice
- 1 tablespoon palm sugar (or brown sugar)
- 1 teaspoon fish sauce
- Pinch of red chili flakes (optional)

Make the Rempah:
Grind galangal, turmeric, lemongrass, shallots, and chilies into a paste (rempah) using a mortar and pestle or food processor.

Toast cashews in a dry pan until fragrant, then grind with shrimp paste (optional) and kaffir lime leaves (pulse briefly) and add to the *rempah*.

Mix *rempah*, coconut cream, kecap manis, soy sauce, palm sugar, and oil. Marinate your protein (chicken, pork, etc.) for at least 30 minutes or overnight.

Thread marinated protein onto soaked skewers.

Grill at medium-high heat for 3-4 minutes per side or until cooked through and charred.

Blend roasted peanuts, coconut milk, kecap manis, lime juice, palm sugar, fish sauce, and chili flakes (optional) for a peanut sauce. Adjust seasonings.

Serve hot satay with peanut sauce and garnish with cilantro.

Note:
The easy *kecap manis* (Indonesian sweet soy sauce) substitute is Soy Sauce + Sugar: This is a quick and easy substitute. Mix equal parts soy sauce and sugar (brown sugar, palm sugar, or maple syrup) to create a similar sweetness level. You might need to adjust the amount of sugar depending on your taste and the recipe's sweetness requirement.

Asam Laksa (Spicy Sour Noodle Soup)

Prep Time: 15-20 minutes
Cooking Time: 20-25 minutes
Servings: 2-3

The Broth

- 4 cups water
- 2 tablespoons tamarind paste
- 1 stalk lemongrass, bruised (or 1 teaspoon lemongrass paste)
- 2 kaffir lime leaves
- 1-2 red chilies, chopped (adjust for spice preference)
- 1 teaspoon palm sugar (or brown sugar)
- 1 tablespoon fish sauce
- 1 cup snow peas, baby *bok choy* and straw mushrooms
- Salt to taste
- 2-3 grilled or pan-fried fish fillets (tilapia, cod, or any firm white fish work well) - OR -
- 1/1 lb of shrimp and 1/2 of mussels (cleaned)
- 150 grams *laksa* noodles (cooked according to package instructions)
- ½ cup shredded red onion
- ½ cup shredded cucumber
- ¼ cup chopped fresh pineapple
- ¼ cup chopped fresh cilantro (or mint if you prefer)
- Lime wedges (for service)

Combine all broth ingredients and vegetables in a large pot. Bring to a boil, then simmer 10 minutes. Season with salt.

-

While broth simmers, cook your chosen protein according to method (grill/pan-fry fish, drain canned fish, or clean and cook shrimp/mussels). Flake fish if using fillets.

-

Divide noodles into bowls. Top with hot broth, protein, vegetables, and herbs.

-

Serve hot with lime wedges.

-

Note:
If you can't find *laksa* noodles, here are some good substitutes for your Asam Laksa:

Rice Vermicelli: These thin rice noodles are widely available and cook quickly. They have a slightly different texture than laksa noodles, but they will still work well in the dish.

Thin Rice Noodles (Pad Thai Noodles): Another readily available option, these noodles have a similar texture to rice vermicelli and will cook quickly.

PENANG MAIN DISHES- STREET

Prep Time: 40-50 minutes. Gathering and measuring ingredients - 5 minutes. Preparing the filling (chopping onion, mincing garlic, etc.) - 5-10 minutes Making the dough (mixing, kneading, resting) - 30-35 minutes

Cooking Time: 20-25 minutes

Servings: 4-6, each 6-8 inches in diameter.

The Dough:

- 2 cups all-purpose flour
- 1 teaspoon sugar
- ½ teaspoon salt
- 1/3 cup melted *ghee* (or vegetable oil, but *ghee* adds a richer flavor)
- ¼ - ½ cup lukewarm water (depending on humidity)
- 2-3 chicken thighs, boneless and thinly sliced (or ground chicken/lamb)
- 1 tablespoon vegetable oil
- 1 medium onion, chopped
- 2 cloves garlic, minced
- 1 teaspoon ginger paste
- 1 teaspoon turmeric powder
- ½ teaspoon ground cumin
- ½ teaspoon coriander powder
- pinch of chili powder (adjust for spice preference)
- ¼ cup water
- Salt to taste
- 1 large egg, beaten

Cooking:
- *Ghee* (essential for that Penang flavor)

Murtabak (Stuffed Flatbread- Penang Hawker Stall Style)

Mix flour, sugar, salt, and melted ghee in a bowl. Gradually add water until a soft, slightly sticky dough forms. Knead for 10 minutes, then let it rest for 30 minutes.

-

Heat oil and saute onions. Add garlic, ginger, spices, and meat (optional). Cook until fragrant and meat is browned. Add water and simmer until thickened.

-

Divide dough, flatten a ball, roll it thin, and spread filling in the center. Brush edges with egg. Fold dough into a square or triangle, sealing edges.

-

Cook folded Murtabak on a hot griddle for 2-3 minutes per side until golden brown. Repeat with remaining dough and filling. Serve hot with curry or *dhal* for dipping.

Roti Canai (Layered Flatbread)

Prep Time: Combining the dough ingredients takes about 5 minutes. Kneading and resting the dough takes 35 minutes. Rolling and shaping the dough balls can be time-consuming, especially for beginners. Estimate 10 minutes for this step.

Cooking Time: Cooking each roti on a griddle takes a few minutes per side. The total cooking time will depend on how many rotis you make. Estimate 10-15 minutes total cooking time.

Servings: The recipe yields enough dough to make 4-6 *roti canai*, each 8-12" in diameter.

The Dough:
- 2 cups all-purpose flour (plus extra for dusting)
- 1 teaspoon sugar
- ½ teaspoon salt
- 1/3 cup melted *ghee* (or vegetable oil, but *ghee* is better.)
- ¼ - ½ cup lukewarm water (depending on humidity)

For Cooking & Serving:
- *Ghee* (essential for that Penang flavor)
- Dhal or Curry of your choice

Mix flour, sugar, salt, and melted *ghee* in a bowl. Add water slowly until a soft dough forms. Knead for 5 minutes and let rest for 30 minutes.

-

Divide dough into balls, roll each ball thin, and drizzle with *ghee*.

(Rolling each ball thin means using a rolling pin to flatten a dough ball into a very thin, large circle, about 12 inches wide. You can almost see through it when held up to light.)

-

Roll this thin disk of dough into a cigar shape, then coil it into a flat spiral.

-

Heat griddle to medium heat with *ghee*. Ideally, the *ghee* should be almost smoking when you place the dough on the griddle.

-

Uncoil dough and cook on both sides until golden brown.

-

Serve hot with *ghee* and curry.

-

Roti Canai Dough Rolling Technique

Imagine a ball of dough like pizza dough. Here's how to turn it into flaky flatbread:

1. Roll it flat: Use a rolling pin to make a large, thin circle of dough.

2. Roll it up tight: Like rolling up a long sheet of paper (jelly roll style), tightly roll up the flat dough into a long, skinny roll.

3. Coil it like a snail: Instead of leaving it rolled up, coil this long roll around itself, tucking the end under the center, similar to a snail shell.

4. Loosen the layers (not unravel): Think of a ball of yarn. You don't want to unravel the entire thing! Instead, gently lift and pull sections of the outside coil upwards slightly, creating a little space between the "windings" of the snail shell, not the layers within the original roll. Do this all around the disc, like peeling back the layers of pastry a little.

5. Flattened with swirls: You'll end up with a flattened disc of dough with visible swirls or lines. These are the separated layers that make your Roti Canai crispy and flaky!

Penang Har Mee (Prawn Broth Soup)

Prep Time: 20-30 minutes
Cooking Time: 20-25 minutes
Servings: 2-3

The Broth

- 6 cups prawn stock (homemade or store-bought)
- 1 cup water
- 2 tablespoons soy sauce
- 1 tablespoon oyster sauce
- 1 tablespoon fish sauce
- 1 tablespoon sugar
- 1 teaspoon white pepper
- Smoky Touch (Choose One):
  ½ teaspoon toasted sesame oil (classic smoky hint)
  OR
  1 chip dried shrimp paste, soaked and mashed (smokier and intense)

The Stir-Fry:

- 16 large prawns (shelled and deveined)
- 1 tablespoon cornstarch (for velveting)
- 2 tablespoons vegetable oil
- 2 shallots, thinly sliced
- 2 cloves garlic, minced
- 1 red chili pepper, deseeded and sliced (adjust for spice preference)
- ½ cup shredded cabbage
- ½ cup bean sprouts
- 100 grams (about ½ block) firm tofu, cut into cubes (optional)
- 250 grams (about 8 oz) thick yellow noodles (fresh or dried)
- 1 green onion, sliced (for garnish)
- Fried shallots (for garnish)

Combine prawn stock, water, soy sauce, oyster sauce, fish sauce, sugar, and white pepper in a pot. Simmer for 10 minutes. (Optional: Add sesame oil or softened shrimp paste for smokiness.)

-

Pat prawns dry, coat with cornstarch, and set aside.

-

Heat oil in a pan. Sear prawns in batches (if needed) for 1 minute per side, then set aside.

-

Saute shallots and garlic in the pan. Add chili pepper (adjust for spice).

-

Stir-fry cabbage and bean sprouts for 2-3 minutes until crisp-tender.

-

Cook noodles according to package instructions (or blanch fresh noodles) and add them to the pan.

-

Pour simmering broth into the pan with noodles and vegetables. Toss to combine.

-

Reduce heat, add prawns and tofu (if using), and heat for 1-2 minutes until cooked through. Season with more white pepper (optional).

-

Plate the *Hokkien Mee* and garnish with green onion and fried shallots.

Simple Prawn Broth

Ingredients:

- Prawn shells and heads (from about 1 pound of prawns)
- Water (around 4 cups)
- 1 onion, roughly chopped (optional)
- 1 carrot, roughly chopped (optional)
- 1 celery stalk, roughly chopped (optional)
- A few peppercorns (whole black peppercorns)
- Salt (to taste)

Instructions:

1. Prep: Peel and devein your prawns, saving the shells and heads for the broth.

2. Simmer: In a large pot, combine the prawn shells and heads, water, and your optional vegetables (onion, carrot, celery). Throw in the peppercorns for a bit of spice. Bring everything to a boil, then reduce heat and simmer for at least 30 minutes, or up to an hour for a richer flavor.

3. Strain: Strain the broth through a fine-mesh sieve to remove the solids. Discard the shells and vegetables.

4. Season: Season your broth with salt to taste. You can also add a squeeze of lemon juice for a touch of brightness (optional).

Tips:
For a more intense prawn flavor, you can lightly toast the prawn shells and heads in a pan before adding them to the water.

f you have some fresh herbs on hand, like bay leaf, thyme, or parsley, you can add them to the pot while simmering for additional flavor.

Otak-Otak (Leaf-wrapped Fish Cakes)

Prep Time: 30 minutes (soaking banana leaves, if needed); 10 minutes (chopping ingredients, making the paste)

Cooking Time: 10-17 minutes total cooking time, depending on grilling options.

Servings: The recipe is for 6-8 medium sized parcels.

The Fragrant Paste:

- ½ pound firm white fish fillets (skinless and chopped)
- ½ cup fresh grated coconut (or unsweetened shredded coconut, soaked in hot water for 15 minutes and drained)
- 2 shallots, finely chopped
- 2 cloves garlic, minced
- 1 lemongrass stalk, bottom white part only, chopped
- 1 inch ginger, peeled and minced
- 2 kaffir lime leaves, thinly sliced (remove central vein)
- 1 stalk galangal (optional, for extra zing)
- 1 red chili pepper, deseeded and finely chopped (adjust for spice preference)
- ½ teaspoon turmeric powder
- ½ teaspoon coriander powder
- ½ teaspoon cumin powder
- ¼ teaspoon shrimp paste (optional, for extra umami)
- Salt and freshly ground black pepper to taste
- 1 tablespoon vegetable oil

The Wrappings:

- Banana leaves, washed and softened (see instructions below)
- Kitchen twine

Soak banana leaves (if stiff) for 30 minutes, then cut into 6-inch squares.

-

Combine fish, coconut, shallots, garlic, spices, and shrimp paste (optional) in a food processor. Pulse until coarsely chopped.

-

Heat oil in a pan, add the paste, and cook for 5-7 minutes, stirring often.

-

Bring water to a boil in a pot. Place steamer basket inside.

-

Divide paste onto banana leaves, fold into parcels, and secure with twine (optional).

-

Steam parcels for 10-15 minutes.

-

Grill parcels for 2-3 minutes per side on a hot grill pan or outdoor grill (optional).

-

Notes:

No banana leaves? Use aluminum foil instead:

Cut squares (slightly bigger than 6 inches) and lightly grease them.

-

Flavor Change: You'll miss the subtle earthiness and faint sweetness from banana leaves.

-

Boost Other Flavors:

Use fresh, high-quality spices like lemongrass and kaffir lime leaves for extra complexity.

Choose fresh, flavorful fish for a delicious filling.

-

Smoky Hint (Optional): If you have a smoker, add banana peels (without flesh) for a short smoke while grilling the parcels.

The focus on spices and fish will create a tasty dish despite the missing banana leaf influence.

PENANG SIDE DISHES- STREET

Pegaga Masak Lemak (Watercress with Coconut & Kaffir Lime)

Prep time: 10 minutes
Cooking time: n/a
Servings: 2-3

For the *Sambal*:
- 2 shallots, thinly sliced
- 2 cloves garlic, thinly sliced
- 1 stalk lemongrass, white part only, thinly sliced
- 2 red chilies, thinly sliced (seeds in for more heat, remove some for less)
- 1 kaffir lime leaf, torn
- 1/2 inch ginger, thinly sliced
- 1 tablespoon vegetable oil

For the Stir-Fry:
- 1 bunch watercress, washed and patted dry
- 1 cup full-fat coconut milk
- 1 tablespoon palm sugar (or brown sugar)
- 1/4 cup lime juice (freshly squeezed)
- 1 tablespoon fish sauce
- Kosher salt, to taste
- Freshly ground black pepper, to taste
- 1 tablespoon vegetable oil
- 1 lime, cut into wedges

Make the Sambal: Heat the vegetable oil in a small pan over medium heat. Add the shallots, garlic, lemongrass, chilies, kaffir lime leaf, and ginger. Sauté for 3-4 minutes, until softened and fragrant.

Grind to a Paste: Transfer the *sambal* ingredients to a mortar and pestle (or food processor) and grind into a fine paste. Set aside.

Blanch the Watercress: Bring a pot of salted water to a boil. Blanch the watercress for 30 seconds to 1 minute, until just wilted. Drain immediately and refresh under cold running water. Squeeze out any excess moisture. Roughly chop the watercress.

In a separate small pan, heat the remaining vegetable oil over medium heat. Add the reserved *sambal* paste and cook for 1 minute, stirring constantly, to release the flavors.

Pour in the coconut milk and bring to a simmer. Reduce heat and simmer for 5 minutes, allowing the flavors to meld.

Add the palm sugar (or brown sugar), lime juice, and fish sauce. Season with salt and pepper to taste. Simmer for another 2 minutes.

Gently fold in the chopped watercress and cook for 1-2 minutes, just until heated through. Be careful not to overcook the watercress, it should retain a vibrant green color and slight bite.

Plate the vibrant *Pegaga Masak Lemak* and garnish with fresh lime wedges.

Kuih Kapit Ikan Bilis Mas (Golden Pinched Anchovy Snacks)

Prep Time: 15 minutes
Cooking Time: 15 minutes
Servings: 25 (depending on size)

- 1 cup flour
- 1/4 cup chopped peanuts
- 1 tbsp anchovy paste
- 1 tbsp *sambal oelek* (adjust for spice- see recipe, above)
- 1/2 tsp black pepper
- 1/4 tsp salt
- 5 tbsp cold butter, cubed
- 2-3 tbsp ice water

Whisk it all: In a bowl, combine flour, peanuts, anchovy paste, sambal oelek, pepper, and salt.

Cut in Butter: Using a fork, cut the cold butter into the dry ingredients until crumbly.

Gradually add ice water, 1 tbsp at a time, tossing with the fork until the dough just comes together. Don't overmix.

Shape dough into a flat disk, wrap in plastic wrap, and refrigerate 30 minutes. Preheat oven to 350°F (175°C). Unwrap and cut dough into thin slices (1/4 inch thick).

Bake to Golden: Arrange slices on a baking sheet lined with parchment paper. Bake 15-20 minutes, or until lightly golden brown and crisp. Let cool completely.

Snack on these or serve with your favorite dipping sauce.

Nasi Lemak Loaf (Savory Coconut Rice Loaf)

Prep time: 10 minutes
Cooking time: 30-25 minutes
Servings: 4-6

- 2 cups cooked jasmine rice (cold, leftover is perfect!)
- 1 cup full-fat coconut milk
- 2 *pandan* leaves (tied into a knot, optional - see substitutions below)
- 1/2 cup chopped roasted peanuts
- 1/4 cup fried shallots
- 1/4 cup chopped *ikan bilis* (dried anchovies)
- 1/2 teaspoon salt
- 1/4 teaspoon freshly ground black pepper

Prep the Aromatics: If using *pandan* leaves, tie them into a knot for easy removal later.

-

In a large bowl, combine the cooked rice, coconut milk, *pandan* leaves (if using), roasted peanuts, fried shallots, ikan bilis, salt, and black pepper. Mix well to ensure everything is evenly distributed.

-

Preheat your oven to 350°F (175°C). Grease a loaf pan and pour the rice mixture into it.

-

Bake the rice loaf for 30-35 minutes, or until heated through and slightly crispy on top.

-

Let the loaf cool slightly before slicing and serving warm as a side dish with curries, stir-fries, grilled meats, or even enjoy it on its own.

-

Pandan Leaves Substitute: Don't have pandan leaves? Here are some substitutes that can add a hint of similar aroma:

Vanilla extract: 1/2 teaspoon of vanilla extract can provide a subtle vanilla flavor.

Pandan essence: If you can find it in Asian grocery stores, a few drops of pandan essence can mimic the pandan aroma.

Lemon zest: Finely grated lemon zest can add a touch of citrusy brightness.

Tamarind Shrimp Rice Balls

Prep Time: 15 minutes
Cooking Time: 25 minutes
Servings: 4-6

For the Fragrant Coconut Rice:
- 1/2 cup jasmine rice
- 1 cup coconut milk (full-fat)
- 1 pandan leaf (tied into a knot, or substitute - see tip, above)
- Pinch of salt

For the Tamarind Sauce:
- 1 small tamarind pod (or 1 tablespoon tamarind paste)
- 2 tablespoons hot water
- 1 tablespoon brown sugar
- 1 tablespoon fish sauce

For the Rice Balls:
- 1 cup cooked fragrant coconut rice (cooled slightly)
- 1/2 cup cooked, chopped shrimp
- 1/4 cup chopped fresh vegetables (peas, carrots, green onions work well)
- 1 tablespoon chopped fresh cilantro
- 1/4 cup panko breadcrumbs
- 1 egg, beaten
- Vegetable oil (for frying)

Make the Sauce: (Skip if using tamarind paste) Soak tamarind pulp in hot water, mash, strain. Combine juice, brown sugar, and fish sauce. (For paste, just whisk together all sauce ingredients)

-

Cook the Rice: Rinse rice, simmer with coconut milk, pandan leaf (optional), and salt until cooked. Discard pandan leaf.

-

Marinate Shrimp: Toss shrimp with soy sauce, ginger, and garlic. Let sit 10 minutes.

-

Assemble & Fry: Combine rice, shrimp (with marinade), veggies, cilantro, and 1 tbsp tamarind sauce. Form balls, dip in egg, then panko. Fry in hot oil until golden brown. Drain on paper towels.

-

Enjoy warm with curries, stir-fries, etc. Dip in remaining tamarind sauce for extra flavor.

Chilled Buttermilk Cucumber Raita Soup

Prep time: 30 minutes
Cooking time: 10 minutes
Servings: 4-6

For the Buttermilk Base:
- 1 cup (240g) full-fat Greek yogurt
- 1/2 cup (120ml) thickened buttermilk
- 1 tablespoon fresh lime juice
- 1/2 teaspoon ground cumin
- 1/4 teaspoon ground coriander
- 1/4 teaspoon smoked paprika
- Pinch of cayenne pepper (adjust for heat)
- 1 tablespoon chopped fresh mint
- 1 tablespoon chopped fresh dill
- 1 tablespoon chopped fresh cilantro
- Salt and freshly ground black pepper, to taste

For the Cucumber Granita:
- 1/2 cup (120ml) water
- 1/4 cup (50g) peeled, seeded, and chopped cucumber
- 1 tablespoon sugar
- 1 tablespoon fresh lime juice
- Pinch of freshly grated ginger

Make the Buttermilk Base:
In a medium bowl, whisk together the Greek yogurt, buttermilk, lime juice, cumin, coriander, smoked paprika, cayenne pepper (adjust to your desired spice level), fresh herbs (mint, dill, cilantro), salt, and pepper. Taste and adjust seasonings as needed. Chill the buttermilk base for at least 30 minutes for the flavors to meld.

Prepare the Granita: Combine water, cucumber, sugar, lime juice, and ginger in a small saucepan. Bring to a simmer over medium heat until the sugar dissolves. Remove from heat and let cool slightly.

Freeze the Granita: Pour the cucumber mixture into a shallow container and freeze for at least 2 hours, or until frozen solid. Scrape the frozen mixture with a fork to create a coarse granita.

Plating Perfection:

1. Ladle the chilled buttermilk base into small serving bowls.

2. Top each bowl with a spoonful of cucumber granita.

3. Garnish with Passion: Don't be shy. Drizzle a touch of high-quality olive oil. Finish with a sprinkle of vibrant garnishes like chopped fresh dill, a pinch of sumac for a touch of tang, and a dollop of vibrant green mint pesto for an extra flavor explosion.

Tips:

Freshness is Paramount: Use the freshest herbs and cucumbers possible for the most vibrant flavor and color.

Acidity Balance: The lime juice adds a necessary brightness to balance the creaminess of the yogurt. Adjust the amount to your preference.

Nasi Impit (Compressed Rice)

Prep Time: 5 minutes
Cooking Time: 20 minutes
Setting Time: At least 2 hour
Servings: 4-6

- 2 cups (400g) jasmine rice, rinsed
- 4 1/4 cups (1.05 liters) water
- 1 pandan leaf, knotted (optional)
- Pinch of salt

Rinse 2 cups jasmine rice. Cook in rice cooker (or pot) with 4 1/4 cups water, pandan leaf (optional), and salt.

Line mold with plastic wrap. Press hot rice firmly into mold. Cover and weight down. Cool at least 2 hours (overnight best).

Slice and enjoy with any Malaysian or Asian-influenced dish.

Notes:
Ideal Molds for *Nasi Impit*:

Square baking dish: An 8x8 inch (20x20 cm) baking dish is a perfect size for this recipe. It allows for shaping a good amount of rice and easily cutting it into squares.

Nasi Impit mold: If you plan on making Nasi Impit regularly, investing in a specific Nasi Impit mold might be worthwhile. These traditional molds come in various sizes and materials like aluminum or plastic.

Acar Rempah Pelbagai Sayur (Penang Pickled Medley)

Prep Time: 5 minutes
Cooking Time: 4 minutes
Servings: 1 Cup

- 1 cup (200g) kohlrabi, peeled and julienned
- 1 cup (200g) jicama, peeled and julienned
- 1 cup (200g) romanesco broccoli, florets cut into bite-sized pieces
- 1/2 cup (100g) green papaya, peeled and julienned (optional - substitute with chayote squash if unavailable)
- 1/4 cup (50g) red bell pepper, thinly sliced
- 1/4 cup (50g) yellow bell pepper, thinly sliced
- 1/4 cup (50g) fresh green beans, trimmed and cut into thin strips

For the Pickling Brine:
- 1 cup (240ml) white vinegar
- 1/2 cup (120ml) water
- 1/4 cup (50g) palm sugar (or substitute with brown sugar)
- 2 tablespoons (30ml) vegetable oil
- 1 tablespoon (15g) ground turmeric

Prepare the Vegetables: Wash and dry all the vegetables. Peel the kohlrabi, jicama, and green papaya (if using) and julienne them into thin strips. Cut the romanesco broccoli florets into bite-sized pieces, slice the bell peppers, and trim and cut the green beans into thin strips.

Combine Vegetables: In a large bowl, combine the julienned kohlrabi, jicama, green papaya (if using), romanesco broccoli florets, sliced bell peppers, and green beans. Toss well to mix.

Prepare the Brine: In a saucepan, combine the white vinegar, water, palm sugar (or brown sugar), vegetable oil, turmeric, mustard seeds, black peppercorns, red chili flakes, and salt. Bring the mixture to a simmer over medium heat, stirring occasionally until the sugar dissolves.

Remove the hot brine from the heat and carefully pour it over the vegetables in the bowl. Ensure all the vegetables are submerged in the brine.

Cover the bowl tightly and let the achar marinate at room temperature for at least 2 hours, or preferably overnight for the flavors to develop fully. Store the pickled vegetables in an airtight container in the refrigerator for up to 2 weeks.

Serving *Achar*:
Enjoy this Achar as a condiment with curries, rice dishes, or grilled meats.

The tangy and crunchy vegetables add a delightful flavor boost to any meal.

Feel free to adjust the vegetables based on your preferences and what's available to you.

Cicah Kari Masam Manis Kelapa (Spicy Sweet Coconut Dipping Sauce)

Prep Time: 10 minutes
Cooking Time: 10 minutes
Servings: 4-6

For the Dip:
- 1 (13.5 oz) can full-fat coconut milk
- 2-3 tablespoons red curry paste (adjust for spice level)
- 1 tablespoon fish sauce
- 1 tablespoon lime juice
- 1 tablespoon palm sugar
- 1 tablespoon soy sauce
- 1 tablespoon minced ginger
- 1 clove garlic, minced
- 1/4 cup chopped fresh cilantro

For the Tropical Garnish
- 1/4 cup (50g) ripe mango, finely chopped
- 1/4 cup (30g) red bell pepper, finely diced
- 1 tablespoon chopped fresh Thai basil

Make the Dip:
In a medium saucepan, whisk together the coconut milk, red curry paste, fish sauce, lime juice, palm sugar, soy sauce, ginger, and garlic.

Heat & Thicken: Over medium heat, bring the mixture to a simmer. Reduce heat and simmer for 5-7 minutes, stirring occasionally, until the flavors meld and the dip thickens slightly.

Remove the pan from heat. aste and adjust seasonings as needed. Stir in the chopped cilantro.

Transfer the dip to a serving bowl. For an optional garnish, create a small mound of the chopped mango and red bell pepper on the side of the bowl. Sprinkle with fresh Thai basil.

Tips:

-Spice Control: Start with 2 tablespoons of red curry paste and taste before adding more.

-Coconut Milk Options: Feel free to use light coconut milk for a slightly less rich dip.

-Leftovers: Store leftover dip in an airtight container in the refrigerator for up to 3 days. Reheat gently on the stovetop before serving again.

Osaka, Japan

Osaka, Japan's culinary heart, pulses with a unique rhythm—a symphony of bold flavors, playful textures, and a relentless pursuit of culinary innovation. This vibrant city, renowned for its vibrant street food scene, serves as a dynamic canvas where tradition meets experimentation. In this section, we invite you to dive into the heart of Osaka's culinary evolution, where classic dishes are transformed with artistic flair and entirely new creations are born from a deep understanding of local ingredients and techniques.

We've curated a collection that celebrates the playful spirit, artful presentation, and culinary intelligence that define Osaka's food culture. You'll discover unexpected twists on familiar favorites, like *takoyaki* reinvented with unique fillings and toppings, and *okonomiyaki* elevated to new heights with unexpected ingredient combinations. We've also delved into the depths of Osaka's culinary heritage, crafting innovative dishes that honor the city's vibrant foodways while pushing the boundaries of flavor and presentation.

This curated collection celebrates Osaka's culinary artistry, showcasing the precision, passion, and playful innovation that define its vibrant street food scene. From evolved classics to bold new creations, each recipe promises to delight and surprise, inviting you on a culinary adventure that tantalizes the senses and awakens the inner gourmet.

Yakitori: A testament to Osaka's mastery of simple yet flavorful grilled dishes, using humble ingredients elevated by precise technique and exquisite seasoning.

Yakisoba: A reflection of Osaka's bustling street food culture, where quick and flavorful stir-fries are a staple for busy urbanites.

Negiyaki with Blue Crab & Shrimp: A luxurious twist on a classic Osaka street food, showcasing the city's innovative spirit and penchant for high-quality seafood.

Negiyaki with Pork Belly, Capicolla & Lardons: A decadent and indulgent take on negiyaki, highlighting Osaka's appreciation for rich flavors and diverse culinary influences.

Sweet Onion, Chili & Garlic Negiyaki Sauce with Sesame: A harmonious blend of sweet, spicy, and savory flavors, exemplifying the complex taste profiles found in Osaka cuisine.

Ribeye Kushikatsu: A testament to Osaka's culinary refinement, elevating humble skewered meat with a crispy panko coating and a flavorful dipping sauce. (Showstopper)

Offal Kushikatsu: A bold and adventurous dish showcasing Osaka's willingness to embrace unconventional ingredients and transform them into delicious street food. (Showstopper)

Okonomiyaki Pork Belly, Choy Sum and Endive Tower: A playful and visually stunning reimagining of the classic okonomiyaki, showcasing Osaka's artistic flair and culinary innovation. (Showstopper)

Clam & Seaweed Takoyaki: A delicate and briny variation on the iconic takoyaki, highlighting Osaka's coastal location and appreciation for seafood.

Spicy Sausage Kimchi Takoyaki: A fiery fusion of Korean and Japanese flavors, reflecting Osaka's multiculturalism and openness to culinary experimentation. (Showstopper)

Shrimp & Sweet Heat Takoyaki: A harmonious blend of sweet and savory flavors, showcasing Osaka's mastery of balanced taste profiles.

Yuzu Watermelon Gazpacho with Pickled Ginger Mignonette: A refreshing and innovative amuse-bouche, blending Japanese citrus with Western culinary techniques.

Sunomono Salad with Radish, Pickled Tomatoes & Sesame Crunch: A vibrant and texturally complex salad, showcasing Osaka's love for fresh, seasonal ingredients.

Roasted Edamame with Pistachio and Balsamic Glaze: A simple yet sophisticated dish, highlighting the delicate flavors of *edamame* with unexpected Mediterranean accents.

Japanese-Style Pear and Sesame Crackers: A delicate and flavorful snack, demonstrating Osaka's appreciation for subtle sweetness and elegant presentation.

Kewpie Potato Salad (Japanese Style): A creamy and comforting side dish, showcasing the ubiquitous Japanese mayonnaise and its unique flavor profile.

Spicy Pickled Walnuts, Garlic, Ginger & Kombu Tsukemono: A tangy and complex pickle, reflecting Osaka's mastery of fermentation and preservation techniques.

Tempura Shiitake with Wasabi Vinaigrette, Toasted Pine Nuts & Citrus Symphony: A harmonious blend of textures and flavors, showcasing Osaka's culinary artistry and appreciation for seasonal produce. (Showstopper)

Miso-Glazed Eggplant with Shichimi Togarashi: A savory and slightly sweet dish, highlighting the umami depth of miso and the complex spice blend of *shichimi togarashi*.

OSAKA MAIN DISHES - STREET

Prep time: 15 minutes
(marinating time not included)
Cooking time: 10-12 minutes
Servings: 4-6

- Skin-on, bone-in chicken thighs, cut into thick chunks (around 1.5 inch pieces)
- 1/4 cup soy sauce
- 1/4 cup mirin
- 2 tablespoons sake
- 2 tablespoons brown sugar
- 1 tablespoon honey
- 1 whole head garlic, roasted until cloves are caramelized
- 1 tablespoon finely grated ginger

Optional garnish:
- Thickly chopped scallions
- Toasted sesame seeds

A+ Yakitori

Combine soy sauce, mirin, sake, brown sugar, and honey in a bowl.

-

Roast garlic head, mash cloves, and add to the marinade with grated ginger.

-

Marinate chicken in the mixture for at least 1 hour (overnight preferred).

-

Preheat grill to high heat (no skewer soaking needed).

-

Thread chicken onto metal skewers and grill for 3-4

minutes per side (until cooked through and charred).

-

Baste chicken with remaining marinade while grilling.

-

Garnish with chopped scallions and toasted sesame seeds.

-

Serve hot and enjoy!

Prep Time: 15 minutes
(marinating time not included)
Cooking Time: 15-20 minutes
Servings: 2-3

- 200g Yakisoba noodles
- 200g boneless, skin-on chicken thighs, cut into thick pieces (around 1.5 inch)
- 1 small onion, thinly sliced
- 1 bell pepper, thinly sliced (any color)
- 1 carrot, julienned
- 1 cup bean sprouts
- 2 cloves garlic, minced
- 2 tablespoons high-heat oil (vegetable or peanut)

For the Sauce:
- 1/4 cup soy sauce
- 2 tablespoons *mirin*
- 2 tablespoons sake
- 2 tablespoons brown sugar
- 1 cup *dashi* (or substitute with 1 cup chicken broth + 1 tsp kelp powder)
- Salt and freshly ground black pepper, to taste

Optional Toppings:
- Aonori (seaweed flakes)
- Katsuobushi (bonito flakes)
- Fried egg
- *Shichimi Togarashi* (Japanese seven-spice powder)

A+ Yakisoba

Boil noodles according to package directions (*al dente*). Drain, rinse, and toss with sesame oil to prevent sticking.

-

In a bowl, toss chicken pieces with a tablespoon of soy sauce, a pinch of sugar, and some freshly ground black pepper. Marinate for 15 minutes while you prepare the vegetables. (Optional step)

-

Whisk together soy sauce, mirin, sake, brown sugar, and dashi (or substitute) in a small bowl.

-

Heat your cast iron pan, or wok, over high heat with a generous amount of oil (coat the bottom).

-

Once the oil is shimmering hot, carefully add the chicken pieces, skin side down. Sear for 2-3 minutes until the skin is golden brown and crispy.

-

Sear chicken (skin-side down) in batches until crispy (juices run clear). Set aside.

-

Add garlic, cook 30 seconds (fragrant).

-

Add onions & peppers, stir-fry 2-3 minutes (softened).

-

Push veggies aside, add noodles & sauce, toss to coat.

-

Add bean sprouts, stir-fry 1 minute (heated through).

-

Return chicken, toss, season with salt & pepper.serving plate.

-

Top with your favorite options like *aonori*, *katsuobushi*, a fried egg, and a sprinkle of *shichimi togarashi* for a touch of heat. (Optional toppings)

Negiyaki with Blue Crab & Shrimp

Prep Time: 15 minutes
Cooking Time: 10 minutes
Servings: 6-8 servings

Dashi Batter:

- 2 cups all-purpose flour
- 1.5 cups strong dashi (homemade or good quality pre-made)
- 2 large eggs
- 2 cups thinly shredded green onions (*negi*)

Blue Crab & Shrimp Filling:

- 1/2 pound cooked blue crab meat, picked clean (around 1 cup)
- 1/2 pound medium shrimp, peeled, deveined, and chopped
- 1 tablespoon olive oil
- 1 clove garlic, minced
- 1/2 red bell pepper, thinly julienned
- 1/4 cup dry white wine
- 1 tablespoon chopped fresh parsley
- Salt and freshly ground black pepper to taste

Toppings (Optional):
- *Takoyaki* sauce (see recipe below)
- Kewpie mayonnaise
- *Aonori* (dried seaweed flakes)
- *Katsuobushi* (bonito flakes)

Dashi Batter:

1. Whisk flour and *dashi* in a bowl until smooth.
2. Add green onions and mix well.
3. In a separate bowl, beat eggs and gently fold them into the flour mixture. Don't overmix.

-

Blue Crab & Shrimp Filling:

1. Heat oil in a pan, add garlic (30 seconds fragrant).
2. Add bell pepper (1 minute softened).
3. Increase heat, add shrimp (2-3 minutes pink & opaque).
4. Deglaze with wine (1 minute scraping browned bits).
5. Add crab, parsley, salt, and pepper (heat 1 minute). Set aside.

-

Cook the *Negiyaki*:

1. Heat a non-stick pan (medium heat), brush with oil.
2. Pour batter, spread into a round pancake.
3. Once batter sets, add filling in the center.
4. Fold batter over filling (half-moon shape).
5. Cook 3-4 minutes per side (golden brown & crispy).

Serve:

Transfer *Negiyaki* to a plate.

Drizzle with *takoyaki* sauce and Kewpie mayo.

Sprinkle with *aonori* and *katsuobushi* (optional).

Takoyaki Sauce

- 2 tbsp concentrated *dashi*
- 2 tbsp *mirin*
- 1 tbsp sake
- 1 tsp rice vinegar
- 1 tbsp soy sauce
- Optional: 1 tsp brown sugar

-

Combine all ingredients (*dashi*, *mirin*, sake, vinegar, soy sauce, optional brown sugar) in a small saucepan.

-

Heat gently over low heat until any sugar dissolves (if using). Don't boil

-

Remove from heat and reserve.

Prep Time: 20-30 minutes
Cooking Time: 20-25 minutes
Servings: 2-3

Negiyaki with Pork Belly, Capicolla and Lardons

The Batter:

- 2 cups all-purpose flour
- 1.5 cups strong dashi
- 2 large eggs, lightly beaten
- 2 cups thinly shredded green onions (*negi*)

The Filling:

Crispy Pork Belly:

- 4 ounces pork belly, thinly sliced (around 1/4 inch)
- 1 tablespoon soy sauce
- 1 tablespoon sake
- 1 tablespoon mirin
- 1 teaspoon brown sugar
- 1 clove garlic, minced
- 1 inch ginger, grated
- splash of Sweet Onion, Chili & Garlic *Negiyaki* Sauce with Sesame (see recipe)
- 1 tablespoon rice vinegar
- Vegetable oil for frying

Lardons:

- 4 ounces thick-cut pork belly, cut into batons (around 1/2 inch thick by 1 inch long)

Capicola:

- 2 ounces capicola, finely diced

Aromatics:

- 1 tablespoon olive oil
- 1 small onion, finely diced
- 2 cloves garlic, minced
- 1/2 cup finely chopped mushrooms (optional, but highly recommended)

Toppings (Optional):

- *Takoyaki* sauce
- Kewpie mayonnaise
- *Aonori* (dried seaweed flakes)
- *Katsuobushi* (bonito flakes)
- Sweet Onion, Chili & Garlic *Negiyaki* Sauce with Sesame (see recipe)

Marinate Pork Belly: Whisk together soy sauce, sake, mirin, brown sugar, garlic, ginger, sriracha, and rice vinegar. Add pork belly slices, coating evenly. Marinate for at least 1 hour, or overnight for maximum flavor.

-

Make Dashi Batter: In a large bowl, whisk flour and dashi until smooth. Add shredded green onions and mix well. Finally, gently fold in the beaten eggs until just combined. Don't overmix.

-

Render Lardons & Sauté Aromatics: Heat a skillet over medium-low heat. Add pork belly batons (lardons) and cook slowly, rendering out the fat and crisping them. Remove and drain on paper towels. Reserve leftover fat in the pan. Increase heat to medium and add a drizzle of olive oil (if needed). Sauté diced onion and garlic until softened. Add chopped mushrooms (optional) and cook until softened.

-

Cook Crispy Pork Belly: Wipe a pan clean (or use a separate one) and heat vegetable oil over medium-high heat. Remove pork belly slices from marinade, pat dry. Sear for 2-3 minutes per side, until golden brown and crispy outside, juicy inside. Drain excess oil.

-

Assemble Filling: In a bowl, combine crispy pork belly slices (cut smaller if desired), diced capicola, cooked lardons, and the sautéed aromatics. Toss everything together gently.

-

Cook the Negiyaki: Heat a non-stick skillet or griddle over medium heat. Brush lightly with oil. Pour a ladleful of batter onto the skillet, spreading it into a round pancake shape.

-

Fill and Flip: Once the batter starts to set, spoon a generous amount of the pork filling in the center. Use a spatula to carefully fold the sides of the batter over the filling to form a half-moon shape. Cook for 3-4 minutes per side, or until golden brown and crispy.

-

Transfer the cooked Negiyaki to a plate and drizzle with *takoyaki* sauce and Kewpie mayonnaise. Sprinkle with *aonori* and dancing *katsuobushi* for an impressive presentation.

-

Drizzle with Sweet Onion, Chili & Garlic *Negiyaki* Sauce with Sesame , or provide on the side. (see recipe)

note

-

Katsuobushi: These are dried, shaved flakes of skipjack tuna. They are a staple ingredient in Japanese cooking, used for their umami flavor and smoky aroma.

'Dancing' *Katsuobushi:* This refers to the visual effect that occurs when *katsuobushi* is placed on hot food. The heat causes the flakes to curl and move slightly, creating a rippling or "dancing" motion.

Sweet Onion, Chili & Garlic Negiyaki Sauce with Sesame

Prep Time: 5 minutes
Cooking Time: 30 minutes

- 1 tbsp avocado oil
- 1/2 tsp toasted sesame oil
- 1 small sweet onion, finely diced
- 3 cloves garlic, minced
- 1 red Fresno chili pepper (seeded and finely minced, adjust for spice preference)
- 1 tbsp tomato paste
- 1/4 cup chicken broth
- 1 tbsp sake
- 1 tbsp mirin
- 1 tbsp soy sauce
- 1 tsp brown sugar
- 1 tbsp rice vinegar
- Pinch of smoked paprika (optional)
- Juice of 1/2 lime (optional, for acidity)
- Salt and freshly ground black pepper

Heat the avocado oil and toasted sesame oil in a pan over medium-low heat. Add the diced onions and cook slowly until caramelized (golden brown and softened), about 15 minutes. Don't rush this step, the caramelization adds sweetness and depth of flavor.

-

Add the minced garlic and cook for another 30 seconds, until fragrant. Be careful not to burn the garlic.

-

Increase the heat to medium. Add the finely minced Fresno chili pepper and cook for an additional minute, allowing the flavors to release.

-

Stir in the tomato paste and cook for a minute, scraping up any browned bits from the bottom of the pan.

-

Deglaze the pan with the chicken broth, sake, and mirin. Bring to a simmer and cook for 2 minutes, letting the alcohol evaporate.

-

Reduce heat to low and add the soy sauce, brown sugar, rice vinegar, and smoked paprika (if using). Season with salt and pepper to taste.

-

Simmer for 15-20 minutes, allowing the sauce to thicken and the flavors to meld. If the sauce becomes too thick, add a splash of water or chicken broth to thin it slightly.

-

Taste and adjust seasonings as needed. A squeeze of fresh lime juice can be added for an optional touch of acidity.

-

Strain the sauce (optional) for a smoother consistency.

-

This sauce can be stored in an airtight container in the refrigerator for up to a week.

-

Notes;
This sauce goes beyond Negiyaki. Here's where it can shine:

Japanese Uses:

Okonomiyaki/Yakisoba: Drizzle thinned sauce for a flavorful twist.

Gyoza Dipping Sauce: Add a touch of sweetness and smokiness.

Donburi Topping: Layer complexity with a small amount of sauce.

Other Cuisines:

Korean BBQ Marinade: Use as a base with a sesame oil twist.

Asian Noodle Salad Dressing: Thin with vinegar and sesame oil for a vibrant option.

Glaze for Grilled Vegetables: Brush for a sweet and savory finish.

Burger Topping: Drizzle for a flavor boost beyond ketchup and mustard.

-

Ribeye Kushikatsu

Prep Time: 20 minutes
Cooking Time: 20 minutes
Servings: 4

- 1 lb *Wagyu* beef or well-marbled ribeye, cut into 1-inch cubes
- Salt and freshly ground black pepper

For the Dipping Sauce:

- 1/4 cup Worcestershire sauce
- 1/4 cup soy sauce
- 2 tbsp rice vinegar
- 2 tbsp brown sugar
- 1/2 cup *dashi* (or substitute with chicken broth)
- 1 tbsp grated ginger
- 1 clove garlic, minced
- Pinch of red pepper flakes

For the Tempura Batter:

- 1 cup all-purpose flour
- 1/2 cup cornstarch
- 1 tsp baking powder
- 1 egg yolk
- 1 cup ice-cold water
- 1 egg white
- Skewers
- Shiitake mushrooms, halved
- Shallots, cut into wedges
- Pickled plums, halved
- Vegetable oil for frying
- *Aonori* (dried seaweed flakes)
- *Katsuobushi* (bonito flakes) (optional)

Marinate the Wagyu beef (or ribeye) in a Yakiniku marinade for 1-2 hours. (see recipe)

-

In a saucepan, whisk all dipping sauce ingredients. Heat until simmering, then remove and cool slightly. Add red pepper flakes (optional).

-

Prepare the tempura batter in two parts: In one bowl, whisk dry ingredients (flour, cornstarch, baking powder). In another bowl, whisk egg yolk with ice water. Gradually add the wet ingredients to the dry ingredients, whisking just until combined. Let the batter rest for 15 minutes. Then, beat the egg white until stiff peaks form and gently fold it into the batter.

-

Thread beef, mushrooms, shallots, and plums onto skewers (assemble).

-

Heat vegetable oil to 350°F (180°C).

-

Dip skewers in the batter, ensuring even coating. Carefully lower them into the hot oil and fry for 3-4 minutes, or until golden brown and crispy. Fry in batches if needed.

-

Remove the fried skewers from the oil and drain on paper towels. While still hot, sprinkle with a touch of additional salt and pepper.

-

Plate the Ribeye *Kushikatsu* and drizzle with the umami-rich dipping sauce. Garnish with *aonori* and dancing *katsuobushi* (optional) for an impressive presentation.

-

Yakiniku Marinade

This flavorful marinade is perfect for elevating your grilled meats, particularly Wagyu beef.

Ingredients:

- 1/4 cup soy sauce
- 1/4 cup mirin
- 2 tbsp sake
- 1 tbsp brown sugar
- 1 tbsp grated ginger
- 1 clove garlic, minced
- 1 scallion, white and light green parts, thinly sliced

Instructions:

1. Combine all ingredients in a bowl.
2. Add your beef cubes or other protein and toss to coat evenly.
3. Marinate for at least 1 hour, or up to 2 hours in the refrigerator, for maximum flavor.

Offal Kushikatsu

Prep Time: 30 minutes (not including marinating chicken livers)

Cooking Time: 15-20 minutes

Servings: 4-6

- 1/2 pound chicken livers, trimmed and cleaned
- 1/2 pound beef tongue, pre-cooked and thinly sliced (available at most Asian grocery stores)
- 1 dozen fresh oysters, shucked (reserve the oyster liquor)
- 8-10 asparagus spears, trimmed
- 8-10 shiitake mushrooms, stems removed
- 8 cherry tomatoes
- 8 quail eggs, hard-boiled and peeled
- 8 cubes of firm tofu, patted dry and cut into bite-sized pieces

Skewers:
- Sturdy metal skewers
- Tempura Batter: (See A+ Ribeye Kushikatsu recipe for instructions)

For the Dipping Sauce:

- 1/2 cup ponzu sauce
- 1/4 cup sake
- 1 tablespoon grated ginger
- 1 tablespoon sriracha (adjust to your spice preference)
- 1 tablespoon mirin
- 1 tablespoon oyster sauce (use the reserved oyster liquor if desired)

For Serving:

- Shichimi Togarashi (Japanese seven-spice powder)
- Aonori (dried seaweed flakes)
- Katsuobushi (bonito flakes)

Soak chicken livers in milk for 15 minutes, drain, and pat dry. Cut thick beef tongue into thinner strips (optional).

-

Prepare a light and crispy tempura batter following the A+ Ribeye Kushikatsu recipe (previous recipe).

-

Assemble skewers creatively, alternating offal, vegetables, tofu, and other fillings.

-

Combine ponzu sauce, sake, grated ginger, sriracha, mirin, and oyster sauce (or liquor) in a saucepan. Heat gently to blend flavors. Remove from heat and reserve.

-

Heat vegetable oil to 350°F (180°C).

-

Dip skewers in batter, coating evenly. Fry in batches: 1-2 minutes for chicken livers/oysters, 2-3 minutes for tongue/vegetables, or until golden brown and crispy.

-

Drain fried skewers on paper towels, cool slightly before serving.

-

Plate skewers, drizzle with dipping sauce. Sprinkle with shichimi togarashi for heat, and add aonori and dancing katsuobushi for presentation.

Okonomiyaki Pork Belly, Choy Sum and Endive Tower

Prep Time: 15 minutes
Cooking Time: 20 minutes
Servings: 2

Batter:
- 1 cup all-purpose flour
- 1 cup dashi stock
- 2 large eggs, whisked
- Pinch of salt

Fillings:
- ¼ pound thinly sliced pork belly (marbled)
- ½ cup chopped choy sum (washed)
- ½ cup thinly sliced endive (white and light green parts)
- Orange zest (freshly microplaned)

Toppings:
- *Okonomiyaki* sauce (see recipe)
- Japanese mayonnaise
- Sesame seeds (black or white)
- Hoisin sauce (optional)

Make the Batter: In a bowl, whisk together flour, dashi stock, eggs, and salt until smooth.

Heat a pan or griddle over medium heat. Add pork belly and cook until crispy on both sides, rendering the fat. Drain excess grease.

Pour half the batter onto the hot griddle, forming a round. Top with half the cooked pork belly, choy sum, endive, and orange zest. Fold the other half of the batter over to enclose the filling, creating a half-moon shape.

Cook the *Okonomiyaki:* Cook for 2-3 minutes per side, or until golden brown and cooked through. Be patient and gentle while flipping to avoid tearing.

Slide the *okonomiyaki* onto a plate. Drizzle with *okonomiyaki* sauce, top with Kewpie mayonnaise, and sprinkle with sesame seeds. Add a drizzle of hoisin sauce (optional) and a finishing touch of freshly grated orange zest.

Okonomiyaki Sauce

- 1 tbsp grapeseed oil
- 1 shallot, finely diced
- 2 cloves garlic, minced
- 1 inch ginger, peeled and grated
- 1/4 cup sake
- 1/4 cup mirin
- 1/2 cup high-quality *dashi*
- 1/4 cup soy sauce (low-sodium preferred)
- 1 tbsp Worcestershire sauce
- 1 tbsp palm sugar (or grated jaggery)
- 1 tbsp concentrated tomato paste
- 1 tbsp rice vinegar
- 1 tsp fish sauce (optional)
- Pinch of red pepper flakes
- Freshly squeezed orange juice (a splash)

1. Heat oil in a saucepan over medium heat. Add shallot, garlic, and ginger. Sauté until softened and fragrant, without browning.

2. Deglaze the pan with sake and mirin, scraping up any browned bits. Allow the alcohol to cook off.

3. Add dashi, soy sauce, Worcestershire sauce, palm sugar, and tomato paste. Simmer for 10 minutes, or until the sauce thickens and reduces by about a third. Adjust seasonings as needed.

4. Stir in rice vinegar, optional fish sauce, red pepper flakes (optional), and a splash of orange juice.

5. The finished sauce should be thick and glossy. If desired, use an immersion blender to achieve a smoother texture.

Tip:
Store leftover sauce in an airtight container in the refrigerator for up to a week.

A+ Takoyaki

Prep Time: 15-20 minutes (not including filling prep time

Cooking Time: 15-20 minutes
Servings: 2-4

Takoyaki Batter:

- 1 cup all-purpose flour
- 1 cup *dashi* stock (or substitute with 1 cup chicken broth + 1 tsp kelp powder)
- 2 large eggs
- Pinch of salt

Filling Options (Choose one):

- **Clam & Seaweed:** Fresh clams and finely chopped *wakame* seaweed add a classic ocean taste with subtle umami, reminiscent of traditional *Takoyaki*.
- 1/2 cup chopped fresh clams (or high-quality canned clams, drained and chopped)
- 1/4 cup finely chopped wakame seaweed

- **Spicy Sausage Kimhi:** Spicy sausage packs a punch, balanced by kimchi's tang and crunch. *Gochujang* adds depth and lets you control the heat.
- 1/2 cup diced spicy sausage
- 1/4 cup kimchi, chopped
- 1 tablespoon *gochujang* Korean chili paste

- **Shrimp & Sweet Heat:** Shrimp stars in this *takoyaki*, its sweetness balanced by onions and garlic. Chili oil brings heat (adjustable!), chives add freshness, and poppy seeds provide a playful textural surprise. (Sophisticated flavors and textures)
- 1 pound jumbo shrimp, peeled, deveined, and finely chopped
- 1/4 cup thinly sliced sweet onions
- 2 cloves garlic, minced
- 1 tablespoon chili oil (adjust to your spice preference)
- 2 tablespoons chopped fresh chives
- 1 tablespoon poppy seeds (well distributed in the final filling mixture)

Whisk flour, dashi, eggs, and salt in a large bowl until smooth. Set aside.

-

Prepare Fillings: Choose your desired filling (Clam & Seaweed, Spicy Sausage Kimchi, or Shrimp & Sweet Heat) and prepare according to separate recipes (not included here).

-

Sauce: Combine soy sauce, mirin, sake, brown sugar, and dashi in a saucepan. Simmer 5 minutes over medium heat until thickened slightly. Adjust consistency with water if needed. Set aside.

-

Heat your takoyaki pan over medium heat, generously greasing the wells with oil.

-

Once hot, carefully pour batter into each well, filling them ¾ full.

-

Gently spoon a small amount of chosen filling into the center of each well.

-

Using a pick or skewer, fold batter edges over the filling to form balls. Rotate frequently for even cooking and browning.

-

Remove cooked, golden brown *takoyaki* from the pan. Drizzle with sauce and mayonnaise, then sprinkle with *aonori* and dancing *katsuobushi*. Enjoy!

Yuzu Watermelon Gazpacho with Pickled Ginger Mignonette (an *Amuse Bouche*)

Prep Time: 15 minutes
Cooking Time: n/a
Servings: 4-6

For the Yuzu Watermelon Gazpacho:
- 2 cups (475ml) seedless watermelon, flesh cut into cubes
- 1/4 cup (60ml) water
- 2 tablespoons (30ml) fresh yuzu juice (or substitute with 1 tablespoon lime juice and 1/2 teaspoon grated yuzu zest)
- 1 tablespoon (15ml) white miso paste
- 1 tablespoon (15ml) mirin
- 1/2 teaspoon (2.5ml) fresh ginger, grated
- Pinch of sea salt

For the Pickled Ginger Mignonette:
- 1/4 cup (60ml) finely chopped pickled ginger
- 1 tablespoon (15ml) finely chopped fresh chives
- 1 tablespoon (15ml) extra virgin olive oil
- Pinch of black pepper

Make the Gazpacho:
In a blender, combine the watermelon cubes, water, yuzu juice (or substitute), miso paste, mirin, ginger, and salt. Blend until smooth and chilled. Strain the mixture through a fine-mesh sieve to remove any solids, if desired, for a silky texture.

Prepare the Mignonette: In a small bowl, combine the chopped pickled ginger, chives, olive oil, and black pepper. Mix well.

Assemble & Serve: For a stunning presentation, use small spoons or shooter glasses. Pour a layer of the yuzu watermelon gazpacho on the bottom. Carefully top with a dollop of the pickled ginger mignonette.

Tips:
- Chilling the Gazpacho: Ensure the gazpacho is well chilled before serving for a refreshing effect.
- Yuzu Substitution: If yuzu juice is unavailable, substitute with a combination of lime juice and yuzu zest as mentioned in the ingredients list.
- Mignonette Variations: You can experiment with different herbs in the mignonette, such as finely chopped shiso leaves for a more pronounced Japanese flavor.
- Compressed Watermelon Option: If you'd like a more compressed watermelon texture, you can explore techniques like wrapping cubed watermelon in cheesecloth and placing a weight on top to extract some moisture before blending. However, the traditional gazpacho approach works well for this recipe.

Sunomono Salad with Radish, Pickled Tomatoes & Sesame Crunch

Prep Time: 10 minutes
Cooking Time: 10 minutes
Servings: 4-6

- 1 large cucumber, thinly sliced
- 1/2 cup (60g) thinly sliced radish (daikon or red radish work well)
- 1/4 cup (60g) pickled cherry tomatoes, halved
- 2 tablespoons (30ml) rice vinegar
- 1 tablespoon (15ml) mirin
- 1 teaspoon (5ml) soy sauce
- 1 teaspoon (5ml) sugar
- Pinch of salt
- 1 tablespoon (15ml) toasted white sesame seeds

Prepare the Vegetables: Thinly slice the cucumber and radish. If using a daikon radish, peel it before slicing. Halve the pickled cherry tomatoes.

Marinate: In a bowl, combine the sliced cucumber, radish, and pickled tomatoes.

Make the Dressing: In a separate bowl, whisk together the rice vinegar, mirin, soy sauce, sugar, and salt. Ensure the sugar dissolves completely.

Combine & Chill: Pour the dressing over the vegetables and gently toss to coat. Cover the bowl and refrigerate for at least 30 minutes to allow the flavors to meld.

Sprinkle the toasted sesame seeds

Tips:
- **Pickled Cherry Tomatoes:** You can find commercially prepared pickled cherry tomatoes at most grocery stores. Alternatively, you can pickle them yourself using a simple vinegar and sugar brine-

1. Boil equal parts vinegar & water with some sugar & *togarashi* (optional).
2. Cool brine & pour over halved tomatoes in jar.
3. Fridge overnight - Pickled!

Roasted Edamame with Pistachio and Balsamic Glaze

Prep time: 10 minutes
Cooking time: 10-12 minutes
Servings: 4-6

- 2 cups (400g) frozen edamame in pods (or shelled)
- 2 tablespoons unsalted butter
- Maldon sea salt, to taste
- 1/4 cup chopped pistachios
- 1/4 cup balsamic vinegar
- 1 tablespoon pure maple syrup

Roast the Edamame:
Preheat your oven to 400°F (200°C). Line a baking sheet with parchment paper. If using frozen edamame in pods, thaw them slightly. Pat them dry with paper towels to remove any excess moisture (Remember, Ramsay hates soggy!). Toss the edamame with a tablespoon of olive oil and spread them out on the baking sheet. Roast for 10-12 minutes, or until slightly browned and crispy.

-

While the edamame roasts, melt the butter in a small pan over medium heat. Once melted, remove from heat.

-

Roughly chop the pistachios using a sharp knife. Aim for a nice, fine consistency, but not a complete dust (No time for food processors here!).

-

Balsamic Reduction: In a separate saucepan over medium heat, combine the balsamic vinegar and maple syrup. Bring to a simmer and cook for 5-7 minutes, or until the mixture thickens slightly and reduces by about half. It should be a nice syrupy consistency, not too thin.

-

Transfer the roasted edamame to a serving dish. Season generously with Maldon sea salt to taste (Let the good ingredients shine!). Drizzle with the melted butter and toss to coat. Finally, sprinkle with the chopped pistachios.

-

Drizzle a TEASPOON (yes, just a teaspoon) of the balsamic reduction on the plate in a swirling pattern for a touch of sweet and tangy magic.

Tips:
- Don't overcook the edamame! You want them slightly browned and crispy, not mushy.
- Don't be shy with the pistachios! This recipe is all about that satisfying crunch.
- Play with the balsamic reduction! You can adjust the amount of maple syrup to find your perfect balance of sweet and tangy.

Japanese-Style Pear and Sesame Crackers

Prep Time: 15 minutes
Cooking Time: 15 minutes
Servings: 4-6

- 1 cup brown rice flour
- 1/2 cup all-purpose flour
- 2 tbsp toasted white sesame seeds
- 2 tbsp toasted black sesame seeds
- 1/4 cup diced Bosc pear
- 2 tbsp white sesame oil
- 2 tbsp soy sauce
- 1 tbsp water (more if needed)
- 1/4 tsp salt
- Pinch black pepper

Whisk dry: Combine flours, white sesame seeds, salt, pepper.

-

Mix wet: Whisk oil, soy sauce, water.

-

Combine: Add wet to dry, mix to soft dough (add water if needed).

-

Fold in pear & black sesame: Gently incorporate pear, sprinkle black sesame on dough.

-

Chill: Wrap, refrigerate 30 min (firms dough).

-

Preheat: Oven to 375°F (190°C). Line baking sheet with parchment paper.

-

Roll & cut: Roll dough 1/4" thick, cut shapes.

Bake: Sprinkle remaining white sesame seeds, bake 12-15 min (golden brown).

-

Cool & enjoy!

Kewpie Potato Salad (Japanese Style)

Prep Time: 15 minutes
Cooking Time: 15-20 minutes
Servings: 4-6

- 2 russet potatoes (about 1 pound), peeled and cut into bite-sized cubes
- 1/4 cup (60ml) frozen peas
- 1 carrot, julienned (thinly sliced into matchsticks)
- 1/4 cup finely chopped red onion (optional)
- 4 hard-boiled eggs, roughly chopped
- 1/2 cup (120ml) Kewpie mayonnaise
- 1 tablespoon (15ml) rice vinegar
- 1 teaspoon (5ml) Dijon mustard
- 1 teaspoon (2.5ml) wasabi paste (adjust to your spice preference)
- 1/2 teaspoon salt
- Pinch of black pepper

Cook the Potatoes:
In a pot of boiling water, cook the potato cubes until fork-tender, about 15-20 minutes. Drain and return to the pot. (Remember, Ramsay wants some texture, so avoid over-mashing!)

Prepare the Vegetables: While the potatoes cook, blanch the frozen peas for a few minutes in boiling water. Drain and rinse under cold water to stop the cooking process. Julienne (matchstick-slice) the carrot and finely chop the red onion (if using).

Using a potato masher, roughly mash the cooked potatoes. Leave some good-sized chunks for a delightful textural experience.

Combine Ingredients: Add the peas, carrots, red onion (if using), and chopped eggs to the mashed potatoes.

Make the Dressing: In a separate bowl, whisk together the Kewpie mayonnaise, rice vinegar, Dijon mustard, wasabi paste (adjust the amount for your desired spice level), salt, and pepper. Ensure the wasabi paste is well incorporated.

Assemble & Chill: Pour the dressing over the potato mixture and gently fold to combine. Ensure everything is evenly coated. Cover and refrigerate for at least 30 minutes to allow the flavors to meld.

Serving Tips:
- Garnish with chopped fresh chives for a pop of color.
- Serve chilled alongside grilled fish, teriyaki chicken, or other Japanese dishes.

Spicy Pickled Walnuts, Garlic, Ginger & Kombu Tsukemono

Prep Time: 15 minutes, total
Cooking Time: 10 minutes, total
Servings: 1-2

- Kombu Tsukemono (high-quality, if possible)
- Pickled Garlic & Ginger (whole cloves)
- Pickled Walnut (finely chopped, a small amount)
- Sesame Seeds (optional)

Important Note: This recipe includes a quick pickling method and may not be suitable for long-term storage. Always ensure proper sterilization techniques for safe food handling.

Arrange *kombu tsukemono* on a plate.

Add whole pickled garlic and ginger cloves for visual appeal.

Sprinkle a small amount of finely chopped pickled walnut for a surprising flavor twist.

Super-Simple Spicy Kombu Tsukemono (Quick Version)

1. Wipe & cut a small kombu piece (3"x4") into thin strips.

2. In a small pan, simmer the kombu strips with 1/4 cup water, 1 tbsp each soy sauce & mirin, and a pinch of sansho pepper (Japanese pepper) for 2-3 mins (softened but chewy). This is your pickling liquid!

3. Let the kombu cool completely in the pan with the pickling liquid.

4. Enjoy! (Store up to 3 days in fridge).

Pickled Walnuts, Garlic & Ginger (Quick Version)

1. Sterilize jars (boil 10 mins).

2. Pack walnuts, garlic & ginger in jars.

3. Boil vinegar, water, sugar, shichimi, & a TINY dab of wasabi.

4. Pour hot brine over ingredients. Seal jars, cool, refrigerate 2+ weeks.

Tempura Shiitake with Wasabi Vinaigrette, Toasted Pine Nuts & Citrus Symphony

Prep time: 20 minutes
Cooking time: 10-12 minutes
Servings: 4-6

For the Tempura Shiitake:
- 4 large shiitake mushrooms, stems removed and caps cleaned
- 1 cup (125g) all-purpose flour
- 1 cup (240ml) chilled club soda
- Vegetable oil for frying

Salad:
- 1/2 cup (75g) fried shallots
- 1 cup (150g) julienned radish (daikon or red radish work well)
- Zest from 1 orange
- 1/4 cup (60ml) pine nuts, toasted

Wasabi Vinaigrette:
- 1/4 cup (60ml) olive oil
- 2 tablespoons (30ml) rice vinegar
- 1 tablespoon (15ml) soy sauce
- 1 teaspoon (2.5ml) wasabi paste (adjust to your spice preference)
- teaspoon (5ml) fresh ginger, grated
- Pinch of salt
- Pinch of black pepper

Prepare the Shiitake: Clean the shiitake mushrooms and remove the stems.

Tempura Batter: In a large bowl, whisk together the flour and club soda until a smooth batter forms. The batter should be slightly thick but still pourable.

Tempura Fry: Heat vegetable oil in a deep pot or wok to 350°F (175°C). Dip the shiitake caps in the batter, coating them completely. Carefully fry the shiitakes for 2-3 minutes, or until golden brown and crispy. Drain on paper towels to remove excess oil.

Wasabi Vinaigrette: In a small bowl, whisk together the olive oil, rice vinegar, soy sauce, wasabi paste, grated ginger, salt, and pepper. Ensure the wasabi paste is well incorporated and adjust the amount for your desired spice level.

Assemble the Salad: In a large bowl, combine the fried shallots, julienned radish, orange zest, and toasted pine nuts.

Just Before Serving: Slice the tempura shiitake into bite-sized pieces and add them to the salad. Drizzle with the prepared wasabi vinaigrette and toss gently to coat.

Miso-Glazed Eggplant with Shichimi Togarashi

Prep Time: 5 minutes
Cooking Time: 4-6 minutes
Servings: 2-3

- 2 eggplants, sliced 1/2" thick
- Oil for grilling/frying
- 2 tbsp each: miso paste, mirin, sake
- 1 tbsp each: brown sugar, water
- Sesame seeds, shichimi togarashi

Grill or Fry: Heat grill/pan. Brush eggplant with oil and cook until tender (grill 2-3 min/side, fry 1-2 min/side).

Miso Glaze: Whisk miso, mirin, sake, sugar, water in a pan. Heat gently until thickened.

Glaze & Serve: Brush eggplant with glaze, sprinkle sesame seeds. Hit it with shichimi and serve.

Mexico City

Mexico City, a sprawling metropolis pulsating with energy, boasts a street food scene as diverse and dynamic as its people. Here, culinary innovation thrives on every corner, where time-honored traditions mingle with a modern sensibility, resulting in a symphony of flavors that both surprise and delight.

In this chapter, we delve into the heart of Mexico City's culinary ingenuity, not by simply replicating classic street eats, but by pushing boundaries and refining them through our idiosyncratic lens of culinary innovation and technique. We've taken beloved staples like *carnitas* and *elote* and infused them with unexpected twists, like the tantalizing sweetness of pineapple in our Pineapple Pork *Carnitas* Tacos and the smoky depth of cast iron in our One Burner Cast Iron *Elote*. We've elevated humble ingredients, transforming *chicharrones* into a crispy, savory canvas for creative toppings and elevating *tlacoyos* with gourmet fillings.

Venturing beyond familiar street food, we've crafted innovative dishes inspired by the rich tapestry of Mexican foodways. From the complex symphony of flavors in Red Mole Boston Butt Tortillas to the sweet-savory-spicy harmony of Guajillo-Braised Turkey Burritos, each recipe celebrates the ingenuity and passion of Mexico City's culinary evolution. Experience the artistry of street food through a modern lens, where every bite is a revelation.

Pineapple Pork Carnitas Tacos: A symphony of sweet and savory, these tacos infuse traditional carnitas with a tropical twist, showcasing Mexico City's openness to culinary experimentation.

One Burner Cast Iron *Elote*: This smoky and charred elote, cooked in a cast iron skillet, elevates a classic street snack with a deeper, more complex flavor profile.

Chicharrones: Crispy, salty, and utterly addictive, our chicharrones take a humble snack and transform it into a gourmet experience with unexpected toppings and flavor combinations. (Showstopper)

***Tlacoyos*:** A canvas for creativity, our tlacoyos feature a blend of traditional masa and innovative fillings, celebrating the versatility of this ancient street food.

Red Mole Boston Butt Tortillas: This dish reimagines the iconic taco by embracing the rich complexity of red mole sauce and tender, slow-cooked pork, creating a culinary masterpiece on a tortilla. (Showstopper)

Burrito with Guajillo-Braised Turkey, Caramelized Plantains, and Chorizo Crema: A symphony of sweet, smoky, and spicy flavors, this burrito takes the humble street food to new heights with unexpected ingredients and refined techniques. (Showstopper)

Mexican-Style Chili Corn Pudding with Roasted *Pepitas*: A comforting and elegant take on traditional esquites, this dish blends the sweetness of corn with the warmth of chili and the crunch of roasted *pepitas*.

Rustic Arborio Rice with Black Beans and Caramelized Plantains: This risotto-inspired dish elevates humble ingredients with creamy arborio rice, earthy black beans, and the caramelized sweetness of plantains. (Showstopper)

Yucatan-inspired Chorizo and Cheese Stuffed Peppers: A fiery tribute to the Yucatan Peninsula's bold flavors, these stuffed peppers are packed with savory chorizo, melty cheese, and a hint of habanero heat.

Citrus-Pickled Red Onions with Jicama & Green Tomato: A refreshing and vibrant appetizer or side dish showcasing the bright, acidic flavors of Mexican cuisine with a modern twist.

Pineapple Pork Carnitas Tacos

Prep Time: 30 minutes, excluding green mole prep

Cooking Time: 45 minutes
Servings: 4-6

Marinate:

- Chopped pineapple (optional)
- Diced tomatoes (optional)
- Garlic, minced
- Achiote paste (or substitute)
- Cumin, ground
- Oregano, dried
- Chipotle chili powder
- Cinnamon, ground
- Salt
- Pepper

Pork:

- 2lbs sliced pork shoulder

Tortillas:

- Flour or corn tortillas

Toppings (Optional):

- Chopped onion
- Cilantro, chopped
- Fresh lime wedges
- Reserved pineapple chunks
- Queso fresco, crumbled
- Guacamole (mashed avocado, lime juice, salt, and pepper)
- Green Mole (see recipe)

In a bowl, combine pineapple (optional), tomatoes (optional), garlic, achiote paste, cumin, oregano, chipotle chili powder (optional), cinnamon, salt, and pepper. Add sliced pork shoulder and ensure it's well coated. Cover and refrigerate.

Sear the Pork (medium heat): Heat a skillet or pan. Cook the marinated pork in batches, avoiding overcrowding, until browned and cooked through (a few minutes per side). Set cooked pork aside.

Warm Tortillas: Warm tortillas directly on the burner flame or in a pan.

Assemble Tacos: Fill tortillas with pork, chopped onion, cilantro, and a squeeze of lime.

Optional Toppings: Add reserved pineapple chunks, crumbled *queso fresco*, or guacamole for extra flavor.

Green Mole

- 1 tbsp avocado oil
- 1 small white onion, diced
- 2 cloves garlic, smashed
- 1 jalapeño, seeded & chopped (adjust for heat)
- ½ cup raw pepitas
- ½ cup cilantro leaves
- ¼ cup parsley leaves
- ½ cup pork cooking liquid (or chicken stock)
- 1 tbsp tomato paste
- Pinch toasted cumin seeds (optional)
- Salt & pepper

1. Sweat the Onion: Heat oil in a pan. Add onion and cook until softened (translucent, not brown).

2. Aromatics: Add garlic and jalapeño. Sauté 1 minute (fragrant, not browned).

3. Toast Pepitas: In a separate pan, toast pepitas until golden brown.

4. Combine & Simmer: Add toasted pepitas, cilantro, parsley, and pork liquid (or stock) to the pan with aromatics. Simmer 10 minutes, reducing liquid slightly.

5. Finish: Add tomato paste and cumin (optional). Season with salt and pepper.

6. Blend: Use a mortar and pestle (preferred) or blender (short pulses) to create a coarse paste.

7. Serve: Drizzle this flavorful sauce over your carnitas tacos. Enjoy!

One Burner Cast Iron Elote

Prep Time: 10 minutes (soaking not included)

Cooking Time: 10-12 minutes

Servings: As many cobs of corn as you like (recipe easily scales)

- Fresh corn on the cob (husks on)
- Real mayonnaise
- Cotija cheese, crumbled (or *queso fresco*)
- Chili powder (smoked paprika optional)
- Fresh limes
- Brown paper lunch bag

Soak corn in husks for 30 minutes in cold water.

-

Rip paper bag pieces to wrap each cob. Lightly dampen the paper.

-

Heat a pan (cast iron preferred) over medium heat.

-

Unwrap a cob, wrap in damp paper (seam side down), and place on the hot pan. Repeat for all cobs.

-

Steam corn for 10-12 minutes, rotating occasionally.

-

Remove hot corn from husks and paper using tongs.

-

Spread mayonnaise on each cob. Sprinkle with cheese, chili powder (smoked paprika optional), and squeeze with fresh lime juice.

Prep Time: 40 minutes
(includes salting time)

Cooking Time: 20-30 minutes
Servings: 4-6

- 2lbs Pork belly (skin on), cut into squares or strips
- Salt
- Lard or vegetable oil
- Paper towels

Optional Seasonings:

- Chili powder
- Smoked paprika
- Cajun seasoning

Chicharrones

Rinse the pork belly skin thoroughly and pat it dry with paper towels. You want it completely dry for maximum crispiness.

Season the pork skin generously with salt. Let it sit for at least 30 minutes to allow the salt to draw out moisture.

In a large Dutch oven, heat lard or vegetable oil to 300°F (use a thermometer).

While the oil heats up, preheat your oven to 200°F.

Fry in Batches (5-10 minutes per batch): Carefully add the pork skin pieces to the hot oil, avoiding overcrowding. Fry for a few minutes per batch until golden brown and curled. Use a slotted spoon to remove them from the oil.

Transfer the fried chicharrones to paper towels to remove excess oil.

Oven-Dry for Extra Crisp (15-20 minutes): Place the fried chicharrones on a baking sheet lined with paper towels. Oven-dry at 200°F for 15-20 minutes to remove any remaining moisture.

Once cool and dry, season with additional salt or your favorite spices like chili powder, smoked paprika, or Cajun seasoning.

A+ Tlacoyos

Prep Time: 30 minutes (mostly for soaking beans and *salsa verde*)

Cooking Time: 37 minutes (includes black bean filling if made from scratch)

Servings: 8 Tlacoyos

Tlacoyo Base:

- 2 cups *masa harina* (corn flour)
- 1 1/4 cups warm water
- 1/2 teaspoon salt

Black Bean Filling:

- 1 cup cooked black beans (rinsed and drained if using canned)
- 1/2 white onion, chopped
- 2 cloves garlic, minced
- 1 chipotle pepper in *adobo*
- Salt and pepper

Toppings (choose your favorites):

- 1 cup crumbled *queso fresco* or ricotta *salata* cheese
- 1/4 cup chopped white onion
- 1/4 cup chopped cilantro
- 1/4 cup chopped parsley
- Sliced avocado (optional)
- *Crema Mexicana* (optional)
- Pickled red onions (optional)

Salsa Verde:

- 6 tomatillos, husked and rinsed
- 1 jalapeño pepper, stemmed and seeded
- 1/4 cup chopped white onion
- 4 cloves garlic, minced
- 1/4 cup chopped cilantro
- 1/4 cup chopped parsley
- Juice of 1 lime
- Salt

Make Black Bean Filling:
If using dried beans: Soak overnight, then simmer with chopped onion, garlic, and chipotle pepper (optional) until tender. Season with salt and pepper. Mash slightly. (To roast for deeper flavour, see notes.)

If using canned beans: Rinse and drain, then mash slightly with seasonings.

Masa Dough:
Combine masa harina, warm water, and salt in a large bowl. Knead until smooth and elastic. Add water by tablespoonfuls if dry.

Form Tlacoyos:
Divide dough into 8 balls. Flatten each ball into a 1/4-inch thick disc.

Place a dollop of black bean filling in the center of each disc.

Pinch the edges of the dough up and around the filling, forming a round, slightly plump shape.

Cook Tlacoyos:
Heat a griddle or skillet over medium heat. Brush lightly with oil (if needed).

Cook Tlacoyos for 3-4 minutes per side until golden brown and crispy.

Salsa Verde:
Boil tomatillos and jalapeño for 5 minutes. Blend with chopped onion, garlic, cilantro, parsley, lime juice, and salt until smooth.

Assemble and Serve:
Arrange cooked Tlacoyos on a platter.

Top with cheese, chopped onion, cilantro, and parsley.

Add avocado, crema, or pickled onions (optional).

Serve with salsa verde on the side.

Notes re: roasting beans.
Roast soaked black beans with spices for 30-40 minutes at 400°F.

Simmer roasted beans with onion, garlic, and chipotle pepper (optional) for 15-20 minutes.

Mash partially, leaving some texture for the filling. Season with salt and pepper.

Traditional *Crema Mexicana* Recipe (with buttermilk)

- 1 cup heavy cream
- 1 tablespoon buttermilk
- 1/2 tablespoon lime juice
- Pinch of salt

Combine heavy cream and buttermilk in a jar or bowl.

Cover tightly and let sit at room temperature for 12-24 hours, or until thickened.

Stir in lime juice (optional) and salt.

Taste and adjust seasonings as desired.

Store in the refrigerator for up to 2 weeks.

Red Mole Boston Butt Tortillas

Prep Time: 40 minutes
(includes salting time)

Cooking Time: 20-30 minutes
Servings: 4-6

Carnitas:

- 4-pound bone-in Boston butt, trimmed (optional)

Rub:
- 2 tablespoons smoked paprika
- 1 tablespoon ground cumin
- 1 tablespoon chili powder
- 1 teaspoon dried oregano
- 1 teaspoon garlic powder
- 1 teaspoon onion powder
- 1/2 teaspoon ground coriander
- Salt and pepper
- 1 tablespoon vegetable oil

Red Mole:

- 4 dried guajillo chilies, stemmed and seeded
- 2 dried ancho chilies, stemmed and seeded
- 1 dried pasilla chili, stemmed and seeded
- 1/2 cup chopped onion
- 4 cloves garlic, minced
- 1/4 cup raw almonds
- 1/4 cup raw pepitas (pumpkin seeds)
- 1/4 cup raw sesame seeds
- 1/4 cup raisins
- 1 small tomato, chopped
- 1 ounce Mexican chocolate, chopped

Spices:

- 1 teaspoon ground cinnamon
- 1/2 teaspoon ground cloves
- 1/2 teaspoon ground allspice
- 2 teaspoons dried oregano
- Pinch of nutmeg (optional)
- 2 cups chicken broth
- 1 tablespoon vegetable oil
- Salt and pepper

Serving:

- Warm corn tortillas
- Chopped fresh cilantro
- Diced white onion
- Crumbled queso fresco
- Lime wedges

Prep Carnitas: Combine rub ingredients. Season Boston butt and coat evenly.

-

Sear Carnitas: Heat oil in a Dutch oven over medium. Sear Boston butt on all sides until golden brown. Remove and set aside.

-

Toast Chilies: In a dry skillet over medium heat, toast chilies for a few minutes until fragrant.

-

Blend Mole Base: Combine toasted chilies, onion, garlic, nuts, seeds, raisins, tomato, chocolate, spices, and 1 cup broth. Blend until smooth.

-

Simmer Mole (Optional): In a saucepan, heat oil and simmer mole sauce 10-15 minutes for richer flavor. (Skip for simpler option)

-

Slow Cook Carnitas: Add remaining broth and seared meat to the Dutch oven. Pour mole sauce over meat. Cover and cook in a preheated oven at 300°F (150°C) for 3-4 hours, or until fork-tender.

-

Shred Carnitas: Remove pot from oven. Shred meat directly in the pot, discarding bone.

-

Serve: Serve carnitas on warm tortillas with desired toppings.

-

Notes:
Boston Butt: Think juicy, flavorful pulled pork. It's the marbled cut from the pig's upper shoulder, perfect for slow-cooking and shredding.

Pork Shoulder: Ideal for *carnitas* or *tacos al pastor*. This is the larger, triangular cut from the lower shoulder, a bit tougher but perfect for braising.

-

Our recipe recommends Boston Butt for *carnitas* because it's the superior cut for shredding:

Marbling: Boston Butt has more marbling (intramuscular fat) than pork shoulder. This fat melts during slow cooking, keeping the meat moist and juicy – perfect for shredding in *carnitas*.

Tenderness: Due to marbling and the specific muscles involved, Boston Butt is naturally more tender than pork shoulder. This makes it easier to shred and ensures a melt-in-your-mouth *carnitas* texture.

Flavor: While both cuts are flavorful, the marbling in Boston Butt contributes to a richer taste profile, ideal for the bold flavors typically found in *carnitas*.

While pork shoulder can be used for *carnitas*, it might require slightly longer cooking for optimal shredding due to its lower fat content.

Burrito with Guajillo-Braised Turkey, Caramelized Plantains, and Chorizo Crema

Prep Time: 30 minutes
Cooking Time: 2- 2.5 hours
Servings: 4 Burritos

Guajillo Braised Turkey:

- 1 bone-in, skin-on turkey thigh (about 1.5 lbs)
- 2 guajillo chilies, stemmed and seeded
- 1 ancho chile, stemmed and seeded
- 1/2 cup chopped white onion
- 4 cloves garlic
- 1 cup homemade or low-sodium chicken broth
- 1 cup dry white wine
- 1 bay leaf
- 1 teaspoon whole black peppercorns
- 1 teaspoon dried thyme
- 1/2 teaspoon ground cumin
- Salt and freshly ground black pepper

Caramelized Plantains:

- 2 very ripe plantains, peeled and halved lengthwise
- 2 tablespoons unsalted butter
- 1/4 cup packed light brown sugar
- 1/4 cup dark rum (optional)

Chorizo Crema:

- 4 ounces Mexican chorizo, casings removed
- 1 cup heavy cream
- 1/4 cup sour cream
- 1 tablespoon lime juice
- 1/4 teaspoon smoked paprika
- Pinch of salt

Assembly:

- 4 large flour tortillas, warmed
- 1 cup crumbled queso fresco or Cotija cheese
- 1/2 cup chopped fresh cilantro
- 1 avocado, thinly sliced
- Pickled red onions (optional)

Braise the Turkey:
Using a sharp knife, carefully remove most of the skin from the turkey thigh, leaving a thin layer for flavor. Season generously with salt and pepper.

In a large Dutch oven, heat a drizzle of olive oil over medium-high heat. Sear the turkey thigh on all sides until golden brown. Remove from the pot and set aside.

-

Toast the guajillo and ancho chilies in a dry skillet over medium heat for a few minutes until fragrant. Soak the toasted chilies in hot water for 15 minutes, then puree with 1/4 cup of the chicken broth in a blender.

Add chopped onion and garlic to the Dutch oven with the remaining oil. Cook until softened, about 3 minutes.

-

Deglaze the pan with white wine, scraping up any browned bits. Add puréed chilies, chicken broth, bay leaf, peppercorns, thyme, cumin, and salt. Bring to a simmer.

-

Return the turkey thigh to the pot, nestling it in the braising liquid. Cover and simmer for 1-1/2 to 2 hours, or until the turkey is very tender and falling off the bone.

-

Caramelize the Plantains:
In a large skillet over medium heat, melt butter. Add the plantains (cut-side down) and cook for 3-4 minutes, or until golden brown.

Flip the plantains and sprinkle with brown sugar. Cook for another 2-3 minutes, or until the sugar melts and starts to caramelize.

-

Optional Flaming Step (for a dramatic presentation): Carefully add the rum (if using) to the pan and tilt slightly to ignite the alcohol. Let the flames subside, then spoon the rum sauce over the plantains.

-

Make the Chorizo Crema:
In a food processor or blender, combine chorizo, heavy cream, sour cream, lime juice, paprika, and salt. Blend until smooth. Taste and adjust seasonings as desired.

-

Assemble the Burritos:
Spread a generous dollop of chorizo crema in the center of each warmed tortilla.

Top with shredded turkey (remove and discard skin and bones), caramelized plantains, cheese, and cilantro.

Add avocado slices and pickled red onions (optional) for extra flavor and texture.

Fold the bottom of the tortilla up and over the filling, then fold in the sides. Roll tightly to enclose the filling.

-

Serve:
Cut the burritos in half and serve immediately. You can garnish with a drizzle of additional crema and a sprinkle of fresh cilantro.

Tips:

This recipe is impressive enough for a dinner party but can also be enjoyed for a satisfying lunch.

Prep time: 30 minutes
Cooking time: 10 minutes
Servings: 4-6

Mexican-Style Chili Corn Pudding with Roasted Pepitas

- 2 cups Corn Kernels
- 1 can (14 oz) Creamed Corn
- 1/2 cup Cornmeal
- 1/4 cup All-Purpose Flour
- 2 Eggs
- 1/2 cup Milk
- 1/4 cup Sour Cream
- 1 can (4 oz) Diced Green Chilies
- 1/2 cup Shredded Cheddar Cheese
- 1/2 cup Cotija Cheese, crumbled
- 1/4 cup Oaxaca Cheese, shredded
- 2 tbsp Chopped Fresh Cilantro
- 2 tsp Chili Powder (recipe below)
- Salt and Pepper to taste
- 1/4 cup Roasted Pepitas (Pumpkin Seeds), for topping

Preheat oven to 375°F (190°C). Grease a baking dish.

Mix all pudding ingredients in a bowl.

Pour mixture into the baking dish.

Bake for 35-40 minutes until set and golden.

Meanwhile, toast *pepitas* in a skillet until browned.

Sprinkle toasted *pepitas* over pudding before serving.

Chili Powder Recipe:
- 1 tbsp Smoked Paprika
- 1/2 tsp Cayenne Pepper
- 1/2 tsp Ground Cumin
- 1/2 tsp Mexican Oregano
- 1/2 tsp Ground Coriander
- 1/4 tsp Ground Cinnamon
- 1/4 tsp Garlic Powder
- 1/4 tsp Onion Powder

Notes on Roasting *Pepitas*:

1. Dry Roast: Spread raw *pepitas* on a skillet over medium heat.

2. Stir Frequently: Stir often to prevent burning and ensure even roasting.

3. Watch Closely: *Pepitas* are ready when golden and fragrant. They can burn quickly is left unattended.

4. Cool Before Use: Transfer to a plate to cool before using.

Following these steps will give you perfectly roasted *pepitas* for your dish.

Prep Time: 15 minutes
Cooking Time: 25-30 minutes
Servings: 4

Yucatan-inspired Chorizo and Cheese Stuffed Peppers

- 4 large *Poblano* Peppers
- 1 lb Mexican *Chorizo*
- 1 cup Cooked Jasmine Rice
- 1 cup Shredded *Queso de Bola* (Edam cheese)
- 1/2 cup *Salsa de Chile Habanero*
- Fresh Cilantro, chopped (for garnish)
- Lime wedges, for serving

Preheat oven to 375°F (190°C).

Char *poblano* peppers over an open flame or broiler until skin is blistered. Let cool, then peel off skin, make a slit, and remove seeds.

Cook Mexican chorizo in a skillet until browned. Mix in cooked jasmine rice and *salsa de chile habanero*.

Stuff each poblano pepper with chorizorice mixture and place stuffed peppers in a baking dish and top with shredded *queso de bola*.

Cover with foil and bake for 25-30 minutes, until peppers are tender and cheese is melted.

Garnish with chopped cilantro. Serve hot with lime wedges on the side.

Simple Salsa de Chile Habanero:

- 4-5 Habanero Peppers
- 2-3 Roma Tomatoes
- 1/2 White Onion
- 2 cloves Garlic
- 1/4 cup Fresh Cilantro
- Juice of 1 Lime
- Salt to taste

Instructions:

1. Blend habanero peppers, tomatoes, onion, garlic, cilantro, and lime juice until smooth.

2. Season with salt to taste.

3. Refrigerate for 30 minutes.

Rustic Arborio Rice with Black Beans and Caramelized Plantains

Prep Time: Overnight soaking for beans + 15 minutes
Cooking Time: 1.5 hours for beans + 30 minutes
Serving Size: 4 portions

- 1 Shallot, finely chopped
- 2 Garlic Cloves, minced
- 1 Fresno Chili, seeded and finely chopped
- 1 Cup *Arborio* Rice
- 4 Cups Low-Sodium Chicken Stock
- 1 Cup Dried Black Beans, soaked overnight
- 1/2 White Onion, diced
- 1 *Chipotle* Pepper in *Adobo* Sauce, finely chopped
- 1 Ripe Plantain, peeled and sliced diagonally
- 2 Tbsp Butter
- 1 Tbsp Jaggery or Brown Sugar
- Pinch of Smoked Paprika
- *Cotija* Cheese, crumbled
- Cilantro, chopped
- Lime Wedges

Prepare Black Beans:
Soak beans overnight, then boil with onion and bay leaf until tender. Mash some beans if desired.

Saute Aromatics: Cook shallot, garlic, and Fresno chili until softened.

Toast Rice: Add *Arborio* rice to pan, toast until slightly translucent.

Cook Rice: Gradually add chicken stock, stirring until absorbed.

Caramelize Plantains: Brown plantain slices in butter, sprinkle with jaggery or brown sugar and paprika.

Combine: Mix cooked beans, plantains, and *chipotle* pepper into rice.

Plate: Serve topped with *Cotija* cheese, cilantro, and lime wedges.

Citrus-Pickled Red Onions with Jicama & Green Tomato

Prep Time: 15 minutes
Cooking Time: 5 minutes
Servings: 4

- 1 Red Onion, thinly sliced
- 1 Lime, thinly sliced
- 1 cup Jicama, diced (optional)
- 1 Green Tomato, diced (substitute with 1 tomatillo or omit if unavailable)
- 1 cup White Vinegar
- 1 cup Water
- 2 tablespoons Sugar
- 1 teaspoon Oregano
- 2 Bay Leaves

In a mixing bowl, combine the thinly sliced red onion, lime slices, diced jicama (if using), and diced green tomato (or substitute).

In a small saucepan, mix together the white vinegar, water, sugar, oregano, and bay leaves. Bring the mixture to a boil, then remove from heat.

Pour the hot vinegar mixture over the onion mixture in the bowl. Make sure all the ingredients are submerged.

Let the mixture cool to room temperature, then cover the bowl and refrigerate for at least 30 minutes, or overnight for best flavor.

Serve the pickled onions with lime, jicama, and green tomato as a tangy and refreshing condiment.

Note:
If green tomatoes are unavailable, you can substitute with tomatillos for a similar tart flavor, or simply omit and proceed with the recipe as usual.

Marrakech, Morocco

Marrakech, a city steeped in history and a crossroads of cultures, has a culinary legacy as rich and diverse as its bustling souks and ornate palaces. Berber traditions, Arab influences, and the echoes of nomadic wanderers have all contributed to the vibrant tapestry of flavors that define Moroccan cuisine.

Centuries of trade and cultural exchange have woven together a unique blend of ingredients and techniques, resulting in a cuisine that is both familiar and exotic. The fragrant spices of North Africa mingle with the sweetness of dried fruits and the savory warmth of tagines, creating a symphony of tastes that tantalize the palate.

In the heart of Marrakech's medina, where narrow alleyways teem with life, street food vendors continue to uphold these time-honored culinary traditions. Their stalls, laden with steaming tagines, sizzling brochettes, and stacks of freshly baked bread, offer a glimpse into the heart of Moroccan food culture.

This chapter pays homage to this rich heritage, while also embracing the spirit of innovation that permeates Marrakech's modern culinary scene. We invite you to explore the flavors of Morocco, from the classic to the contemporary, and discover the magic that unfolds when tradition meets creativity.

Moroccan-Inspired Skewers with Chermoula Drizzle: A vibrant fusion of North African flavors, these grilled skewers capture the essence of Moroccan street food with a fragrant chermoula marinade. (Showstopper)

Grilled Eggplant Salad (Zaalouk) with Charred Peppers and Toasted Spices: A classic Moroccan mezze, this smoky eggplant salad is elevated with charred peppers and a symphony of warm spices.

Moroccan Flatbread: A staple of Moroccan cuisine, this simple yet versatile flatbread is the perfect vessel for scooping up flavorful dips and tagines.

Tomatillo Harira with Crispy Duck and Herb Gremolata: A creative twist on the traditional Harira soup, this innovative recipe blends Moroccan spices with the tangy brightness of tomatillos and the rich flavor of crispy duck. (Showstopper)

Preserved Lemons: A quintessential ingredient in Moroccan cooking, these preserved lemons offer a unique salty, tangy flavor that brightens up tagines, salads, and stews.

Moroccan Honey Glazed Sweet Potato Rounds: A sweet and savory side dish inspired by Moroccan flavors, showcasing the natural sweetness of sweet potatoes enhanced with warm spices and a touch of honey.

Khobz dyal Zraa (Barley Bread): A rustic, wholesome bread deeply rooted in Moroccan tradition, made with simple ingredients like barley flour, yeast, and water.

Harissa-Spiked Carrot & Cannellini Bean Dip with Toasted Pine Nuts: A modern mezze inspired by Moroccan flavors, this vibrant dip balances the sweetness of carrots with the heat of harissa and the creamy texture of cannellini beans. (Showstopper)

Moroccan-Inspired Skewers with Chermoula Drizzle

Prep Time:
15 minutes
(not including marinating time)

Cooking Time: 10-12 minutes
Servings: 4-6

For the Skewers:

- 1 pound boneless, skinless chicken thighs, cut into bite-sized chunks
- 1 pound merguez sausages, casings removed and formed into bite-sized pieces
- 1 red bell pepper, cut into chunks
- 1 yellow bell pepper, cut into chunks
- 1 red onion, cut into wedges
- 1 zucchini, cut into chunks
- 1 pint cherry tomatoes
- Metal skewers

For the Marinade:

- 1 cup whole-milk yogurt
- 1/4 cup extra virgin olive oil
- 2 tablespoons harissa paste (adjust to your spice preference)
- 2 tablespoons freshly squeezed lemon juice
- 1 tablespoon grated cumin
- 1 tablespoon grated coriander
- 1 teaspoon smoked paprika
- 1/2 teaspoon cayenne pepper (optional)
- 1/4 teaspoon ground cinnamon
- 1/2 teaspoon salt
- Freshly ground black pepper
- 1/4 cup chopped fresh mint
- 1/4 cup chopped fresh parsley

For the Chermoula Drizzle:

- 1/2 cup chopped fresh flat-leaf parsley
- 1/4 cup chopped fresh cilantro
- 2 cloves garlic, minced
- 1 tablespoon freshly squeezed lemon juice
- 1/4 cup extra virgin olive oil
- Salt and freshly ground black pepper to taste

Mix yogurt, olive oil, harissa paste, lemon juice, spices, salt, pepper, mint, and parsley in a bowl.

Add chicken, sausage, peppers, onion, and zucchini. Marinate for at least 2 hours (overnight is best) in the fridge.

Preheat grill to medium-high. Thread chicken, sausage, peppers, onion, and zucchini onto skewers.

Brush grill with oil. Grill skewers 10-12 minutes, turning often, until cooked through and slightly charred.

While grilling, blend parsley, cilantro, garlic, lemon juice, olive oil, salt, and pepper into a sauce.

In the last few minutes of grilling, add cherry tomatoes to the grill.

Plate skewers and tomatoes. Drizzle generously with sauce.

Prep Time: 10 minutes
Cooking Time: 40-45 minutes
Servings: 4-6 people

Grilled Eggplant Salad (Zaalouk) with Charred Peppers and Toasted Spices

- 2 large eggplants
- 2 tablespoons olive oil
- 3 cloves garlic, minced
- 1 red bell pepper, roughly chopped
- 1 yellow bell pepper, roughly chopped
- 1/2 red onion, thinly sliced
- 2 large tomatoes, seeded and chopped
- 1 tablespoon freshly squeezed lemon juice
- 1 tablespoon pomegranate molasses (optional)
- 1 teaspoon ground cumin
- 1 teaspoon ground coriander
- 1/2 teaspoon smoked paprika
- 1/4 teaspoon cayenne pepper
- 1/4 teaspoon ground cinnamon
- Salt and freshly ground black pepper to taste
- 1/4 cup chopped fresh parsley
- 2 tablespoons chopped fresh mint
- Extra virgin olive oil for drizzling
- Toasted pita bread or crackers for serving

Preheat oven to 400°F (200°C).

-

Pierce the eggplants in a few places with a fork. Drizzle with olive oil and roast for 30 minutes, or until tender.

-

While the eggplants roast, heat olive oil in a pan over medium heat. Add garlic, peppers, and onion. Sauté for 5 minutes, or until softened.

-

Add chopped tomatoes, lemon juice, pomegranate molasses (if using), cumin, coriander, smoked paprika, cayenne pepper (if using), and cinnamon. Season with salt and pepper. Simmer for 5-7 minutes.

-

Once the eggplants are cooked, remove them from the oven and let them cool slightly. Scoop out the flesh and add it to the pan with the cooked vegetables.

-

Use a fork to mash the eggplant flesh and combine it with the other ingredients.

-

Taste and adjust seasonings as needed.

-

Garnish the dip with chopped parsley, mint, and a drizzle of olive oil.

-

Serve with toasted pita bread or crackers.

Moroccan Flatbread

Prep Time: 10 minutes (mixing dough, doesn't include rising time)

Cooking Time: 4-6 minutes per flatbread
Servings: 8

- 2 cups all-purpose flour, plus extra for dusting
- 1 teaspoon active dry yeast
- 1 teaspoon sugar
- 1 teaspoon salt
- 1 tablespoon olive oil
- 3/4 cup warm water (about 105°F/40°C)
- Olive oil or vegetable oil for cooking

Combine warm water, sugar, and yeast in a large bowl. Let it sit until foamy.

Add flour, salt, and olive oil to the yeast mixture. Mix until a shaggy dough forms. Knead on a floured surface until smooth and elastic (add more flour if sticky).

Form the dough into a ball, place it in an oiled bowl, and cover it with plastic wrap. Let it rise in a warm place until doubled in size.

Punch down the dough and divide it into 8 equal pieces. Roll each piece into a ball.

On a floured surface, roll each ball into a round flatbread, about 1/4-inch thick.

Heat a large skillet or griddle over medium heat with a thin layer of oil.

Place a dough round on the griddle and cook for 2-3 minutes per side, or until golden brown and puffed up.

Wrap cooked flatbreads in a clean kitchen towel to keep them warm. Repeat with remaining dough.

Serve warm with your favorite Moroccan dishes or a drizzle of olive oil and herbs.

Prep Time: 10 minutes
Cooking Time: 40-45 minutes
Servings: 4-6 people

Tomatillo Harira with Crispy Duck and Herb Gremolata

For the Flavor Base:

- 2 tablespoons olive oil
- 1 large onion, finely chopped
- 2 cloves garlic, minced
- 1 tablespoon freshly grated ginger
- 1 teaspoon freshly grated turmeric
- 1/2 teaspoon ground cinnamon
- 1/4 teaspoon cayenne pepper (optional)
- 1 teaspoon paprika
- Pinch of saffron threads
- 1 teaspoon salt
- 1/2 teaspoon black pepper

For the Broth:

- 2 cups chicken broth
- 2 cups homemade duck stock (or substitute chicken broth)

For the Stew:

- 1 cup dried brown lentils, rinsed
- 1 cup dried chickpeas, rinsed
- 4 large tomatillos, husked and halved

For the Duck:

- 2 cooked duck breasts (skin on)
- 1 tablespoon olive oil

For the Herb Gremolata:

- 1/4 cup chopped fresh cilantro
- 1/4 cup chopped fresh flat-leaf parsley
- 1/4 cup chopped fresh mint
- 1 tablespoon lemon zest
- 1 tablespoon olive oil
- Salt and freshly ground black pepper to taste

For Serving:

- Cooked couscous or crusty bread

Heat oil in a large pot and cook chopped onion until softened (about 5 minutes).

-

Add minced garlic, ginger, spices (except saffron), and cook with the onion for another minute, stirring constantly.

-

Pour in chicken broth and duck stock (or just chicken broth). Bring to a simmer, then add rinsed lentils, chickpeas, halved tomatillos, and saffron threads. Cover the pot and simmer for 30-40 minutes, or until the lentils and chickpeas are tender.

-

While the stew simmers, heat olive oil in a separate pan over medium-high heat. Sear the cooked duck breasts skin-side down for 5-7 minutes, then flip and cook for another 2-3 minutes until cooked through. Remove the duck from the pan, let it rest for a few minutes, and then shred it.

-

Once the stew is finished simmering, add the shredded duck meat back to the pot and season with salt and pepper to taste.

-

(Optional) Make the gremolata by combining chopped cilantro, parsley, mint, lemon zest, olive oil, salt, and pepper in a small bowl.

-

Serve the hot stew over cooked couscous or crusty bread. Top with the gremolata if using.

Prep Time: 10 minutes
Cooking Time: n/a
Servings: Makes enough preserved lemons for multiple uses

- 4 Lemons (mix Meyer & regular for best results)
- 1/2 cup Kosher Salt (coarse)
- 1/4 cup Extra Virgin Olive Oil
- 2 Bay Leaves
- A few cracks of Black Pepper
- 1/2 teaspoon Coriander Seeds (whole)
- 1/2 teaspoon Fennel Seeds (whole)
- Pinch of Dried Thyme
- 1 Dried Chili Flake (or to taste)

Preserved Lemons

Scrub & Slice: Wash the lemons throughly. Cut 'em open book-style, leaving the blossom end attached.

Salt & Spice: Pack those lemons with salt, don't be shy! Stuff the cavity with bay leaves, pepper, coriander seeds, fennel seeds, thyme, and the chili flake (if using).

Jar & Oil: Squeeze those stuffed lemons into a jar. Pour olive oil over them, make sure they're submerged.

Seal & Wait: Tight lid on that jar! Stash it away in a cool, dark place for at least 4 weeks, but ideally 6-8 for maximum flavor.

Prep Time: 5 minutes
Cooking Time: 20-25 minutes
Servings: 2-3

- 2 Large Sweet Potatoes
- 2 Tbsp Olive Oil
- 1/2 tsp Ground Cumin
- 1/2 tsp Ground Coriander
- 1/4 tsp Ground Ginger
- Pinch of Smoked Paprika
- Pinch of Cayenne Pepper (optional, for a kick)
- Pinch of Ground Black Pepper
- Salt to taste
- 1/4 cup Honey
- 2 Tbsp Orange Juice (or water)
- Pinch of Ground Cinnamon
- Fresh Chopped Herbs (optional, for garnish) - Try parsley, chives, or cilantro.

Moroccan Honey Glazed Sweet Potato Rounds

Cut the sweet potatoes 1/2 inch thick rounds.

Mix olive oil, cumin, coriander, paprika, salt, and cayenne pepper (if using) in a bowl. Toss the sweet potato slices in the spice mix to coat them well.

Roast: Heat oven to 450°F (230°C). Spread the sweet potatoes on a baking sheet and roast for 20-25 minutes, flipping halfway through, until tender and crispy on the edges.

Honey Glaze: In a small pan, simmer honey and orange juice (or water) for a few minutes until slightly thickened. Add cinnamon (if using) for extra flavor.

Brush the warm honey glaze on the roasted sweet potatoes. Garnish with fresh herbs (optional) and serve.

Khobz dyal Zraa (Barley Bread)

Prep Time: 20-30 minutes
Cooking Time: 25-30 minutes
Servings: a single loaf

- 2 cups barley flour
- 1 cup warm water (approximately, may need slight adjustment)
- 1 teaspoon active dry yeast
- 1 teaspoon sugar
- 1 teaspoon salt

Combine warm water, sugar, and yeast in a small bowl. Let it sit for about 5 minutes until foamy.

-

In a large bowl, combine the barley flour and salt. Add the activated yeast mixture and start mixing. Gradually add more water as needed to form a soft, slightly sticky dough.

-

Knead the dough on a lightly floured surface for 5-7 minutes until smooth and elastic.

-

Place the dough in a lightly oiled bowl, cover with a towel, and let it rise in a warm place for about an hour, or until doubled in size.

-

Punch down the dough and form it into a round loaf. Place on a baking sheet lined with parchment paper.

-

Cover the loaf loosely with a towel and let it rise for another 30-40 minutes.

-

Preheat oven to 450°F (230°C). Score the top of the loaf with a sharp knife.

-

Bake for 25-30 minutes, or until golden brown and hollow-sounding when tapped.

Harissa-Spiked Carrot & Cannellini Bean Dip with Toasted Pine Nuts

Prep Time: 15-20 minutes
Cooking Time: 20-25 minutes
Servings: 2 Cups; 4-6

- 2 large carrots, peeled and roughly chopped
- 1 (15 oz) can cannellini beans, drained and rinsed
- 1/4 cup olive oil
- 3-4 tablespoons harissa paste
- 2 cloves garlic, minced
- 1 whole lemon, juiced
- 1 tablespoon ground cumin
- 1/3 cup chopped fresh cilantro
- Salt and freshly ground black pepper
- 1/4 cup labneh or thick Greek yogurt
- 2 tablespoons toasted pine nuts

Preheat oven to 400°F (200°C). Toss the carrots with 1 tablespoon olive oil, salt, and pepper. Roast for 20-25 minutes, or until tender and slightly browned.

-

Combine beans, remaining olive oil, harissa paste, garlic, lemon juice, and cumin in a food processor. Process until mostly smooth, with some texture remaining.

-

Add roasted carrots to the food processor. Pulse a few times to combine, leaving a slightly chunky texture. Season generously with salt and pepper.

-

Transfer dip to a serving bowl. Top with labneh or Greek yogurt, fresh cilantro, and toasted pine nuts. Serve with warm pita bread, crackers, crudités and/or sliced *Khobz dyal Zraa*.

Lima, Peru

Lima, often overshadowed by the culinary prowess of its Andean neighbors, holds a vibrant and deeply rooted culinary tradition that is ripe for rediscovery. Rooted in ancient Inca practices and enriched by the confluence of Spanish, African, Chinese, and Japanese influences, Peruvian cuisine is a testament to the country's multicultural history.

Traditional dishes like *aji de gallina*, a creamy chicken stew infused with the vibrant *aji amarillo* chili, and *lomo saltado*, a fiery stir-fry born from the fusion of Chinese and Peruvian techniques, reveal the ingenuity and adaptability of Lima's cooks. Hearty stews like *cau cau* and *aji de pallares* showcase the resourcefulness of using simple, local ingredients to create deeply satisfying meals. And the ubiquitous *papas a la huancaína*, potatoes bathed in a creamy, spicy sauce, exemplify the Peruvian love for bold flavors and contrasting textures.

In this chapter, we delve into the heart of these traditional recipes, honoring their authentic roots while adding a touch of modern flair. Expect to find subtle elevations in techniques and presentations, creating dishes that are both familiar and surprising. Alongside these classics, we introduce innovative creations inspired by the diverse flavors and ingredients of Lima's street food scene. Whether it's a playful twist on *arroz chaufa* or a gourmet take on *torrejas de choclo*, each recipe is a testament to Lima's culinary legacy and its potential for modern innovation. Prepare to be delighted by the unexpected as we explore the rich tapestry of flavors that make Peruvian cuisine a true hidden gem.

Ají de Gallina: A creamy, comforting stew where shredded chicken meets the vibrant, slightly spicy aji amarillo pepper, embodying the fusion of indigenous and European influences that define Peruvian cuisine. (Showstopper)

Lomo Saltado (Stir-Fried Beef): A wok-tossed symphony of tender beef, onions, tomatoes, and soy sauce, lomo saltado reflects the dynamic fusion of Chinese and Peruvian culinary traditions. (Showstopper)

Anticuchos de Pescado: Grilled fish skewers marinated in aji panca and lime, these anticuchos offer a lighter, coastal take on a traditional Peruvian street food.

Cau Cau: A creamy potato stew with a rich turmeric hue, showcasing the versatility of humble ingredients and the comforting warmth of Peruvian home cooking.

Arroz Chaufa: A flavorful fried rice dish that reflects the significant Chinese influence on Peruvian cuisine, incorporating soy sauce, ginger, and other aromatic spices.

Papas a la Huancaína: Creamy, spicy, and utterly satisfying, this classic appetizer features boiled potatoes smothered in a vibrant aji amarillo and cheese sauce. (Showstopper)

Ají de Pallares: A hearty stew made with lima beans, aji amarillo paste, and a medley of spices, representing the indigenous roots of Peruvian cuisine and its reliance on local ingredients.

Torrejas de Choclo: Sweet corn fritters, a beloved street food snack, showcasing the natural sweetness of Peruvian corn and the simplicity of traditional frying techniques.

Prep Time: 15 minutes
Cooking Time: 45-50 minutes
Servings: 4-6

Ají de Gallina: Peruvian Poached Chicken in Vibrant Aji Amarillo Sauce

The Poached Chicken:

- 4 boneless, skinless chicken breasts
- 1 onion, quartered
- 2 carrots, roughly chopped
- 1 celery stalk, roughly chopped
- 6 black peppercorns
- 4 bay leaves
- Salt

The *Aji Amarillo*:

- 2 tablespoons olive oil
- 1 onion, finely diced
- 4 cloves garlic, minced
- 2 *aji amarillo* peppers, seeded and finely chopped (start with 2, adjust for spice preference)
- 2 cups chicken broth
- 1 cup heavy cream
- 1/2 cup grated Parmesan cheese
- 1 teaspoon freshly ground black pepper (plus more to taste)
- 1 tablespoon green peppercorns in brine, drained

Finishing:

- Fresh cilantro leaves for garnish
- Cooked white rice or potatoes for serving

Poach chicken breasts with quartered onion, chopped carrots, celery, peppercorns, bay leaves, and salt in a large pot. Cover with cold water, simmer 15-20 minutes (165°F internal temp). Let chicken cool slightly in the poaching liquid.

-

Sauté diced onion in olive oil until softened (5 minutes) in a large skillet. Add minced garlic, cook 1 minute more.

-

Add chopped *aji amarillo* peppers to the skillet and cook for 5-7 minutes, letting their flavor develop (don't burn).

-

Pour in chicken broth and scrape browned bits from the bottom of the pan. Simmer 20-30 minutes, allowing peppers to soften and infuse the broth.

-

Remove simmered broth from heat and let cool slightly. Blend the mixture until smooth and velvety using an immersion blender or regular blender. Season with 1 teaspoon black pepper (adjust later).

-

Return blended sauce to the pot, add heavy cream and grated Parmesan cheese. Whisk until combined and sauce thickens slightly.

-

Stir in drained green peppercorns and adjust black pepper for desired heat. Taste and add more if needed.

-

Shred cooked chicken breasts into bite-sized pieces, discarding any fat. Add shredded chicken to the creamy aji amarillo sauce and stir gently to coat.

-

Serve Ají de Gallina over cooked white rice or potatoes. Garnish with fresh cilantro leaves (optional) for a pop of color. Enjoy the Peruvian flavors with a peppery surprise!

Lomo Saltado (Stir-Fried Beef)

Prep Time: 15 minutes
Cooking Time: 15-20 minutes
Servings: 4 people

- Flank steak: 1 pound, thinly sliced against the grain

Marinade:

- Soy sauce: 1/4 cup
- Red wine vinegar: 1/4 cup
- Aji amarillo paste (or 1/2 tsp powder): 1 tablespoon
- Olive oil: 1 tablespoon
- Garlic (minced): 1 clove
- Cumin: 1/2 teaspoon
- Black pepper: 1/4 teaspoon

Stir-Fry:

- Vegetable oil: 2 tablespoons
- 1 Red onion (thinly sliced)
- 2 Tomatoes (seeded and diced)
- 1 Yellow bell pepper (thinly sliced, optional)
- Aji amarillo pepper (seeded and thinly sliced, optional): 1
- Chopped cilantro: 1/2 cup
- Salt and freshly ground black pepper

Marinate Beef: Combine soy sauce, vinegar, aji amarillo, olive oil, garlic, cumin, and pepper in a bowl. Add steak, coat well, and refrigerate for at least 30 minutes, or up to 2 hours.

-

While beef marinates, slice onion, dice tomatoes, and thinly slice bell pepper and aji amarillo (if using). Chop cilantro.

-

Optional Searing (for enhanced flavor): Heat a grill pan or cast iron skillet with oil. Sear marinated beef strips for 1-2 minutes per side.

-

Stir-Fry: Heat oil in a wok or skillet over medium-high heat. Sauté onion until softened (2-3 minutes). Push onions aside and add marinated beef. Cook for 2-3 minutes per side to desired doneness (beef will continue cooking slightly after removal).

-

Transfer beef to a plate. Stir-fry tomatoes, bell pepper, and aji amarillo (if using) for 3-4 minutes (slightly softened but crisp).

-

Return beef to the pan with vegetables. Add any leftover marinade. Season with salt and pepper.

-

Garnish with cilantro and serve over cooked white rice or french fries.

Anticuchos de Pescado: Grilled Fish Skewers

Prep Time: 15 minutes (excluding marinading time)
Cooking Time: 10-12 minutes
Servings: 4

Fish (choose one):

- 1 pound grouper, cut into 1-inch cubes
- 1 pound mahi-mahi, cut into 1-inch cubes

Marinade:

- 2 tablespoons *aji amarillo* paste (or 1 teaspoon powder + 3 teaspoon Guajillo Chile Paste (see recipe)
- 1/4 cup each: fresh orange juice, fresh lime juice
- 2 tablespoons olive oil
- 2 cloves garlic, minced
- 1 red onion, finely chopped (reserve some for garnish)
- 1 teaspoon cumin
- 1/2 teaspoon each: dried oregano, smoked paprika
- 2 Tbs Chia Seeds
- Salt and freshly ground black pepper

Optional *Aji Amarillo* Glaze:

- 1/4 cup *aji amarillo* paste
- 2 tablespoons olive oil
- 1 tablespoon each: soy sauce, honey, lime juice
- Pinch of salt

Garnish: Chopped fresh cilantro, reserved red onion, aji amarillo slices (optional), lime wedges

Marinate the Fish:
Combine marinade ingredients in a bowl. Add fish, coat evenly, cover, and refrigerate for 2 hours (or overnight for stronger flavor).

Thread fish cubes onto skewers. Cut large cubes in half for easier skewering. Aim for similar-sized pieces for even cooking.

Preheat grill or grill pan to medium-high. Grill skewers for 3-4 minutes per side, or until cooked through and slightly charred. Avoid overcooking to prevent dryness.

Optional Glaze: Whisk glaze ingredients in a small bowl. Brush glaze over the fish during the last minute of cooking for added flavor and shine.

Plate the skewers and garnish with chopped cilantro, reserved red onion and a squeeze of lime for a refreshing touch. Absolutely! Here's a recipe for a Guajillo Chile Paste with Fresh Herbs that you can use for your fish skewers and other dishes:

Guajillo Chile Paste with Fresh Herbs

- 3 dried guajillo chiles, stemmed and seeded
- 1/2 cup water
- 2 cloves garlic
- 1/2 red onion, chopped
- 1 tablespoon olive oil
- 1/2 teaspoon ground cumin
- 1/4 teaspoon dried oregano
- 1 tablespoon chopped fresh cilantro
- 1 tablespoon chopped fresh parsley
- Salt and freshly ground black pepper to taste

1. Rehydrate the Chiles: In a small saucepan, combine the dried *guajillo* chiles with the water. Bring to a simmer and cook for 15 minutes, or until the chiles are softened. Remove from heat and let sit for 10 minutes.

2. Blend the Paste: While the chiles are soaking, heat the olive oil in a pan over medium heat. Add the garlic and red onion and cook until softened, about 5 minutes.

3. Transfer and Blend: Carefully transfer the softened chiles and their soaking water, along with the cooked garlic and onion, to a blender or food processor. Add the cumin, oregano, cilantro, parsley, salt, and pepper. Blend until you get a smooth paste. You may need to add a little more water if the mixture is too thick.

4. Taste and Adjust: Taste the paste and adjust seasonings with additional salt, pepper, or herbs if desired.

Storage:

Store leftover Guajillo Chile Paste in an airtight container in the refrigerator for up to a week. You can also freeze it in portions for longer storage (up to 3 months).

Prep Time: 10 minutes
Cooking Time: 25-30 minutes
Servings: 4-6

Cau Cau: Creamy Peruvian Potato Stew

Base:

- 2 tablespoons vegetable oil
- 1 yellow onion, finely chopped
- 4 cloves garlic, minced
- 1 *ají amarillo* pepper, seeded and finely chopped (or 1/2 teaspoon *aji amarillo* paste, pinch cayenne pepper)
- 1/2 cup chopped fresh cilantro, divided
- 1 cup evaporated milk
- 1/2 cup heavy cream
- 1 cup chicken broth
- Salt and freshly ground black pepper

Vegetables:

- 1 pound yellow potatoes, peeled and cut into bite-sized cubes
- 1/2 cup frozen peas
- 1/2 cup chopped green beans (optional)

Sauté Aromatics:
Heat oil in a large pot or Dutch oven over medium heat. Add onion and cook until softened and translucent (5 minutes). Add garlic and cook for 1 minute more.

-

Add *ají amarillo* pepper (or substitute) and cook for 2-3 minutes, releasing its flavor. Avoid burning to prevent bitterness.

-

Pour in evaporated milk, heavy cream, and chicken broth. Season with salt and pepper. Bring to a simmer, cook for 5 minutes to meld flavors.

-

Add potatoes, partially cover pot, and simmer for 15-20 minutes, or until fork-tender.

-

Once potatoes are nearly cooked, stir in peas and green beans (if using) and cook for 2-3 minutes, or until heated through.

-

Reserve some cilantro for garnish. Stir in most of the remaining cilantro. Taste and adjust seasonings. Ladle stew into bowls and garnish with reserved cilantro.

Arroz Chaufa (Peruvian Fried Rice)

Prep Time: 5 minutes (assuming cooked rice is already available)
Cook Time: 10-12 minutes
Serving Size: 2-3 servings

- Cold, cooked white rice (2 cups)
- Vegetable oil (2 tablespoons)
- Red bell pepper, diced (1)
- Onion, chopped (1/2 cup)
- Garlic, minced (4 cloves)
- Ginger, minced (1 tablespoon)
- Protein (diced chicken breast, shrimp, tofu - your choice)
- Soy sauce (1/4 cup)
- Oyster sauce (optional, 1 tablespoon)
- Egg, beaten (1)
- Scallions, chopped green parts only (1/2 cup)
- Salt & pepper
- Cilantro (optional, for garnish)

Heat oil in a wok or pan (medium-high).

Sauté bell pepper & onion until softened (3-4 minutes).

Add garlic & ginger, cook 30 seconds.

Push ingredients to side, cook protein until browned.

Add soy sauce & oyster sauce (if using), stir-fry 1 minute.

Push ingredients to side, scramble egg in center, then mix in.

Add cold rice, break up clumps with spatula, toss to combine.

Season with salt & pepper, stir-fry 2-3 minutes until heated through.

Mix in scallions, garnish with cilantro (optional).

Serve hot.

Papas a la Huancaína (Potatoes in Spicy Huancaína Sauce)

Prep Time: 15 minutes
Cook Time: 30 minutes
Serving Size: 4

- 8 medium potatoes, peeled
- 1 tablespoon olive oil
- 1 onion, sliced
- 3-4 aji amarillo chiles, halved and seeded (or 1/2 cup jarred *aji amarillo* paste)
- 1/4 teaspoon turmeric (optional)
- 2 garlic cloves, mashed
- 2 cups queso fresco, crumbled
- 1/4 cup vegetable oil
- 2 teaspoons salt
- 1/4 teaspoon black pepper
- 1/3 cup evaporated milk
- 8 lettuce leaves
- 4 hard-boiled eggs, halved lengthwise
- 8 black olives, pitted and halved

Cook the potatoes: Place the potatoes in a large pot and cover with water. Bring to a boil over medium-high heat and cook until tender when pierced with a fork, about 15-20 minutes. Drain the potatoes and let them cool.

Make the sauce: While the potatoes are cooking, prepare the sauce. Heat the olive oil in a medium saucepan over medium heat. Add the onion and cook until softened, about 5 minutes.

Add the *aji amarillo* chiles (or paste) and turmeric (if using) and cook for 1 minute more. Add the garlic, *queso fresco*, vegetable oil, salt, and pepper. Blend the mixture until smooth with an immersion blender or transfer it to a regular blender and blend until smooth. Add the evaporated milk and blend until the sauce is creamy.

Assemble the dish: Slice the potatoes and arrange them on top of the lettuce leaves. Pour the sauce over the potatoes and garnish with the hard-boiled eggs and black olives.

Tips:
-For a spicier sauce, add more aji amarillo chiles.
-If you don't have queso fresco, you can substitute with feta cheese.
-You can also garnish the dish with chopped fresh cilantro.

Ají de Pallares (Lima Bean Stew)

Prep Time: 15 minutes (including soaking time instructions)
Cook Time: 45-50 minutes (soaking time not included)
Serving Size: 4-6 servings

- 1 cup dried lima beans (soaked overnight, at least 12 hours)
- 1 tablespoon olive oil
- 1 white onion, finely chopped
- 3 garlic cloves, minced
- 1 tablespoon *aji amarillo* paste (or 1 teaspoon *aji amarillo* powder + 1/2 teaspoon ground turmeric)
- 1 teaspoon ground cumin
- 1/2 teaspoon dried oregano
- Salt and freshly ground black pepper (to taste)
- 4 cups vegetable broth
- 1/2 cup evaporated milk (or heavy cream for extra richness)
- 1/4 cup chopped fresh cilantro
- 1/4 cup grated Parmesan cheese (optional)
- Sliced avocado (for garnish, optional)
- Cooked white rice (for serving)

Soak the Beans: For optimal results, soak the lima beans in water for at least 12 hours, or overnight. Rinse them thoroughly before proceeding.

-

Sauté the Aromatics: Heat the olive oil in a large pot or Dutch oven over medium heat. Sauté the chopped onion until softened and translucent. Add the minced garlic and cook for an additional minute, allowing the fragrance to develop.

-

Incorporate the *aji amarillo* paste (or substitute), cumin, and oregano. Let them sizzle with the garlic to awaken their flavors.

-

Simmer the Beans: Add the rinsed and drained lima beans along with the vegetable broth.

Season generously with salt and freshly ground black pepper. Bring to a boil, then reduce heat, cover, and simmer for 30-40 minutes, or until the beans are tender but not mushy. Check for doneness with a fork.

-

Creamy Enrichment: For a lighter touch, use evaporated milk. Heavy cream provides richness, but be mindful of the calorie content. Simmer for a few minutes to allow the sauce to thicken as desired.

-

Freshness and Depth: Stir in the chopped cilantro for a burst of freshness that complements the richness. Parmesan cheese adds an optional layer of salty complexity.

-

Serve the stew atop fluffy white rice.

Torrejas de Choclo (Sweet Corn Fritters)

Prep Time: 15 minutes
Cooking Time: 10 minutes
Servings: 4-6

- 1 cup fresh corn kernels (or frozen kernels, thawed)
- 1/2 cup shredded mozzarella cheese (or *queso fresco* for a more authentic flavor)
- 1/4 cup chopped red onion
- 1/4 cup chopped fresh cilantro
- 1 large egg
- 1/3 cup all-purpose flour
- 1/3 cup cornmeal (coarse or medium grind)
- 1/4 cup cooked *kiwicha* (amaranth) or cooked *kañiwa* (canahua) - both ancient Peruvian grains
- 1/2 teaspoon baking powder
- Pinch of salt
- Vegetable oil for frying

Combine corn, cheese, onion, cilantro, egg, flour, cornmeal, cooked grain, baking powder, and salt in a bowl.

-

Heat oil in a large skillet or frying pan over medium-high heat. You want the oil to be hot but not smoking. To test the temperature, you can dip the tip of a chopstick into the oil. If it bubbles rapidly, the oil is hot enough.

-

Make small patties from batter and fry until golden brown (2-3 minutes per side). Drain on paper towels.

Hanoi, Vietnam

Hanoi, the ancient capital of Vietnam, is a city where the past and present intertwine, and its culinary landscape is no exception. A symphony of flavors unfolds on the streets, where fragrant herbs, fiery chilies, and umami-rich broths mingle to create a unique culinary identity. In this chapter, we invite you to savor the essence of Hanoi's street food, a vibrant tapestry woven from centuries of tradition and a modern spirit of innovation.

Unlike its southern counterpart, Ho Chi Minh City, Hanoi's cuisine is characterized by a delicate balance of flavors, with a focus on fresh herbs, subtle sweetness, and a hint of sourness. It's a cuisine that celebrates simplicity and resourcefulness, transforming humble ingredients into dishes that nourish both body and soul.

Our curated selection of seven Hanoi street food recipes offers a glimpse into this vibrant culinary world. You'll find beloved classics like *Bún Chả* (Grilled Pork with Vermicelli Noodles) and *Bánh Mì* (Vietnamese Sandwich), with modern twists that elevate their flavors and presentation. We've also ventured beyond the familiar, crafting innovative dishes inspired by Hanoi's rich culinary heritage, such as the unexpected fusion of dragonfruit and cucumber in our "*Dưa Leo Thanh Long Lạc*" salad.

While Ho Chi Minh City's cuisine is often characterized by its bold, sweet, and richer flavors, Hanoi's culinary traditions lean towards a lighter, more balanced approach. However, both cities share a deep love for fresh ingredients, fragrant herbs, and a vibrant street food culture that is a feast for the senses.

Join us as we embark on a culinary adventure through the streets of Hanoi, where each bite tells a story of history, culture, and a passion for food that is both timeless and ever-evolving.

Bún Chả **with Pickled Peppers and Chiles:** A symphony of textures and flavors, this iconic Hanoian dish showcases the delicate balance of sweet, savory, and spicy notes, with grilled pork patties and vermicelli noodles bathed in a tangy dipping sauce, punctuated by the heat of pickled peppers and chilies.

Beef and Oyster *Banh Mi* **with Deep Roasted Garlic & Chili Paste Sauce:** A playful twist on the classic Banh Mi, this creation fuses Vietnamese street food with a touch of decadence, featuring tender beef, succulent oysters, and a fiery, umami-rich sauce. (Showstopper)

Our A+ *Bánh Gối* **(Crispy Fried Wontons):** These golden, crispy wontons filled with a savory blend of pork and mushrooms offer a delightful taste of Hanoi's rich culinary heritage, where simple ingredients are transformed into irresistible snacks.

Our A+ *Bò Nướng Xả* **(Grilled Lemongrass Beef):** Fragrant lemongrass and a medley of spices infuse these grilled beef skewers with a smoky, aromatic complexity, a testament to the vibrant flavors of Vietnamese street food.

Canh Chua **Hanoi-Style:** This sweet and sour soup, a Hanoi staple, harmonizes the flavors of fresh fish, tamarind, tomatoes, pineapple, and vegetables, embodying the delicate balance of Vietnamese cuisine.

Hanoi-Inspired *Đồ Chua* **Arancini with a Kick:** This fusion dish takes a classic Italian concept (arancini) and fills it with the unexpected, tangy flavors of Đồ Chua, a traditional Vietnamese pickle. The presentation is also unique, making it a standout dish that showcases culinary creativity. (Showstopper)

Sweet, Sour, & Spicy Vietnamese Salad with Peanuts: This refreshing salad celebrates the vibrant flavors of Hanoi, combining fresh herbs, crisp vegetables, and a tangy dressing with a satisfying crunch from peanuts.

Bun Cha with Pickled Peppers and Chiles

Prep Time: 10 minutes
Cooking Time: 15 minutes total
Servings: 4

- 250g each ground chicken & pork
- 100g shiitake mushrooms, chopped
- 50g dried tree ears (or water chestnuts), chopped (soaked if using tree ears)
- 50g bamboo shoots, chopped
- 2 cloves garlic, minced
- 1 shallot, minced
- Seasonings: fish sauce, soy sauce, sugar, pepper
- Oil for cooking
- Rice noodles (cooked)
- Fresh herbs (mint, cilantro, basil)
- Sliced cucumber & carrot (optional)

Make the Patties: Mix all patty ingredients (except oil) and form into small patties.

-

Heat oil in a pan. Cook patties 3-4 minutes per side until golden brown.

-

Divide noodles in bowls. Top with patties, fresh herbs, and veggies (if using).

-

Enjoy with your favorite Nuoc Cham dipping sauce and Pickled Chiles.

-

Authentic Vietnamese Pickled Peppers and Chiles- *Nhanh Gon*

Prep Time: 10 minutes
Total Time: 30 minutes (including pickling time)
Servings: 4

- 1 cup assorted peppers and chilis (red bell pepper, jalapenos, serranos, Thai chilies, etc.), thinly sliced (adjust spice level with chili choice)
- ½ cup rice vinegar
- ¼ cup water
- 1 tablespoon sugar
- 1 tablespoon fish sauce
- 1 garlic clove, thinly sliced
- 1 small carrot, julienned
- 1 small shallot, thinly sliced
- ½ teaspoon whole black peppercorns

Instructions:

1. Combine Wet Ingredients: In a saucepan, combine rice vinegar, water, sugar, and fish sauce. Bring to a simmer over medium heat until the sugar dissolves.

2. Add Aromatics: Remove the pan from heat and add the sliced garlic, shallot, and whole black peppercorns.

3. Pickle the Vegetables: Add the sliced peppers and carrot (if using) to the hot pickling liquid. Let the mixture cool slightly.

4. Transfer to Jar: Transfer the pickled vegetables and liquid to a clean, airtight jar.

5. Pickle: Seal the jar tightly and refrigerate for at least 30 minutes, or preferably overnight, to allow the flavors to develop.

Use a variety of peppers and chilis for a rainbow of colors and a range of spice levels.

You can substitute lime juice for some of the rice vinegar (1 tablespoon) for a brighter flavor.

Prep Time: 10 minutes
Cooking Time: 25-30 minutes
Servings: 4-6

Beef and Oyster Banh Mi with Deep Roasted Garlic & Chili Paste Sauce

Nuoc Cham Sauce:

- 5 dried guajillo chiles, roughly torn (seeds optional for heat)
- 1 inch ginger, peeled and chopped
- 2 cloves garlic, unpeeled
- 1 shallot, chopped
- 1 tablespoon neutral oil (grapeseed or vegetable)
- 1/2 cup water
- 1/4 cup fresh lime juice
- 1/4 cup sugar (palm sugar preferred, but white sugar works too)
- 1 tablespoon fish sauce
- 1 tablespoon light soy sauce
- 1 red bird's eye chili, seeded and finely chopped (adjust for heat)
- 1 clove garlic, minced
- 1/2 red onion, thinly sliced
- 1 tablespoon chopped fresh cilantro
- 1 tablespoon chopped fresh mint

Beef:

- 300g thinly sliced beef tenderloin
- 2 cloves garlic, minced
- 2 tablespoons soy sauce
- 1 tablespoon fish sauce
- 1 tablespoon oyster sauce
- 1 tablespoon brown sugar
- 1 tablespoon vegetable oil

Oysters:

- 200g shucked oysters
- 2 tablespoons cornmeal
- Salt and pepper to taste
- Vegetable oil for frying

Pickled Vegetables (optional):

- 1 carrot, julienned
- 1 daikon radish, julienned
- ½ cup rice vinegar
- ¼ cup sugar
- 1 tsp salt
- 1 red chili pepper, thinly sliced (optional)

Banh Mi:

- 1 baguette, freshly baked
- Mayonnaise (optional)
- Hoisin sauce

Make the Nuoc Cham:
Heat a dry pan over high heat. Add chiles, ginger, unpeeled garlic clove, and shallot. Char them until blackened and fragrant, stirring occasionally. Add oil and cook for another minute. Transfer everything to a pot with water. Simmer for 15 minutes.

-

In a separate bowl, whisk together lime juice, sugar, fish sauce, and soy sauce.

-

Strain the broth from the pot into the bowl with the wet ingredients.

-

Add chopped bird's eye chili (be careful, it's spicy!), minced garlic, and sliced red onion.

-

Let the sauce cool completely. Taste and adjust seasonings with lime juice or sugar as needed. Fold in chopped cilantro and mint before serving.

-

Marinate the Beef: In a bowl, combine thinly sliced beef with minced garlic, soy sauce, fish sauce, oyster sauce, and brown sugar. Mix well and marinate for at least 30 minutes.

-

Prepare the Pickled Vegetables (optional): If using, combine julienned carrot, daikon radish, rice vinegar, sugar, salt, and sliced red chili pepper (optional) in a bowl. Stir well and let pickle for at least 30 minutes, preferably longer.

-

Fry the Oysters: Pat the shucked oysters dry with paper towels. Season with salt and pepper, then lightly coat them in cornmeal. Heat vegetable oil in a skillet over medium-high heat. Fry the oysters until golden brown and crispy, about 2-3 minutes per side. Drain on paper towels.

-

Cook the Beef: Heat vegetable oil in a skillet or grill pan over medium-high heat. Cook the marinated beef slices for 1-2 minutes per side to your desired doneness. Set aside.

-

Assemble the Banh Mi: Slice the baguette lengthwise, but not all the way through. Spread a thin layer of mayonnaise (optional) on one side and drizzle hoisin sauce on the other.

-

Layer the cooked beef slices, fried oysters, and pickled vegetables (if using) inside the baguette.

-

Top with fresh cilantro, mint, and enjoy immediately with the Nuoc Cham dipping sauce on the side. Optionally, wrap the Banh Mi in parchment paper or foil for easier handling.

Tips:

Use high-quality, fresh oysters for the best flavor.

A freshly baked baguette with a nice crust is essential for a perfect Banh Mi.

Adjust the amount of bird's eye chili in the Nuoc Cham according to your spice preference.

Prep Time: 10 minutes
Cooking Time: 15 minutes total
Servings: 4

A+ Banh Goi (Crispy Fried Wontons)

Filling:

- Aromatics: garlic (1 clove, minced), ginger (1 tbsp, minced), galangal (1tbsp, minced)
- 2 cups cooked, ground chicken or turkey (or a combination)
- 2 cups cooked, ground pork sausage (casings removed)
- 1 cup chopped shrimp
- 1 cup roughly chopped scallops
- 1 cup chopped shiitake mushrooms
- 1/2 cup chopped watercress
- 1/2 cup chopped bamboo shoots

Seasonings:
- 3 tablespoons soy sauce
- 2 tablespoons fish sauce
- 1 tablespoon oyster sauce
- Salt, pepper to taste

Sauté Aromatics: Heat oil in a pan over medium heat. Add garlic, ginger, and galangal (if using) - 30 seconds or until fragrant.

-

Add chicken & sausage, cook 2-3 minutes, breaking up meat. Add shrimp, scallops, cook until pink and opaque (2-3 minutes).

-

Add mushrooms, watercress, and bamboo shoots. Cook 2-3 minutes. Stir in soy sauce, fish sauce, oyster sauce. Season to taste. Cool slightly.

-

Assemble & Fry (use store-bought wonton wrappers):

Place filling in wrapper center, brush edges with water.

Fold diagonally into triangle, seal tightly. Repeat.

-

Heat oil in a pan (medium heat). Fry Banh Goi in batches until golden brown & crispy (2-3 min/side).

-

Drain on paper towels and serve.

A+ Bo Nuong Xa (Grilled Lemongrass Beef)

Prep Time: 20 minutes (including marinating time)
Cooking Time: 10 minutes
Servings: 4

Marinade:

- 2 cloves garlic, minced
- 2 stalks lemongrass, white bulb only, minced
- 1 shallot, thinly sliced
- 2 tablespoons fish sauce (adjust to taste)
- 1 tablespoon soy sauce
- 1 tablespoon jaggery, grated (or substitute with palm sugar)
- 1-2 teaspoons powdered seaweed (optional)
- (Optional) Toasted peanuts, finely ground (to taste)
- 1 teaspoon freshly ground black pepper
- 1/4 teaspoon ground coriander
- 1 tablespoon vegetable oil

Beef:

- 1 pound flank steak, thinly sliced against the grain (1/8 inch thick)

Accompaniments:

- Bún (rice vermicelli noodles), soaked according to package instructions
- Lettuce leaves (butter lettuce or romaine)
- Fresh herbs (mint, cilantro, basil, Thai basil - optional)
- Nuoc cham (dipping sauce)

Heat a pan with a little oil over medium heat. Add the garlic and shallot and cook until caramelized, about 3-4 minutes. This adds a deeper flavor to the marinade. Transfer the caramelized garlic and shallot to a bowl with the remaining marinade ingredients (except oil).

-

Add the sliced beef to the marinade and toss to coat evenly. Cover and refrigerate for at least 2 hours, or ideally overnight for maximum flavor.

-

Soak rice vermicelli according to package instructions. Wash and pat dry the lettuce leaves. Arrange the fresh herbs on a platter.

-

Preheat your grill to high heat. Thread the marinated beef onto skewers, making sure the slices are fanned out slightly to prevent curling. Discard any leftover marinade.

-

Grill the skewers for 2-3 minutes per side, or until cooked through to your desired doneness (around 145°F for medium-rare). Use a thermometer for best results.

-

Place some rice vermicelli on a lettuce leaf, add a few slices of grilled beef, and top with fresh herbs. Drizzle with *nuoc cham*.

-

Tips:

Slicing the beef thinly against the grain ensures a more tender texture when cooked.

Adjust the amount of fish sauce to your taste preference.

Toasted peanuts add a nutty flavor to the marinade, but are optional.

Prep Time: 20 minutes (including marinating time)
Cooking Time: 10 minutes
Servings: 4

Canh Chua Hanoi-Style

For the Broth:
- 2 unripe green mangoes
- 1/2 cup dried bamboo shoots, rehydrated and thinly sliced
- 3 tamarind pods
- 1 stalk lemongrass, bruised and toasted
- 2 shallots, thinly sliced
- 2 cloves garlic, minced
- 1/2 inch ginger, thinly sliced
- 1 tablespoon *nuoc leo* (clear fish sauce)
- 8 cups water
- Salt to taste

For the Vegetables:
- 1 cup baby corn
- 1 inch ginger, bruised
- 1 star anise pod
- 1 cup water spinach

For the Protein:
- 1/2 pound white fish fillets (cut into bite-sized pieces) - traditional Hanoi uses freshwater fish like *tra* (catfish) or basa
- 1 tablespoon vegetable oil

For Assembly:
- Thai basil leaves, chiffonade
- Rice paddy herb (*ngo om*), chiffonade (a Hanoi specialty)
- Crispy shallots (recipe below)
- *Nuoc mam* (fish sauce)
- Calamansi limes, wedges
- Crispy Shallots (optional)

Hanoi-Style Broth: Follow steps 1 from the previous recipe, charring the mangoes and simmering them with the tamarind pods, lemongrass, shallots, garlic, and ginger. Instead of sun-dried tomatoes, use the rehydrated and thinly sliced bamboo shoots for a distinct earthy flavor. Season with nuoc leo (clear fish sauce) instead of regular salt for a cleaner taste.

-

Blanch the baby corn and steam the water spinach for 1-2 minutes, just until wilted. This leafy green adds a slightly bitter note that complements the sour broth, a common feature in Hanoi cuisine.

-

Heat vegetable oil in a pan over medium heat. Saute the white fish pieces for 2-3 minutes per side until cooked through and flaky.

-

In a shallow serving dish, arrange the baby corn, water spinach, and cooked fish pieces. Ladle the hot broth over the ingredients.

-

Garnish with a chiffonade of Thai basil and the unique rice paddy herb (*ngo om*), a Hanoi specialty with a slightly peppery aroma. Sprinkle with crispy shallots for texture. Add a touch of *nuoc mam* (fish sauce) for umami depth, and a squeeze of calamansi lime for a final burst of citrus.

-

Notes:
No *ngo om*?

Lime Zest + Chopped Fresh Herbs: Combine lime zest with a small amount of chopped fresh herbs like mint or Thai basil. This provides a combination of citrus and a hint of herbaceousness, mimicking some aspects of *ngo om*.

Nuoc leo is like the refined older brother of regular fish sauce. Made from fermented fish, it undergoes filtration for a crystal clear appearance and milder flavor. Regular fish sauce has a stronger umami punch and a darker color due to the presence of sediment.

-

No *nuoc leo*?

Nuoc leo shines in delicate dishes where a hint of umami is desired without overpowering other flavors. It's a staple in Hanoi-style cuisine for broths and dipping sauces.

Finding *nuoc leo* can be tricky outside of Asian grocery stores. Here's the short-cut:

Substitute: Use regular fish sauce sparingly (half the amount) and taste as you go. Expect a slightly stronger, fishier taste.

Online: Search for "nuoc leo" or "Vietnamese clear fish sauce" from Asian ingredient retailers.

-

No water spinach?
For a well-rounded substitution, combine a leafy green with a hollow stem vegetable. Try Swiss Chard + Celery: Swiss chard provides the bitterness, while celery adds a similar crunchy stem texture.

Hanoi-Inspired Đồ Chua Arancini with a Kick

Prep Time- Đồ Chua: 5 minutes active prep + at least 2 hours resting time (ideally overnight)

Prep Time- Arancini Filling & Assembly: Approximately 20-25 minutes

Cook Time: 5-7 minutes per batch
Serving Size: 12-15 *Arancini*

Đồ Chua (Vietnamese Pickled Carrots & Daikon):
- 1 large carrot, peeled and cut into matchsticks
- 1/2 daikon radish, peeled and cut into matchsticks
- 1 cup white vinegar
- 1 cup water
- 2 tbsp sugar
- 1 tsp salt

Filling:
- 1 cup cooked sticky rice
- 1/4 cup cooked ground pork
- 1 tbsp grated fresh ginger

Arancini:
- 1/2 cup all-purpose flour
- 1 egg, lightly beaten
- 1/2 cup panko breadcrumbs
- Vegetable oil for frying

In a jar, combine carrots, daikon, vinegar, water, sugar, and salt. Seal tightly and refrigerate for at least 2 hours, ideally overnight.

Combine sticky rice, 1/2 cup of the Đồ Chua (drained), ground pork, ginger, and a pinch of salt.

Form small balls of rice mixture, pressing a bit of extra Đồ Chua into the center of each. Seal the rice around the filling.

Dredge each rice ball in flour, then beaten egg, then panko breadcrumbs.

Heat 1 inch of oil in a skillet. Fry arancini in batches until golden brown. Drain on paper towels.

Whisk together *hoisin* sauce, chopped chilies, lime juice, chili oil, rice vinegar, and cilantro.

Arrange arancini on a platter and serve with the dipping sauce on the side.

For the Dipping Sauce:
- 3 tbsp *hoisin* sauce
- 1-2 fresh red chilies, finely chopped
- 1 tbsp lime juice
- 1 tsp chili oil
- 1 tsp rice vinegar
- Handful fresh cilantro, finely chopped

Sweet, Sour, & Spicy Vietnamese Salad with Peanuts

Prep Time: 15 minutes
Cooking Time: n/a
Servings: 4 sides or 2 mains

- 1 cucumber, thinly sliced into matchsticks
- 1/2 cup shredded green mango
- 1/2 cup shredded green papaya
- 1/4 cup bean sprouts
- 1/4 cup thinly sliced red onion (optional)
- 1/4 cup chopped roasted peanuts
- 3 tbsp fresh cilantro, chopped
- 2 tbsp fresh mint, chopped
- 2 tbsp fresh basil, chopped (or Thai basil if available)

Dressing:
- 2 tbsp fish sauce
- 2 tbsp lime juice
- 1 tsp sugar
- 1/2 tsp chili flakes (or more to taste)

Combine cucumber, green mango, green papaya, bean sprouts, and red onion in a large bowl.

Whisk together fish sauce, lime juice, sugar, and chili flakes to create the dressing.

Toss salad with the dressing until evenly coated.

Just before serving, stir in the chopped peanuts and fresh herbs.

Ho Chi Minh City, Vietnam

Ho Chi Minh City, the vibrant heart of Southern Vietnam, is a culinary melting pot where tradition meets innovation, where French colonial influences mingle with the vibrant flavors of Southeast Asia. The city's streets pulse with energy, a symphony of sizzling woks, fragrant herbs, and the tantalizing aroma of street food.

Unlike Hanoi's more delicate flavors, Ho Chi Minh City's cuisine is bolder, sweeter, and richer, reflecting its diverse cultural influences and love for indulgence. Here, you'll find a symphony of tastes and textures, from the rich coconut milk curries to the crispy, savory *bánh xèo* (Crispy Coconut Crepes).

This chapter offers a curated glimpse into the culinary landscape of Ho Chi Minh City. You'll find beloved classics like *Bún Bò Huế* (Grilled Beef Soup) and *Cơm Tấm* (Broken Rice with Grilled Pork) - Ho Chi Minh City Style, reimagined with a smoky twist and modern flair. We'll delve into the comforting warmth of *Canh Thi* (Winter Melon Soup), offering variations to savor in every season. And we'll explore the delicate balance of sweet, sour, and spicy in *Gỏi Cuốn* (Spring Rolls) with a Spicy Peanut Dipping Sauce.

Our curated selection of recipes will take you on a culinary adventure through the city's vibrant food scene, where tradition meets innovation. Discover the bold flavors, unique ingredients, and culinary ingenuity that make Ho Chi Minh City a true foodie paradise.

Our A+ Mi Quang (Turmeric Noodle Soup) - Ho Chi Minh City Style: Unlike Hanoi's lighter broths, this vibrant noodle soup boasts a rich turmeric-infused broth, showcasing the Southern Vietnamese penchant for bolder flavors and a wider array of textures.

Bun Bo Hue with Smoky Twist-(Grilled Beef Soup): A bolder, spicier rendition of the beloved Hue beef noodle soup, infused with a smoky char from grilled beef, reflecting Ho Chi Minh City's embrace of intense flavors. (Showstopper)

Our A+ Com Tam (Broken Rice with Grilled Pork) - Ho Chi Minh City Style: This iconic street food dish features fragrant broken rice topped with succulent grilled pork, a fried egg, and a medley of pickled vegetables, representing the quintessential flavors of Ho Chi Minh City. (Showstopper)

Goi Cuon (Spring Rolls) with Spicy Peanut Dipping Sauce - Ho Chi Minh City Style: These delicate rice paper rolls filled with fresh herbs, shrimp, and pork, served with a spicy peanut dipping sauce, showcase the balance of fresh, vibrant flavors typical of Southern Vietnamese cuisine.

Canh Thi (Winter Melon Soup) with variations for all seasons: This versatile soup, traditionally made with winter melon, is reimagined for year-round enjoyment, showcasing the adaptability of Vietnamese cuisine with seasonal variations.

Bánh Xèo (Crispy Coconut Crepes): These crispy, savory crepes filled with shrimp, pork, and bean sprouts are a testament to Ho Chi Minh City's love for contrasting textures and bold flavors.

Cơm Lam (Bamboo Rice): This aromatic sticky rice, traditionally cooked in bamboo tubes, represents the ingenuity of Vietnamese cuisine and its resourceful use of natural materials.

Prep Time: 15 minutes
Cooking Time: 1.5 Hours
Servings: 4

A+ Mi Quang (Turmeric Noodle Soup) - Ho Chi Minh City Style

Broth:
- 1 whole chicken (about 3 lbs)
- Vegetables: 1 onion, 2 carrots, 1 rib of celery, 4 garlic cloves, 1 inch of fresh ginger, sliced
- Spices: 1 star anise pod, 4 cloves, 1/2 cinnamon stick
- Water
- Salt

Aromatics:
- 1 tablespoon oil
- 1 large shallot, thinly sliced
- 2 cloves garlic, minced
- 1 inch ginger, minced
- 1 stalk lemongrass, white part only, thinly sliced

Soup:
- 4 cups reserved chicken broth
- 1 tablespoon fish sauce
- 1 teaspoon ground turmeric
- ½ teaspoon paprika (optional)
- ¼ teaspoon ground coriander (optional)
- ¼ teaspoon black pepper
- Salt, to taste
- 1 teaspoon sugar (optional)

Toppings:
- Marinated pork belly (optional, recipe below) or cooked shrimp
- 50g (1.75 oz) rice vermicelli noodles, soaked in hot water for 10 minutes, drained
- 1 cup bean sprouts
- Fresh herbs (cilantro, mint, basil) - chopped
- ¼ cup roasted peanuts (chopped)
- Lime wedge
- 1 package (150g) yellow turmeric rice noodles (or regular rice noodles)

Combine chicken, vegetables, spices, and water in a pot. Bring to a boil, then simmer for 1.5 hours (or until chicken is cooked). Strain, season with salt.

-

Optional Pork Belly Marinade: Follow separate recipe (recommended for extra flavor) or simply cook shrimp.

-

Sauté shallot, garlic, ginger, lemongrass in oil.

-

Combine broth, aromatics, fish sauce, turmeric, paprika (optional), coriander (optional), and pepper. Simmer 10 minutes. Adjust seasonings with salt and sugar (optional) to taste.

-

Cook shrimp separately. Sear pork belly or shrimp (if using). Cook noodles according to package directions.

-

Assemble: Place noodles in bowls. Top with shrimp/pork, broth, bean sprouts, herbs, peanuts. Squeeze lime wedge over soup.

Bun Bo Hue with Smoky Twist- (Grilled Beef Soup)

Prep Time: 15 minutes
Cooking Time: 1 hour 15 minutes (mostly simmering)
Servings: 4

Broth:

- 1 lb beef bones (marrow bones work well)
- 1 tablespoon oil
- Chopped shallot & ginger
- 1 lemongrass stalk (white part, optional)
- Spices: 1 star anise pod, 1/2 cinnamon stick, 10 peppercorns, 1 bay leaf
- 8 cups water
- Seasonings: fish sauce, sugar, salt

Grilled Toppings:

- 300g, or approx. 3/4lb, thinly sliced beef (flank or sirloin)
- Marinade: oil, soy sauce, brown sugar, black pepper, coriander, chili flakes
- 1 red & 1 yellow bell pepper, sliced
- 1 red onion, cut into wedges
- Optional: sliced chilies for extra heat

Serving:

- Rice vermicelli noodles (soaked for 10 minutes)
- Bean sprouts
- Fresh herbs (mint, basil)
- Lime wedges

Marinate the Beef (while broth simmers): Combine sliced beef with marinade ingredients and let sit for at least 30 minutes (or overnight for best flavor).

-

Brown the Bones:
Heat oil in a pot and brown the beef bones.

-

Sauté Aromatics: Add shallot, ginger, and lemongrass (if using) and cook until fragrant.

-

Add spices, water, and bring to a boil. Reduce heat and simmer for 1 hour, skimming scum occasionally. Strain & season with fish sauce, sugar, and salt.

-

Slice bell peppers, red onion, and optional chilies.

-

Preheat a burner to high heat. Sear the marinated beef strips for 1-2 minutes per side to desired doneness. Alternatively, use a grill pan.

-

Use a separate burner or grill pan to char the bell peppers, onion wedges, and optional chilies.

-

In bowls, combine noodles and bean sprouts. Ladle hot broth over them.

-

Arrange grilled beef and charred vegetables on top. Garnish with fresh herbs and a squeeze of lime.

-

Technique for Achieving Smoky Flavours:

Charred Scallions: You can achieve a similar smoky hint by charring the scallions (white and light green parts) over an open flame or grill pan until slightly blackened. Then add them to the broth with the other aromatics.

Smoked Paprika: A sprinkle of smoked paprika (½ teaspoon or to taste) added with the other spices can also impart a smoky note to the broth, though the flavor will be slightly different from cold smoking.

-

Smoking Gun: This is a handheld device that produces cold smoke, perfect for infusing delicate ingredients like aromatics without cooking them.

To smoke lemongrass with a Smoking Gun for Bun Bo Hue:

1. Prep: Wash, dry lemongrass stalk. Cut into 1-2 inch pieces.

2. Smoke the Lemongrass: Place the lemongrass pieces in a separate chamber (usually above the wood chips) and smoke them for a short time (30 seconds to 1 minute) until fragrant.

3. Smoke: Ignite wood chips, smoke lemongrass for 30 seconds to 1 minute (until fragrant).

4. Use: Add smoked lemongrass with shallot and ginger to the broth.

To avoid mishap, be sure to follow all manufacturer instructions when using a Smoking Gun.

A+ Com Tam (Broken Rice with Grilled Pork) - Ho Chi Minh City Style

Prep Time: 20 minutes
(not including marinating time)

Cooking Time: 20-30 minutes total
Servings: 4-6

Rice
- 2 cups jasmine rice
- 1.5 cups water
- 1 tablespoon vegetable oil

Marinated pork

- 500g, or approx 1lb, pork shoulder or belly, thinly sliced
- Garlic, shallot, lemongrass (minced) - 2 cloves, 1 shallot, 1 tablespoon
- Fish sauce, soy sauce, oyster sauce - 1 tablespoon each
- Brown sugar - 1 tablespoon
- Black pepper - 1/2 teaspoon
- Ground coriander (optional) - 1/4 teaspoon

Accompaniments (some optional)

- Fried eggs - 2 eggs
- Shredded pork rind (store-bought or fried from dried pork rind)
- Pickled vegetables (carrots, daikon radish)
- Fresh herbs (mint, cilantro, basil)
- Nuoc Cham dipping sauce
- Toasted shallots (optional)

Marinate the pork: Mix garlic, shallot, lemongrass, fish sauce, soy sauce, oyster sauce, brown sugar, black pepper, and coriander (if using) in a bowl. Add pork and stir to coat. Cover and refrigerate for at least 2 hours, or overnight.

-

Cook the rice: Rinse rice, then cook with water and oil in a rice cooker or saucepan according to instructions.

-

Prepare accompaniments:
Pickled vegetables: Julienne carrots and radish, then soak in hot vinegar, water, sugar, and salt mixture for at least 30 minutes (or overnight).

Shredded pork rind (optional): Soak dried pork rind, then fry until crispy. Shred.

Fry eggs and toast shallots (optional) if desired.

Serve rice with marinated pork, accompaniments, and dipping sauce.

-

Rice Info:

Using Broken Rice: If you can find broken rice, particularly medium-grain, rinse it briefly in a strainer under cold running water until the water runs mostly clear. Add the rinsed rice, 1 1/2 cups of water, and a drizzle of oil to a rice cooker or saucepan.

Follow the cooking instructions for your specific appliance or stovetop method for medium-grain rice. During the last 5 minutes of cooking, lift the lid slightly to allow some steam to escape. This drying step helps prevent the broken rice from becoming mushy and sticking together too much.

-

Substitute with Regular Rice:

If broken rice isn't available, use pulsed jasmine rice. Rinse the pulsed rice briefly and cook it according to package instructions for jasmine rice, adjusting the water amount as needed based on the texture of your rice. Short version:

-

Making Pulsed Jasmine Rice (Broken Rice Substitute):

1. Add jasmine rice (up to 2 cups) to a food processor in batches.

2. Pulse a few times each batch, checking for a mix of whole and broken kernels (no rice flour).

3. Rinse (optional) and cook according to broken rice instructions in your Com Tam recipe.

Prep Time: 20 minutes (including marinating time)
Cooking Time: 10 minutes
Servings: 4

Goi Cuon (Spring Rolls) with Spicy Peanut Dipping Sauce - Ho Chi Minh City Style

Marinade:

- 2 cloves garlic, minced
- 2 stalks lemongrass, white bulb only, minced
- 1 shallot, thinly sliced
- 2 tablespoons fish sauce (adjust to taste)
- 1 tablespoon soy sauce
- 1 tablespoon jaggery, grated (or substitute with palm sugar)
- 1-2 teaspoons powdered seaweed (optional)
- (Optional) Toasted peanuts, finely ground (to taste)
- 1 teaspoon freshly ground black pepper
- 1/4 teaspoon ground coriander
- 1 tablespoon vegetable oil

Beef:

- 1 pound flank steak, thinly sliced against the grain (1/8 inch thick)

Accompaniments:

- *Bún* (rice vermicelli noodles), soaked according to package instructions
- Lettuce leaves (butter lettuce or romaine)
- Fresh herbs (mint, cilantro, basil, Thai basil - optional)
- *Nuoc cham* (dipping sauce)

Heat a pan with a little oil over medium heat. Add the garlic and shallot and cook until caramelized, about 3-4 minutes. This adds a deeper flavor to the marinade. Transfer the caramelized garlic and shallot to a bowl with the remaining marinade ingredients (except oil).

-

Add the sliced beef to the marinade and toss to coat evenly. Cover and refrigerate for at least 2 hours, or ideally overnight for maximum flavor.

-

Soak rice vermicelli according to package instructions. Wash and pat dry the lettuce leaves. Arrange the fresh herbs on a platter.

-

Preheat your grill to high heat. Thread the marinated beef onto skewers, making sure the slices are fanned out slightly to prevent curling. Discard any leftover marinade.

-

Grill the skewers for 2-3 minutes per side, or until cooked through to your desired doneness (around 145°F for medium-rare). Use a thermometer for best results.

-

Place some rice vermicelli on a lettuce leaf, add a few slices of grilled beef, and top with fresh herbs. Drizzle with *nuoc cham*.

-

Tips:

Slicing the beef thinly against the grain ensures a more tender texture when cooked.

Adjust the amount of fish sauce to your taste preference.

Toasted peanuts add a nutty flavor to the marinade, but are optional.

Prep Time: 10 minutes
Cook Time: 20-25 minutes
Serving Size: 4 servings

Canh Thi (Winter Melon Soup)

- 4 cups vegetable broth
- 2 cups peeled and chopped winter melon
- 1 carrot, julienned
- 1/2 cup sliced mushrooms (white, shiitake, or your preference)
- 1 tablespoon vegetable oil
- 1 shallot, thinly sliced
- 2 cloves garlic, minced
- 1 teaspoon salt
- 1/2 teaspoon freshly ground black pepper
- Chopped fresh herbs (cilantro, scallions - for garnish)

With this versatile recipe, you can enjoy *Canh Thi* all year round, making it a staple in your healthy and flavorful meal rotation.

Heat the vegetable oil in a pot over medium heat. Add the shallot and cook until softened, about 3 minutes.

Add the garlic and cook for another minute, releasing its fragrance.

Add the chopped winter melon, carrot, and mushrooms. Saute for 2-3 minutes, allowing the vegetables to soften slightly.

Pour in the vegetable broth, season with salt and pepper, and bring to a boil.

Reduce heat and simmer for 15-20 minutes, or until the vegetables are tender.

Taste and adjust seasonings if needed.

Turn off the heat and stir in a squeeze of fresh lime juice (optional - for a brighter flavor).

Ladle the soup into bowls and garnish with chopped fresh herbs.

Seasonal Variations:

Winter:
- Stick with the classic winter melon, carrots, and mushrooms.
- Consider adding shredded chicken or tofu for a more substantial meal.
- Include ginger and chilies for a warming kick.

Spring:
- Swap winter melon for green beans, asparagus, or sugar snap peas.
- Add fresh herbs like mint, basil, or cilantro for a light and refreshing touch.
- Consider using a vegetable broth for a lighter base.

Summer:
- Substitute winter melon with cucumber or zucchini for a cooler base.
- Add a squeeze of lime juice or a splash of fish sauce for a bright and refreshing acidity.
- Include shrimp, scallops, or tofu as your protein.

Fall:
- Roast butternut squash or sweet potatoes and add them to the soup for sweetness and earthiness.
- Include spices like cinnamon, star anise, or cloves for a warm and comforting aroma.
- Swirl in some coconut milk or heavy cream for a touch of richness.

Tips:

- Adjust the amount of water depending on your desired consistency.
- Experiment with different vegetables and garnishes to create your own variations.
- Feel free to adjust the spice level by adding more chilies or using a spicier broth.

No Winter Melon?

Using a half and half mixture of daikon radish and yellow squash is a fantastic way to substitute winter melon in your *Canh Thi* soup. This combination offers a great balance of textures and flavors:

Daikon: Provides a mild flavor with a slightly sharper bite, similar to winter melon.

Yellow Squash: Offers a refreshing sweetness and cooks quickly, adding a delightful textural contrast.

Banh Xeo (Crispy Coconut Crepes)

Prep Time:
15 minutes (excluding marinating time)
Cook Time: 10-12 minutes per crepe
Servings: 4

Crepe Batter:
- 1.5 cups brown rice flour
- 0.5 cup tapioca flour (or extra brown rice flour for gluten-free)
- 2 cups coconut milk
- 1 tsp turmeric
- 0.5 tsp white pepper
- Pinch saffron (optional)
- 2 scallions, sliced

Seafood Filling:
- 8 prawns, cleaned, deveined
- 4 baby scallops, cleaned
- 2 oz monkfish tail, thinly sliced
- 1 tbsp Shaoxing wine (or substitute)
- 1 tbsp light soy sauce
- 0.5 tsp white pepper
- Nuoc Cham (Dipping Sauce)
- Mung bean sprouts, rinsed
- Pea shoots (optional)
- Fresh herbs (cilantro, mint, Thai basil) - for garnish (optional)

Batter: Mix brown rice flour, tapioca flour (or extra brown rice flour for gluten-free), coconut milk, turmeric, white pepper, saffron (optional), scallions. Rest batter in fridge (2+ hours, ideally overnight).

-

Seafood: Toss prawns, scallops, monkfish with Shaoxing wine, soy sauce, white pepper. Marinate 30 minutes.
3. Nuoc Cham Twist: Simmer pineapple juice, water, palm sugar, fish sauce, lime juice, chili pepper, garlic. Strain.

-

Heat cast iron skillet. Oil it.

Swirl batter for thin crepe. Add seafood in center.

-

Add oil next to crepe, sear seafood 1 minute per side.

-

Top seafood with bean sprouts, pea shoots (optional).

-

Fold crepe over filling. Cook covered 1-2 minutes until crispy.

Cơm Lam (Bamboo Rice)

Prep Time: 15 minutes
Cooking Time: 30-35 minutes
Servings: 4

- 2 cups jasmine rice
- 1 cup water
- 1/2 teaspoon salt
- 1 stalk lemongrass, white part only, chopped (optional)
- 1 shallot, thinly sliced (optional)
- Banana leaves (optional, for presentation)
- Aluminum foil

Wash and soak the rice:
Rinse the jasmine rice in cold water until the water runs clear. Soak the rinsed rice for at least 30 minutes, or up to an hour.

-

Season the rice: Drain the soaked rice and combine it with the water, salt, chopped lemongrass (if using), and sliced shallots (if using). Stir well to distribute the flavors.

-

Prepare the "bamboo" substitute: Cut squares of aluminum foil large enough to wrap individual portions of rice.

-

Wrap the rice: Place a portion of seasoned rice (around 1/2 cup) in the center of each aluminum foil square. Fold the foil upwards around the rice, creating a pouch with a small opening at the top.

-

Optional Banana Leaf Presentation (if available): Cut banana leaves into squares slightly larger than the aluminum foil squares. Wrap the aluminum foil pouches with the banana leaves, securing them with toothpicks or kitchen twine. This step is optional but adds a traditional touch.

-

Steaming: Place the wrapped rice packets in a steamer basket over simmering water. Steam for 30-35 minutes, or until the rice is cooked through and fluffy.

-

Carefully unwrap the rice packets and enjoy the fragrant *Cơm Lam* with your favorite Vietnamese dishes.

Los Angeles, California

Los Angeles, a city synonymous with reinvention and cinematic dreams, is a sprawling culinary landscape where innovation knows no bounds. The food truck phenomenon, born from a collision of cultures, entrepreneurial spirit, and a hunger for the new and exciting, has evolved into a cornerstone of LA's gastronomic identity. From Kogi BBQ's groundbreaking Korean-Mexican tacos to Coolhaus's architecturally inspired ice cream sandwiches, these kitchens-on-wheels have shattered culinary boundaries and ignited a passion for unexpected flavor combinations.

The history of LA's food trucks is a story of resourcefulness and creativity. In the early 2000s, a wave of ambitious chefs and entrepreneurs, limited by financial constraints and traditional restaurant models, took to the streets, transforming humble trucks into mobile culinary laboratories. This democratization of fine dining allowed for bold experimentation, resulting in a culinary revolution that transformed LA's street food scene.

Inspired by this spirit of culinary audacity, our chefs have embraced the "anything goes" mentality of LA's food trucks, pushing the boundaries of flavor and creating a collection of truly unique dishes. While not replicating specific food truck creations, we've channeled the city's boundless creativity to develop unexpected and exhilarating culinary mashups. Each recipe is a testament to the power of culinary fusion, showcasing the harmonious marriage of seemingly disparate ingredients and techniques.

Hokkaido-Inspired Tempura & Roe with Pear Fusion Tortillas: This dish is a showstopper due to its innovative fusion of Japanese and Mexican culinary traditions. Crispy tempura-battered tortillas are generously topped with delicate roe and sweet pear slices, offering a surprising yet harmonious blend of textures and flavors. (Showstopper)

Burmese Bowl with Duck: A vibrant tapestry of Burmese flavors and textures, this bowl showcases tender duck curry alongside fragrant coconut rice and a colorful array of pickled vegetables, inviting a culinary adventure into Southeast Asia's rich culinary heritage.

Ethiopian Chicken & Berbere Fusion Burrito: This dish boldly combines the rich spices of Ethiopian cuisine with the familiar comfort of a burrito, resulting in a unique and flavorful experience that is sure to surprise and delight. (Showstopper)

The Krimson Karenderia: A California Filipino Fusion Burrito: This innovative burrito, inspired by the vibrant food truck culture of Los Angeles, fuses Filipino flavors like *adobo* and *Recado* Paste with the fresh, vibrant ingredients of California cuisine. (Showstopper)

Joojeh, Stone Fruit & Grilled Serrano Skewers with Dual Dips: A symphony of sweet, savory, and spicy notes, these grilled skewers pay homage to Persian culinary traditions while embracing the global flavors of stone fruit and chiles, accompanied by a vibrant duo of dipping sauces. (Showstopper)

Yuzu Kosho Brussels Sprouts: A tantalizing combination of East and West, these crispy Brussels sprouts, tossed in a zesty yuzu kosho sauce, deliver a unique and unexpected flavor experience.

Kimchi Gazpacho: This unexpected combination of Korean kimchi and Spanish gazpacho creates a refreshing and tangy cold soup with a spicy kick, showcasing the versatility of fermented flavors and global culinary influences. (Showstopper)

Prep Time: 25 minutes
Cooking Time: 15 minutes
Servings: 4

Hokkaido-Inspired Tempura & Roe with Pear Fusion Tortillas

For the Tempura Batter:
- 1 cup all-purpose flour
- 1/2 cup cornstarch
- 1/2 teaspoon baking powder
- 1 cup cold water (plus extra if needed)

For the Tempura Vegetables:
- 1 cup assorted vegetables (such as asparagus spears, thinly sliced sweet potato, maitake mushrooms)
- 1 Japanese pear (or 1 Bartlett pear if unavailable), julienned very thinly
- 1/2 pound (225 g) shrimp, cleaned and deveined (or scallops, sliced)
- Vegetable oil for frying

For the Yuzu Kosho Mayo:
- 1/4 cup mayonnaise
- 1-2 teaspoons yuzu kosho (Japanese citrus chili paste) - adjust to your spice preference
- 1 tablespoon soy sauce
- 1 tablespoon toasted sesame seeds

For Serving:
- 8 small corn tortillas, warmed
- Pickled vegetables (such as julienned carrots, daikon radish)
- Fresh cilantro or shiso leaves (optional)
- Lime wedges
- vegetable, salmon or flying fish roe (tobilko)

Prep:
1. Batter: Mix flour, cornstarch, baking powder in a bowl. Slowly whisk in cold water until smooth and slightly thick. Let it rest for 15 minutes.

2. Veggies & Seafood: Cut asparagus, sweet potato, mushrooms into bite-size pieces. Julienne the pear thinly. Pat shrimp (or scallops) dry.

3. Heat Oil: Heat enough oil in a pot to 350°F (175°C).

-

Tempura:
1. Dip each veggie, pear piece, and seafood in batter.

2. Carefully fry them in hot oil for 1-2 minutes until golden brown and crispy. Watch pear and seafood as they cook faster. Drain on paper towels.

-

Sauce & Toppings:
1. Mix mayonnaise, yuzu kosho (start with 1 tsp, adjust for spice), and soy sauce.

2. Warm tortillas.

-

Assemble & Serve:
1. Put some tempura veggies, pear, and seafood on each tortilla.

2. Top with yuzu kosho mayo, sesame seeds, pickled veggies. Gently place 1/2 teaspoon of roe across the top of the filling.

3. Garnish with cilantro or shiso leaves (optional).

4. Squeeze fresh lime juice on top before serving.

Burmese Bowl with Duck

Prep Time: 15-20 minutes
Cooking Time: 25-30 minutes
Servings: 2

For the Fragrant Burmese Curry:

- 1 tablespoon vegetable oil
- 1 shallot, thinly sliced
- 1 inch ginger, peeled and minced
- 1 garlic clove, minced
- 1/2 teaspoon turmeric powder
- 1/4 teaspoon ground coriander
- 1/4 teaspoon ground cumin
- 1 tablespoon sambal oelek (adjust for spice preference)
- 1 (13.5 oz) can coconut milk
- 1/2 cup vegetable broth
- 1 tablespoon soy sauce
- 1 tablespoon brown sugar
- 1/2 cup cooked chickpeas
- 1 cup shredded cooked duck (skin optional, for extra richness)
- Salt and freshly ground black pepper to taste

For the Crispy Shallots:
- 1 shallot, thinly sliced
- Vegetable oil for frying

For the Burmese Bowl Assembly:
- 2 cups cooked jasmine rice
- 1/2 cup shredded red cabbage
- 1/4 cup thinly julienned carrots
- 1/4 cup chopped fresh cilantro
- 1/4 cup chopped fresh mint
- Lime wedges
- Optional: Toasted peanuts, a drizzle of toasted sesame oil

In a large pot, heat oil over medium heat. Add sliced shallot and cook until softened (3 minutes). Stir in ginger and garlic, cook for another minute.

-

Add sambal oelek (adjust for spice).

-

Add turmeric, coriander, and cumin. Cook for 30 seconds, stirring constantly.

-

Pour in coconut milk and broth. Simmer for 5 minutes, then stir in soy sauce and brown sugar.

-

Add chickpeas and duck (or chicken). Season with salt and pepper. Simmer 10-15 minutes.

-

While the curry simmers, heat oil in a small pan. Fry thinly sliced shallots until golden brown and crispy. Drain on paper towels.

-

Divide cooked rice between bowls. Top with curry, shredded cabbage, julienned carrots, cilantro, and mint.

-

Sprinkle with crispy shallots, lime juice (optional: toasted peanuts, sesame oil, fried egg).

Ethiopian Chicken & Berbere Fusion Burrito

Prep Time: 30-45 minutes
Cooking Time: 45 minutes total
Marinating Time: At least 30 minutes, ideally overnight

Servings: 4-6

- 1 lb boneless, skinless chicken thighs or breasts, cut into 1-inch pieces
- Berbere spice mix (store-bought or homemade)
- Olive oil
- 1 onion, diced
- 1 red bell pepper, diced
- 1 carrot, diced
- 2 cloves garlic, minced
- 1 (15oz) can diced tomatoes, undrained
- 1 (15oz) can pinto beans, drained and rinsed
- 1 cup chicken broth
- 1/2 cup cooked chickpeas
- 1/2 cup chopped green beans
- 1/4 cup chopped fresh cilantro
- 1/4 cup chopped fresh mint
- 1/4 cup dried currants
- 1/4 cup toasted pine nuts
- 1/4 cup crumbled feta cheese
- 1/4 cup diced red onion
- 1/2 avocado, sliced (optional)
- Tortillas (warmed)

Spiced Yogurt:

- 1/2 cup plain yogurt
- 1/4 tsp berbere spice mix
- 1/4 tsp ground cumin
- Pinch of salt
- Pomegranate seeds, for garnish

Marinate chicken in berbere spice mix and olive oil for at least 30 minutes.

Preheat oven to 400°F (200°C). Toss diced onion, bell pepper, and carrot with olive oil, salt, and pepper. Roast for 20-25 minutes, or until tender.

While vegetables roast, cook chicken in a skillet over medium-high heat until browned on all sides. Remove from pan and set aside.

In the same skillet, sauté garlic for 30 seconds until fragrant.

Add diced tomatoes, pinto beans, and chicken broth to the skillet. Bring to a simmer and cook for 15 minutes.

Stir in roasted vegetables, chickpeas, green beans, and cooked chicken. Simmer for 5 minutes, or until heated through.

While stew simmers, soak dried currants in hot water for 10 minutes. Drain.

Warm tortillas. Spread a thin layer of spiced yogurt on each tortilla. Top with stew, drained currants, pine nuts, feta, red onion, and avocado (if using). Roll up and serve.

Simplified Berbere Spice Mix:

- 2 tablespoons paprika (sweet or smoked)
- 1 tablespoon ground coriander
- 1 tablespoon ground cumin
- 1 teaspoon ground cardamom
- 1/2 teaspoon cayenne pepper (adjust to your spice preference)
- 1/2 teaspoon ground ginger
- 1/4 teaspoon ground cloves
- 1/4 teaspoon ground cinnamon

Instructions:

1. Toast the Spices: In a small dry skillet over medium heat, toast the coriander, cumin, and cardamom for 1-2 minutes, or until fragrant, stirring constantly.

2. Grind (Optional): If using whole spices instead of ground, let the toasted spices cool slightly, then grind them in a spice grinder or mortar and pestle.

3. Combine: In a small bowl, combine the toasted (or ground) spices with the remaining ingredients (paprika, cayenne pepper, ginger, cloves, and cinnamon).

4. Store: Transfer the spice mix to an airtight container and store in a cool, dark place for up to 3 months.

Tips:

Customization: Feel free to adjust the amount of cayenne pepper to suit your spice preference. You can also add a pinch of ground nutmeg or allspice for additional complexity.

Whole vs. Ground Spices: Using whole spices and toasting/grinding them yourself will result in a fresher, more vibrant flavor. However, using pre-ground spices is a convenient shortcut.

This simple recipe captures the essence of Berbere spice, a vibrant and complex blend that adds depth and warmth to a variety of dishes. It's a versatile spice mix that can be used in stews, rubs, marinades, or even sprinkled over roasted vegetables for a flavorful kick.

Prep Time: 20 minutes
Cooking Time: 20 minutes
Servings: 1

The Krimson Karenderia: A California Filipino Fusion Burrito

Base:
- 1 large flour tortilla (heat it in a pan or microwave for a few seconds until warm and slightly crisp)

Spicy Shrimp:
- 1 pound medium shrimp, peeled and deveined
- 2 tablespoons mild Recado paste (adjust based on spice preference, start with less and add more to taste)

Coconut Noodles:
- 8 ounces rice noodles (or udon or chow mein)
- 1 cup coconut milk

Vegetables:
- 2 cups shredded iceberg lettuce
- 1/2 cup chopped red onion
- 1 cup chopped cauliflower florets
- 1 cup chopped bok choy
- 1 cup snap peas, trimmed

Sweet:
- 1 ripe banana, sliced thin
- Vegetable oil for frying

Crunch:
- 1 tablespoon roasted sesame seeds
- 1 tablespoon amaranth seeds - toast them in a dry pan over medium heat for a few minutes until fragrant (like popcorn.)

Sauce:
- 2 tablespoons soy sauce
- 1 tablespoon rice vinegar
- 1 tablespoon chopped garlic
- 1/2 teaspoon grated ginger
- 1-2 tablespoons water
- A few drops of *achiote* oil (look for it in the ethnic section of your grocery store)

Marinate the Shrimp:
In a bowl, toss the shrimp with the *Recado* paste. Cover and refrigerate for at least 30 minutes, or up to 2 hours for deeper flavor.

-

Cook the Noodles: In a saucepan, heat the coconut milk over medium heat until simmering. Add the noodles and cook according to package instructions, or until tender. Drain the noodles and set aside.

-

Wash and chop the lettuce, onion, cauliflower florets, bok choy, and snap peas.

-

Heat a couple tablespoons of oil in a pan or wok over medium-high heat. Add the cauliflower, bok choy, and snap peas. Cook for 3-4 minutes, stirring occasionally, until slightly softened and crisp-tender. Set aside.

-

Fry the Banana: Heat a thin layer of oil in a separate pan over medium heat. Fry the banana slices until golden brown and crispy, about 1-2 minutes per side. Drain on paper towels to remove excess oil.

-

Cook the Shrimp: If using *achiote* oil, add a few drops to a pan or wok over medium-high heat. Otherwise, just use a regular cooking oil. Saute the marinated shrimp for 2-3 minutes per side, or until pink and cooked through.

-

Make the Sauce: In a small bowl, whisk together the soy sauce, rice vinegar, garlic, and ginger. Add water, 1 tablespoon at a time, until the sauce reaches a slightly thick consistency that can coat the ingredients.

-

Assemble the Burrito: Spread the shredded lettuce on the warmed tortilla. Top with the cooked shrimp, stir-fried vegetables, and coconut milk noodles. Drizzle with the sauce. Add the fried banana slices and sprinkle with the roasted sesame seeds and amaranth seeds (if using).

-

Fold the bottom edge of the tortilla over the filling, then fold in the sides. Roll up tightly to secure the fillings. Slice in half and serve.

-

Simple Homemade *Recado* Paste (Mild)

- 2 tablespoons annatto seeds
- 1/2 cup hot water
- 5 cloves garlic, smashed
- 1/2 onion, chopped
- 1 tablespoon dried oregano
- 1 teaspoon ground allspice
- 1.5 teaspoons black pepper
- 1/2 cup mild chili powder
- 1 tablespoon salt
- 1/4 cup vinegar

Instructions:

1. Soak annatto seeds in hot water for 30 minutes.

2. Toast garlic and onion in a pan until softened (15-20 minutes).

3. Combine all ingredients in a blender and blend until smooth.

4. Taste and adjust seasonings (salt, pepper, vinegar).

5. Store in an airtight container in the fridge (up to 1 week) or freeze for longer storage.

Joojeh, Stone Fruit & Grilled Serrano Skewers with Dual Dips

Prep Time: 20-25 minutes
Marinate Time: Minimum 30 minutes, ideally overnight

Cooking Time: 10-15 minutes
Servings: 4-6 skewers

Joojeh Marinade:
- 1 lb boneless, skinless chicken thighs, cut into 1-inch cubes
- 1/2 cup Greek yogurt (full fat)
- Generous pinch of saffron threads, soaked in 2 tbsp warm water
- Juice and zest of 1 lemon
- 4 cloves garlic, finely minced
- 1 tbsp ground cumin
- 1 tbsp ground coriander
- 1 tsp smoked paprika
- 1/2 tsp salt
- 1/4 tsp black pepper
- 2 tbsp honey
- 2 tbsp soy sauce
- 1 tbsp grated ginger

Skewers:
- 4-6 firm plums (Santa Rosa or similar), halved and pitted
- 4-6 apricots, halved and pitted
- 2-3 serrano peppers, seeded and halved lengthwise
- Skewers (soaked in water if wooden)

Roasted Red Pepper *Harissa* Dip:
- 1/2 cup jarred roasted red peppers, drained
- 2 tbsp *harissa* paste
- 2 tbsp extra-virgin olive oil
- 1 tbsp pomegranate molasses
- 1/2 tsp ground cumin
- Pinch of salt

Spiced Banana Ketchup Dip:
- 2 ripe bananas, mashed
- 1/4 cup tomato paste
- 2 tbsp apple cider vinegar
- 2 tbsp coconut sugar
- 1/4 tsp chili flakes
- 1/2 tsp grated ginger
- 4-5 pitted Medjool dates, chopped
- 1/4 tsp ground cinnamon
- 1 tbsp dark rum (optional)

Garnish:
- Fresh mint leaves
- Chopped cilantro
- Edible flowers (optional)

Combine all marinade ingredients in a bowl. Add chicken and toss thoroughly to coat. Marinate for at least 2 hours, ideally overnight in the refrigerator.

Thread chicken onto skewers, alternating with plum halves, apricot halves, and serrano pepper pieces.

Preheat grill or broiler to high heat. Grill or broil skewers until chicken is cooked through, the fruit is caramelized, and peppers are slightly blistered, about 5-7 minutes per side.

Make Dips:
- Harissa:

Blend all ingredients in a food processor until smooth. Adjust seasoning to taste.

- Banana Ketchup:

In a small saucepan, combine all ingredients and simmer over low heat until thickened and fragrant, about 10 minutes. Let cool slightly.

Plating Notes:
Arrange skewers artfully on a serving platter. Drizzle with any remaining marinade. Serve with both dipping sauces, garnished with fresh mint, cilantro, and edible flowers for an elegant touch.

Chef's Tip: For a smoky flavor, grill the fruit and chilies separately from the chicken.

Yuzu Kosho Brussels Sprouts

Prep Time: 5 minutes
Cook Time: 10-12 minutes
Servings: 2-3 as a side dish

- 1 lb Brussels sprouts, trimmed
- 1 tablespoon olive oil
- Pinch of salt
- 1-2 tablespoons Yuzu Kosho paste (optional)

Parboil the Brussels Sprouts: Fill a large pot with water and add a pinch of salt. Bring to a boil over high heat. Add the Brussels sprouts and cook for 3-4 minutes, or until tender but still slightly firm. Drain them well in a colander.

-

Dry It Out: Spread the cooked Brussels sprouts on a paper towel-lined plate. Pat them gently to remove any excess moisture. You can also let them sit for a few minutes to allow some of the moisture to evaporate naturally.

-

Searing: Heat the olive oil in a large skillet over medium-high heat. Once hot, add the dried Brussels sprouts in a single layer (don't overcrowd the pan). Let them sear undisturbed for 2-3 minutes, or until golden brown on the bottom.

-

Gently toss the Brussels sprouts and continue cooking for another 2-3 minutes, or until they are browned and crispy on all sides.

-

Yuzu Kosho Glaze (optional): If you're feeling adventurous, drizzle the Brussels sprouts with 1-2 tablespoons of Yuzu Kosho paste and toss to coat. Be careful, a little goes a long way!

-

Enjoy these delicious Brussels sprouts hot as a side dish or appetizer.

Kimchi Gazpacho

Prep Time: 10 minutes
Cooking Time: n/a
Servings: 2-3

For the Gazpacho:
- 2 cups kimchi, roughly chopped (save some juice for later)
- 1 cucumber, seeded and finely diced
- 2 ripe tomatoes, finely diced
- 1 clove garlic, minced
- 1/2 cup vegetable broth
- 2 tablespoons olive oil
- 1 tablespoon rice vinegar (or more to taste)
- Salt and freshly ground black pepper to taste

For the Smoky Paprika Aioli:
- 1/2 cup mayonnaise
- 2 tablespoons lemon juice
- 1-2 tablespoons smoked paprika (depending on desired smokiness)
- Pinch of cayenne pepper
- Salt and freshly ground black pepper to taste

Gazpacho:

1. Roughly chop kimchi (save juice!), dice cucumber & tomatoes.

2. Add garlic, broth, olive oil, vinegar. Blend (not mush!), season aggressively. Add kimchi juice for an extra kick if needed. Chill (30 min).

Smoky Aioli:

1. Whisk mayo, lemon juice, 1-2 tbsp smoked paprika (be bold!), cayenne (adjust heat). Season and taste.

Serve:

1. Chilled gazpacho in bowls. Swirl in smoky aioli.

BEACH

Beachfront dining has always been a hallmark of luxury travel, a symphony of culinary indulgence set against the backdrop of breathtaking ocean views and the rhythmic lull of crashing waves. From the glamorous French Riviera to the sun-drenched shores of Hawaii, beachfront resorts have long been a playground for discerning travelers seeking both relaxation and epicurean delights.

The evolution of beachside cuisine mirrors the changing tides of culinary trends. In the early days, menus leaned towards the familiar and conservative, catering to the palates of well-heeled travelers who sought comfort in the familiar. However, as the world became more interconnected and adventurous, so too did the palates of beach-goers. Chefs began experimenting with local ingredients, blending traditional techniques with global influences, and creating dishes that reflected the unique terroir of each destination.

Today, beachside dining is a global culinary adventure. In Oahu, Hawaiian cuisine dances with Asian influences, resulting in innovative dishes like our Huli Huli Chicken with Grilled Spicy Pineapple Skewers and a tropical slaw that sings with freshness. In San Sebastian, the Basque Country's rich culinary heritage takes center stage, with elevated tapas like *Atun Ahumado con Tomate Fresco* showcasing the region's passion for seafood and simple yet elegant flavors.

In Playa del Carmen, the fiery spirit of Mexican cuisine comes alive in dishes like Campfire *Papadzules* and Yucatan-Inspired Tacos, where ancient Mayan flavors mingle with modern techniques. The sun-drenched shores of Cottesloe Beach in Perth inspire unique culinary creations like Vegemite Grilled Cornbread and the Ultimate Aussie Fusion Burger, showcasing the bold flavors and innovative spirit of Australian cuisine.

Venture to Bali, where Indonesian spices and aromatics infuse dishes like Balinese *Pepes Ikan* and *Mie Goreng*, inviting you to savor the exotic flavors of the tropics. And in Phuket, Thailand, the fragrant curries and noodle dishes like *Pad See Ew* and *Tom Yum Goong* will tantalize your taste buds with their harmonious blend of sweet, sour, salty, and spicy notes.

This chapter is a culinary journey across the globe, a celebration of the diverse flavors and innovative spirit found in beachside restaurants worldwide. We invite you to explore these recipes, inspired by the rich culinary traditions of each destination, and discover the magic that unfolds when exceptional cuisine meets the breathtaking beauty of the ocean.

Oahu, Hawaii

Oahu's culinary scene is a vibrant tapestry woven from the threads of diverse cultures and a rich history. As a culinary traveler, you'll discover a unique fusion of flavors that reflects the island's Polynesian roots, Asian influences, and the innovative spirit of its chefs.

The native Hawaiian diet, once centered around taro, sweet potato, breadfruit, and seafood, has evolved over centuries, embracing the culinary traditions of immigrant communities from China, Japan, Korea, and the Philippines. This blending of cultures has given rise to dishes like the iconic "plate lunch," a hearty combination of rice, macaroni salad, and a protein like teriyaki chicken or *kalua* pig.

Today, Oahu's culinary scene is a dynamic blend of tradition and innovation. Chefs are reimagining classic Hawaiian dishes with modern techniques and global flavors, while also championing local ingredients and sustainable practices. From the freshest poke bowls bursting with ahi tuna and vibrant seasonings to farm-to-table restaurants showcasing the bounty of Oahu's farms and fisheries, the island offers a diverse and exciting culinary landscape.

In this section, we invite you to explore Oahu's unique foodways, both on the bustling streets and in the refined ambiance of its upscale restaurants. You'll savor the sweet and tangy flavors of traditional Hawaiian cuisine, like *kalua* pig and poi, alongside innovative creations that push the boundaries of flavor. Discover the freshest seafood, the most flavorful fruits, and the unique culinary traditions that make Oahu a true foodie paradise.

Hawaiian Poke: A vibrant and refreshing dish showcasing the freshest, sashimi-grade ahi tuna, diced avocado, crisp vegetables, and a symphony of spices, this iconic Hawaiian staple is a testament to the island's bountiful ocean harvest and love for simple yet flavorful ingredients.

Huli Huli Chicken with Grilled Spicy Pineapple Skewers and Tropical Slaw: Inspired by the smoky flavors of traditional Hawaiian barbecue, this dish features succulent grilled chicken glazed with a tangy huli huli sauce, perfectly paired with the sweet heat of grilled pineapple and a refreshing tropical slaw.

Our A+ Hawaiian Spiced Pork Skewers with Spicy Pickled Pineapple, Plums & Hearts of Palm: Elevating the beloved Hawaiian tradition of grilling, these skewers feature tender pork infused with local spices, accompanied by a medley of pickled fruits and vegetables that add a tangy, vibrant counterpoint to the smoky meat. This innovative combination of flavors and textures makes it a true showstopper. (Showstopper)

Hawaiian-Inspired Chicken & Shrimp Bowl with Lilikoi Vinaigrette: A modern take on Hawaiian plate lunch, this vibrant bowl combines grilled chicken, succulent shrimp, and fresh, seasonal vegetables, all drizzled with a fragrant lilikoi vinaigrette for a taste of the islands.

A Simple & A Complex (double chicken broth) Saimin: A beloved noodle soup deeply rooted in Hawaiian comfort food culture, this dish offers two variations, showcasing the versatility of both a simple, everyday broth and a more complex, deeply flavorful double chicken broth. (the Complex Broth is the real Showstopper, here)

Lau Lau **(Hawaiian Steamed Parcels):** A testament to the resourcefulness of Hawaiian cuisine, these steamed bundles of pork and fish, wrapped in taro leaves, offer a unique and satisfying culinary experience that connects diners to the island's history and traditions.

Fire-Kissed Hawaiian Steak with Mango Salsa and Macadamia Butter: Indulge in the flavors of Hawaii with this succulent grilled steak, adorned with a vibrant mango salsa that bursts with tropical sweetness and a decadent macadamia nut butter that adds a luxurious touch. This dish's rich, indulgent flavors and upscale presentation make it a true showstopper. (Showstopper)

Our A+ Kulolo (A Cherished Hawaiian Dessert): A cherished dessert with deep cultural significance, this sweet and creamy pudding, made from taro, coconut milk, and sugar, offers a taste of traditional Hawaiian flavors and hospitality.

Hawaiian Sweet Rolls: Soft and fluffy, these sweet rolls, infused with the flavors of pineapple and coconut, evoke the warmth and generosity of the islands, perfect for breakfast or a sweet afternoon snack.

Spicy Pineapple Boat: A playful and innovative twist on the classic fruit salad, this dish features a hollowed-out pineapple filled with a fiery shrimp and pineapple mixture, showcasing the bold and unexpected flavors of Hawaiian cuisine. (Showstopper)

Cucumber Salad with Sesame Ginger: A refreshing and light side dish, highlighting the crispness of cucumbers with a subtle Asian influence, this salad complements the rich flavors of many Hawaiian dishes, offering a harmonious balance of taste and texture.

Prep Time: 10-15 minutes
Cooking Time: n/a
Servings: 2-3

Hawaiian Poke

The Poke:
- 1 pound sashimi-grade ahi tuna (cubed) - Freshness is key for taste and safety.
- 1/2 cup thinly sliced red onion
- 1 avocado, diced
- 1 cup chopped cucumber
- 1/2 cup chopped fresh pineapple
- 1/4 cup chopped fresh cilantro

The Sauce:
- 2 tablespoons tamari sauce
- 2 tablespoons fresh lime juice
- 1 tablespoon toasted sesame oil
- 1 tablespoon grapeseed oil

The Spice Mix:
- 2 tablespoons ground ginger
- 2 tablespoons garlic powder
- 2 tablespoons onion powder
- 1 tablespoon ground turmeric
- 1 tablespoon smoked paprika
- 1/2 tablespoon ground cinnamon
- 1 teaspoon togarashi powder
- 1 tablespoon ground coriander
- 1 tablespoon crumbled Nori seaweed
- 1 teaspoon cayenne pepper
- 1 teaspoon sea salt (adjust to taste)

The Garnish:
- Toasted sesame seeds
- Thinly sliced red chili pepper (optional, for an extra fiery kick)
- Wontons or crispy seaweed salad

Prepare the Poke:
Combine the cubed ahi tuna, diced avocado, red onion, cucumber, pineapple, and chopped cilantro in a large bowl.

-

Make the Sauce: In a separate bowl, whisk together the soy sauce, lime juice, toasted sesame oil, vegetable oil, poke spice mix, and optional cayenne pepper. Adjust the seasonings to your taste for desired saltiness, acidity, and spice level.

-

Assemble and Serve: Drizzle the sauce over the poke mixture and toss gently to coat everything evenly. Spoon the poke mixture into individual bowls.

-

Garnish (Optional): Sprinkle with toasted sesame seeds for a nutty crunch. For additional heat, garnish with thinly sliced red chili pepper. For textural variety, consider adding crispy wonton strips or seaweed salad (both optional).

Prep Time: 15-20 minutes
Cooking Time: 25-30 minutes
Servings: 2

Huli Huli Chicken with Grilled Spicy Pineapple Skewers and Tropical Slaw

For the Huli Huli Chicken (makes 4 servings):

- 1 pound boneless, skinless chicken thighs (cut into bite-sized pieces)
- 1/4 cup low-sodium soy sauce
- 2 tablespoons brown sugar
- 1 tablespoon rice vinegar
- 1 tablespoon grated ginger
- 1 clove garlic, minced
- 1 teaspoon sesame oil
- Pinch of red pepper flakes
- 1 tablespoon vegetable oil (for grilling)

For the Huli Huli Glaze:

- 1/4 cup low-sodium soy sauce
- 2 tablespoons brown sugar
- 1/4 cup fresh pineapple juice
- 1 tablespoon cornstarch
- 2 tablespoons water

For the Spicy Pineapple Skewers (makes 4 servings):

- 1 fresh pineapple, cut into 1-inch cubes
- 2 tablespoons brown sugar, melted
- 1 tablespoon lime juice
- 1 teaspoon Sweet Garlic, Hot Mango & Chia Seed Sauce
- Pinch of ground cumin

For the Tropical Slaw (makes 4 servings):

- 2 cups shredded green cabbage
- 1 cup shredded carrots
- 1/2 cup chopped red bell pepper
- 1 cup chopped fresh pineapple
- 1/4 cup chopped fresh cilantro
- 2 tablespoons lime juice
- 1 tablespoon olive oil
- 1 tablespoon honey
- 1/4 cup mango puree
- 1/4 jalapeno, seeded and finely chopped
- Salt and black pepper to taste

Marinate the Chicken:
Combine soy sauce, brown sugar, rice vinegar, ginger, garlic, sesame oil, and red pepper flakes in a large bowl. Add the chicken pieces and toss to coat evenly. Marinate for at least 30 minutes, or up to overnight for deeper flavor.

-

Prepare the Huli Huli Glaze: In a separate bowl, whisk together soy sauce, brown sugar, pineapple juice, cornstarch, and water. Set aside.

-

Assemble the Pineapple Skewers (Optional): Whisk together melted brown sugar, lime juice, sriracha, and cumin in a small bowl. Thread pineapple cubes onto skewers and brush generously with the mixture.

-

Prepare the Slaw (Optional): In a large bowl, combine shredded cabbage, carrots, red bell pepper, pineapple, and cilantro. Whisk together lime juice, olive oil, honey, mango puree (if using), jalapeno (if using), salt, and black pepper in a separate bowl. Pour the dressing over the slaw and toss to coat.

-

Grill the Chicken and Pineapple (Optional): Preheat your grill to medium-high heat. Brush the chicken with oil and grill for 5-7 minutes per side, or until cooked through and slightly charred.

-

Baste the chicken with the Huli Huli Glaze during the last few minutes of grilling. Grill the pineapple skewers alongside the chicken, for 2-3 minutes per side, or until slightly caramelized and warmed through (steps can be done in a grill pan if needed).

-

Plate the grilled Huli Huli Chicken and spicy pineapple skewers (if using) with a generous helping of the tropical slaw.

-

Sweet Mango Chili Sauce with Chia Seeds

Ingredients:

- Garlic (2 cloves, sliced)
- Olive Oil (1 tbsp)
- Mango (1 ripe, chopped)
- Lime Juice (1/4 cup)
- Honey (2 tbsp)
- Fresno Chili (1/2 red, seeded, sliced) - adjust for spice
- Water (1/4 cup)
- Chia Seeds (1 tbsp)
- Salt & Pepper (to taste)

Instructions:

1. Sweat garlic in olive oil (medium-low heat, 1-2 min).

2. Blend garlic, mango, lime juice, honey/maple syrup, chili, water until smooth.

3. Strain (optional) for a finer texture.

4. Stir in chia seeds, let sit 5-10 min (thickens slightly).

5. Season and reserve.

-

Prep Time: 20-30 minutes
Cooking Time: 20-25 minutes
Servings: 4-6

A+ Hawaiian Spiced Pork Skewers with Spicy Pickled Pineapple, Plums & Hearts of Palm

For the Spiced Coconut Pork Skewers:
- 1 pound boneless, skinless pork shoulder (cut into 1-inch cubes)
- 1/4 cup low-sodium soy sauce
- 1/4 cup unsweetened coconut milk
- 2 tablespoons lime juice
- 1 tablespoon grated ginger
- 1/2 teaspoon red pepper flakes (adjust for desired heat)
- 1 clove garlic, minced
- 1/2 teaspoon ground cumin
- 1/4 teaspoon ground coriander
- 1/2 teaspoon Hawaiian sea salt (or kosher salt)
- Pinch of black pepper

For the Spicy Pickled Pineapple:
- 1 fresh pineapple, cut into 1-inch chunks
- 1/2 cup rice vinegar
- 1 tablespoon sliced red chili pepper (seeds removed for less heat)
- 1 whole star anise (optional, for a touch of licorice flavor)
- 1 small cinnamon stick (optional, for a touch of warmth)

For the Pickled Plums:
- 2 ripe plums, thinly sliced
- 1/4 cup rice vinegar
- 1/4 cup water
- 1 tablespoon granulated sugar
- 1/2 teaspoon whole black peppercorns

For the Hearts of Palm (Optional):
- 1 (14-ounce) can hearts of palm, drained and cut into 1-inch slices

For Serving:
- 1/2 cup chopped fresh mint
- Grilled pineapple slices
- Coconut Crema (optional):

Marinate Pork:
Combine marinade ingredients in a bowl. Add pork cubes, toss to coat, and marinate for 1-hour minimum (overnight for deeper flavor).

-

Pickle Pineapple & Plums: Prepare pickling solutions (see recipe) and pickle pineapple and plums for 30 minutes to 1 hour (instructions not included here).

-

Assemble Skewers: Thread marinated pork cubes, pickled pineapple, plums, and hearts of palm (if using) onto soaked skewers.

-

Grill the Skewers: Preheat grill to medium-high. Grill skewers for 5-7 minutes per side, until cooked through and slightly charred.

-

Optional Sides (Prepare While Grilling): Grill pineapple slices and whisk together coconut milk, lime juice, and sugar for the crema (if desired).

-

Plate grilled pork skewers with remaining pickled pineapple and plums, fresh mint, grilled pineapple slices (if using), and a dollop of coconut crema (if using).

-

Quick Pickled Pineapple & Plums for Skewers

1 cup water
1/2 cup white wine vinegar (or rice vinegar)
1/4 cup sugar
4 black peppercorns
2 cloves
1 star anise (optional)
1 inch ginger, sliced (optional)
1/2 scotch bonnet pepper, sliced (optional)
1/2 vanilla bean, split (optional)
1 tablespoon honey
1 tablespoon lime juice
Pineapple chunks
Plum slices

Instructions:

1. Combine everything in a pot (except fruits) and simmer for 10 minutes.

2. Let cool completely.

3. Divide liquid into two containers, add pineapple to one and plums to the other.

4. Refrigerate at least 30 minutes.

-

Easy Coconut Crema

1/2 cup full-fat coconut milk (chilled)
1 tablespoon lime juice
Pinch of salt

Instructions:

1. In a small bowl, whisk together chilled coconut milk, lime juice, and salt until smooth and slightly thickened.

2. Enjoy immediately drizzled over grilled skewers, vegetables, or fish.

Hawaiian-Inspired Chicken & Shrimp Bowl with Lilikoi Vinaigrette

Prep Time: 15-20 minutes
Cooking Time: 25-30 minutes
Servings: 2

For the Marinated Chicken and Shrimp:
- 1 pound boneless, skinless chicken thighs (cut into bite-sized pieces)
- 1 pound medium shrimp, peeled and deveined
- 1/4 cup low-sodium soy sauce
- 2 tablespoons granulated sugar
- 1 tablespoon pineapple juice
- 1 tablespoon grated ginger
- 1 clove garlic, minced
- 1/2 teaspoon Hawaiian sea salt
- 1/4 teaspoon black pepper
- Pinch of ground allspice
- 1 tablespoon vegetable oil (for searing)

For the Lilikoi Vinaigrette (Choose One Option):

Option 1 (Sweet and Tangy):
- 1/2 cup fresh lilikoi (passion fruit) pulp (or substitute with 1/4 cup orange juice and 1 tablespoon passion fruit syrup)
- 2 tablespoons olive oil
- 1 tablespoon rice vinegar
- 1 teaspoon honey
- 1 tablespoon guava paste
- Pinch of salt and black pepper

Option 2 (Sweet and Sour):
- 1/2 cup fresh lilikoi (passion fruit) pulp (or substitute with 1/4 cup orange juice and 1 tablespoon passion fruit syrup)
- 2 tablespoons olive oil
- 1 tablespoon rice vinegar
- 1 teaspoon honey
- 1 tablespoon freshly squeezed lime juice
- 1/4 cup chopped fresh pineapple
- Pinch of salt and black pepper

For the Bowl:
- 2 cups cooked black rice (or white rice, if preferred)
- 1 cup mixed greens (combination of baby spinach and arugula)
- 1/2 cup chopped red onion
- 1/4 cup chopped fresh cilantro
- 1 ripe plum, thinly sliced
- Lime wedges

Marinate Chicken & Shrimp: Combine marinade ingredients in a bowl. Add chicken and shrimp, tossing to coat. Marinate for 30 minutes to 1 hour.

-

Prepare Vinaigrette: While chicken marinates, choose your vinaigrette option: blend lilikoi pulp (or substitute), olive oil, rice vinegar, honey, chosen sweetener/acid (guava paste/lime juice), salt, and pepper until smooth. Adjust sweetness and acidity to taste.

-

Sear Chicken & Shrimp: Heat oil in a large skillet over medium-high heat. Sear chicken in batches until browned (2-3 minutes per side). Set aside. Cook shrimp in the same pan until pink and cooked through (2-3 minutes per side).

-

Assemble Bowls: Divide rice between bowls. Top with mixed greens, chicken, shrimp, red onion, cilantro, and plum. Drizzle generously with chosen vinaigrette.

-

Serve: Garnish with a lime wedge (optional).

Simple & Complex Saimin

Prep Time (simple): 5-10 minutes
Cooking Time (simple): 10-15 minutes
Servings (simple): 2

- 4 cups chicken broth (low-sodium or double broth- see recipe)
- 1/2 cup dried thin wheat noodles (soba noodles work well)
- 1 green onion, thinly sliced
- 1 slice kamaboko (fish cake), or substitute with a few cooked shrimp
- 1 large egg
- 1/2 teaspoon soy sauce
- Pinch of freshly ground black pepper

Optional toppings: chopped fresh cilantro, sliced green chili pepper (seeds removed for less heat), sesame oil

Homemade Kamaboko (Fish Cake):

- 1 lb white fish (cod, haddock)
- 1/4 cup cold water
- 1 tbsp soy sauce
- 1 tbsp sake
- 1 tsp sugar
- 1/2 tsp salt
- Pinch white pepper
- 1.5 tbsp potato starch (adjust for firmness)

Instructions:

1. Pulse fish in a food processor until a fine paste.

2. Mix in water, soy sauce, sake, sugar, salt, pepper (optional ginger).

3. Gradually add potato starch until sticky and holds shape.

4. Form a log or decorative shapes (optional) on a steamer basket lined with parchment paper.

5. Steam 20-25 minutes until firm. Cool, slice, serve.

Heat the Broth:
In a small saucepan, heat the chicken broth over medium heat until simmering.

Cook the Noodles: While the broth simmers, bring a separate pot of water to a boil. Add the noodles and cook according to package instructions (typically 3-5 minutes). Drain thoroughly.

Fry the Egg (Optional): Heat a thin layer of oil in a small non-stick pan over medium heat. Crack the egg and fry to your desired doneness.

Assemble the Saimin: Divide the hot chicken broth between two bowls. Add the cooked noodles to each bowl. Top with a fried egg (if using).

Garnish and Season: Garnish each bowl with sliced green onion, kamaboko (or cooked shrimp, if using), and a drizzle of soy sauce. Season with a pinch of black pepper.

If making the Double Chicken Broth, the chicken meat from the final broth can be used in various ways:

Shredded: Shred the cooked chicken and use it in soups, stews, salads, or dumplings.

Flaked: Flake the chicken for sandwiches, tacos, or pot pies.

Deboned: Remove the bones entirely and use the chicken meat in casseroles, quiches, or croquettes.

Double Chicken Broth:

Initial Broth:
- 1 pound chicken necks, gizzards, and backs (cleaned)
- 1lb of chicken wings
- 2 quarts cold water
- 1 tablespoon whole black peppercorns
- 2 bay leaves
- 1 medium onion, finely diced
- 1 carrot, finely diced
- 1 celery stalk, finely diced

Final Broth:
- 1 whole chicken (around 3-4 lbs)
- Strained initial broth (reserve all)
- 1 medium onion, finely diced
- 1 carrot, finely diced
- 1 celery stalk, finely diced
- 4 scallions, green parts only, chopped
- 2 inches ginger, thinly sliced
- 2 cloves garlic, smashed
- 2 whole cloves

Intense Base: Bring to a boil then simmer chicken parts with aromatics (peppercorns, bay leaves) and mirepoix for 3 hours. Strain and reserve broth.

Rich Final Broth: Combine whole chicken, strained broth, fresh mirepoix, scallions, ginger, garlic, and cloves. Bring to a boil then simmer 2-3 hours, skimming scum.

Clarify Broth:
Whisk 2-3 egg whites with a splash of cold water in a small bowl. Gently stir the egg whites into the simmering broth. As the whites cook, they will trap impurities, leaving a clear broth. Once the whites rise to the surface and solidify, strain the broth again through cheesecloth for a crystal-clear finish.

Let the broth cool completely, then skim off any remaining fat from the surface. Store in an airtight container in the refrigerator for up to 5 days or freeze for longer storage.

Lau Lau (Hawaiian Steamed Parcels)

Prep Time: 15-20 minutes
Cooking Time: 25-30 minutes
Servings: 2

- 1 pound firm white fish fillets (cod, mahi-mahi, halibut)
- Taro leaves (or banana leaves, if unavailable)
- 1 tablespoon neutral oil (avocado or grapeseed)

Simplified Spice Mix (makes about 4 tablespoons):
- 2 tablespoons ground ginger
- 2 tablespoons garlic powder
- 1 tablespoon ground coriander
- 1 tablespoon smoked paprika
- 1 teaspoon Hawaiian sea salt
- 1/2 teaspoon freshly ground black pepper
- Pinch of cayenne pepper (adjust for desired spice level)

Optional additions:
- Small piece of butterfish or pork belly (for added richness)
- 1 tablespoon chopped green onions (for garnish)

Marinate the Fish: Toss the fish pieces with olive oil and the spice mix in a bowl. Marinate for at least 15 minutes, or up to 30 minutes for deeper flavor.

Prepare the Leaves: Wash the taro leaves thoroughly and remove the stems. If using banana leaves, cut them into squares large enough to wrap the fish.

Assemble the Lau Lau: Place a seasoned fish piece in the center of a leaf square. Add a piece of butterfish or pork belly (optional) on top for extra richness. Fold the leaf edges over the fish, creating a secure packet. Use skewers to pin the sides closed.

Fill a large pot with a few inches of water. Place a steaming rack or metal colander inside. Bring the water to a simmer.

Steaming: Arrange the wrapped fish packets on the rack, ensuring they don't touch. Cover the pot tightly and steam for 15-20 minutes, or until the fish flakes easily with a fork.

Carefully remove the cooked Lau Lau packets with tongs or a spatula. Serve hot, either unwrapped on steamed rice or directly in the leaves. Garnish with chopped green onions (optional).

Fire-Kissed Hawaiian Steak with Mango Salsa and Macadamia Butter

Prep Time: 20-30 minutes
Cooking Time: 15-20 minutes total
Servings: 1-2

- 2 pounds high-quality ribeye steak (or your preferred cut, trimmed of excess fat)

Mango Salsa:
- 1 ripe mango, peeled, seeded, and diced
- 1/2 red onion, finely diced
- 1/4 cup chopped fresh cilantro
- 1 tablespoon fresh lime juice
- 1 jalapeno pepper, seeded and finely minced (adjust for desired heat)
- 1 tablespoon olive oil
- 1 teaspoon finely grated lemon zest
- Salt and freshly cracked black pepper, to taste

Macadamia Butter:
- 1/2 cup unsalted macadamia nuts, toasted
- 4 tablespoons unsalted butter, softened
- 1 tablespoon honey
- Pinch of sea salt

For Finishing:
- Black lava sea salt or Hawaiian black sea salt
- Freshly chopped chives

Make the Mango Salsa: In a bowl, combine the diced mango, red onion, chopped cilantro, lime juice, jalapeno (adjusted for spice preference), olive oil, lemon zest, salt, and pepper. Set aside to allow the flavors to meld.

-

Macadamia Butter: Utilizing a food processor, pulse the toasted macadamia nuts until finely ground. Subsequently, incorporate the softened butter, honey, and sea salt. Process meticulously until a smooth and creamy texture is achieved. Transfer the macadamia butter to a small bowl and set aside.

-

Optional Marinade: While not mandatory, marinating the steak for 30 minutes to an hour can significantly enhance its flavor profile. To implement this optional step, whisk together olive oil, soy sauce, minced garlic, and grated ginger in a bowl. Introduce the steak and toss thoroughly to ensure complete coating. Cover the marinated steak and refrigerate for 30 minutes to 1 hour.

-

Grill Preheating: Preheat your grill or grill pan to a high heat setting. Season the steak generously with both salt and freshly cracked black pepper.

-

Searing: Place the seasoned steak on the preheated grill and sear it for 2-3 minutes per side to create a caramelized crust.

-

Internal Temperature Control: Reduce the heat to medium-high and cook the steak for an additional 4-6 minutes per side for a medium-rare doneness. Alternatively, adjust cooking time to achieve your desired level of doneness. Utilize a meat thermometer to verify the internal temperature, targeting 125°F for medium-rare.

-

Resting Period: Once cooked, transfer the steak to a cutting board and allow it to rest for 5-10 minutes. This resting period is essential for facilitating the redistribution of juices within the steak, resulting in a more tender and flavorful final product.

-

Slicing: Slice the rested steak against the grain into thin strips for optimal presentation.

-

Plating: Arrange the sliced steak on a serving platter. Top each serving with a generous dollop of the vibrant mango salsa. Drizzle the steak with a flavorful measure of the macadamia butter.

-

Presentation: For an elegant touch and a burst of salinity, sprinkle the plated steak with black lava sea salt or Hawaiian black sea salt. Fresh chives may be added as an optional garnish for a pop of color.

-

Broiler Option:

1. Preheat broiler to high, rack 4-6 inches from heat.
2. Sear seasoned steak in hot cast iron skillet (2-3 min/side).
3. Broil on baking sheet 3-5 min/side for medium-rare (125°F internal temp).
4. Rest steak 5-10 min for tenderness & flavor. (Monitor closely to avoid overcooking)

A+ Kulolo (A Cherished Hawaiian dessert)

Prep Time: 15-20 minutes
Cooking Time: 2-3 hours (steaming)
Servings: 6-8
(depending on ramekin size)

Taro Root Option:
- 2 pounds taro root (peeled and grated) - Tip: Wear gloves when handling raw taro to avoid skin irritation.

or

Yam Option:
- 2 pounds yam (peeled and grated)

then

- 1 pound sweet potato (peeled and grated)
- 2 cups coconut milk (full-fat, well-shaken)
- 1 cup granulated sugar (or ½ cup brown sugar for a deeper caramel flavor)
- ½ teaspoon Hawaiian sea salt
- 1 teaspoon vanilla extract
- Ti leaves (for wrapping, rinsed and softened - optional)
- Banana leaves (for wrapping, rinsed and softened - optional)
- Aluminum foil (for wrapping, if not using leaves)

Grate Vegetables:
Utilize a food processor or box grater to finely grate the peeled taro root and sweet potato into a large bowl.

-

Combine Wet Ingredients: In a separate bowl, employ a whisk to thoroughly combine the coconut milk, sugar, Hawaiian sea salt, and vanilla extract (if used).

-

Unify the Mixture: Gently pour the wet ingredients over the grated root vegetables. Utilize a spoon or spatula to meticulously combine all elements, ensuring uniform distribution.

-

Wrapping Options:

Traditional Method: (Optional) For those using ti leaves or banana leaves, cut them into squares sufficiently large to accommodate a generous portion of the Kulolo mixture. Line a steamer basket with the leaves, leaving excess for folding. Spoon the Kulolo mixture onto the leaves, allowing space for expansion during steaming. Fold the overhanging leaves over the mixture to create a secure packet.

Modern Method: Alternatively, aluminum foil can be used for individual portions. Divide the Kulolo mixture equally into small oven-safe ramekins or baking dishes. Tightly cover each ramekin or dish with aluminum foil, meticulously crimping the edges to form a seal.

-

Steaming Process: Fill a large pot or Dutch oven with a few inches of water. Carefully place a steamer basket (or trivet if using ramekins) inside the pot, ensuring it doesn't come into contact with the water. Bring the water to a simmering state.

-

Steaming the Kulolo: Arrange the wrapped Kulolo packets (or ramekins) cautiously within the steamer basket. Cover the pot with a tight-fitting lid and steam for 2-3 hours, or until the Kulolo sets and a toothpick inserted in the center emerges clean.

-

Cooling: Once complete, carefully remove the Kulolo packets (or ramekins) from the pot using tongs and allow them to cool entirely at room temperature for at least 3 hours, or ideally overnight, permitting the flavors to further develop.

-

Unwrap the Kulolo packets (if using leaves) or remove the foil from the ramekins. Serve the Kulolo chilled or at room temperature.

Hawaiian Sweet Rolls

Prep Time: 10 minutes
Cook Time: 15-20 minutes
Serving Size: 12 rolls

- 1/2 cup (120ml) warm milk (around 105°F / 40°C)
- 1/2 cup (120ml) canned pineapple juice (warmed to lukewarm)
- 1 tablespoon active dry yeast
- 1/4 cup granulated sugar
- 2 1/2 cups (315g) all-purpose flour, plus extra for dusting
- 1/2 teaspoon salt
- 3 tablespoons unsalted butter, softened
- 1/4 cup finely chopped canned pineapple chunks (drained)

Mix warm liquids, yeast, and sugar.

Let it sit (5-10 min) until bubbly. In a separate bowl, whisk flour and salt.

Combine wet and dry ingredients. Add butter and knead (5-7 min) until smooth.

Let dough rise in a greased bowl (1-2 hours) until doubled.

Punch down dough and roll into a rectangle (don't stress perfection!).

Sprinkle with pineapple.

Cut into squares and roll up each one. Place rolls on a baking sheet and let rise again (30 min).

Bake at 375°F (190°C) for 15-20 minutes (golden brown).

Garlic Parmesan Roasted Green Beans

Prep Time: 5 minutes
Cook Time: 15-20 minutes
Serving Size: 4-6, as a side dish

- 1 pound fresh green beans, trimmed
- 1 tablespoon olive oil
- 1/2 teaspoon garlic powder
- 1/4 teaspoon smoked paprika (optional, for a smoky twist)
- 1/4 teaspoon kosher salt
- 1/4 teaspoon black pepper
- 1/4 cup grated Parmesan cheese
- 1/4 cup chopped macadamia nuts, toasted (optional, for added crunch)

Heat oven to 425°F (220°C), line a baking sheet with parchment paper.

Toss green beans with olive oil, garlic powder, salt & pepper. Spread beans on the baking sheet and roast 15-20 minutes (tender-crisp & browned).

Remove from oven (optional): sprinkle with Parmesan cheese & macadamia nuts.

Broil 2-3 minutes (optional): melt cheese & get a little nutty crunch.

Serve hot.

Spicy Pineapple Boat

Prep Time: 15 minutes
Cook Time: 20-25 minutes
Serving Size: 2-4 servings

- 1 ripe pineapple (around 3 lbs)
- 1/2 cup cooked, shredded white or dark chicken or tofu (optional)
- 1/4 cup chopped red bell pepper
- 1/4 cup chopped green bell pepper
- 1/4 cup chopped red onion
- 1/4 cup chopped green onion
- 1 jalapeno pepper, seeded and minced (adjust for desired heat)
- 1 clove garlic, minced
- 1/4 cup chopped fresh cilantro
- 2 tablespoons soy sauce
- 1 tablespoon brown sugar
- 1 tablespoon rice vinegar
- 1 tablespoon toasted sesame oil
- 1/2 teaspoon crushed red pepper flakes (adjust for desired heat)
- 1/4 teaspoon ground ginger
- Pinch of cayenne pepper (optional)
- Salt and freshly ground black pepper to taste

Prep:
- Heat oven to 375°F (190°C).
- Cut top off pineapple, save leafy top.
- Scoop out pineapple flesh (leave a border) and chop.
-
Sauté:
- Heat a pan, cook peppers & onion (5 min).
- Add garlic, cook 1 min more.
-
Mix & Fill:
- In a bowl, combine cooked veggies, chopped pineapple, protein (optional), cilantro, soy sauce, brown sugar, vinegar, sesame oil, red pepper flakes, ginger, salt, pepper.
- Stuff pineapple with mixture.

Bake:
- Cover pineapple boat with foil and bake 20-25 min (heated filling, soft pineapple).

Serve:
- Let cool slightly, garnish with cilantro and the leafy top (optional).

Cucumber Salad with Sesame Ginger Dressing

Prep Time: 10 minutes
Cooking Time: n/a
Servings: 2

- 2 large cucumbers (around 1.5 lbs)
- 1/4 cup granulated sugar (or substitute with honey or maple syrup)
- 3 tablespoons seasoned rice vinegar (for extra *umami*)
- 1 tablespoon soy sauce
- 1 tablespoon roasted sesame oil
- 1 generous thumb of ginger, grated
- 1 clove garlic, minced
- 1/4 teaspoon black pepper (more to taste)
- 2 tablespoons toasted sesame seeds (for garnish)
- 1/4 cup chopped fresh cilantro

Prep:
- Wash & slice cucumbers (ribbons, rounds, or half-moons - be consistent)
- Salt cucumbers - rinse well after 10 min
-
Dressing:
- Whisk sugar (or substitute), seasoned vinegar, soy sauce, toasted sesame oil, grated ginger, garlic, pepper. Taste & adjust.
-
Assemble:
- Toss cucumbers with dressing. Chill 30 min.
-
Serve:
- Garnish with toasted sesame seeds & a sprinkle of cilantro.

San Sebastian, Spain

San Sebastián, a sun-kissed jewel on Spain's rugged Basque coast, isn't just a city for food lovers—it's a culinary playground where tradition and innovation dance a tantalizing tango. Born from a rich history of communal cooking and a deep connection to both land and sea, this gastronomic paradise beckons you to explore its vibrant tapestry of flavors.

Get ready to be swept away by the smoky aroma of sizzling pintxos in bustling bars, where miniature culinary masterpieces showcase the artistry of Basque cuisine. From the freshest seafood plucked from the Cantabrian Sea to locally-sourced produce bursting with flavor, every bite is a celebration of the region's bountiful harvest.

But San Sebastián isn't just about preserving the past; it's about pushing culinary boundaries with bold new creations. Michelin-starred restaurants and innovative chefs are constantly reimagining traditional Basque dishes with a modern twist, resulting in a culinary scene that is both exciting and deeply satisfying.

This chapter invites you on an unforgettable journey through San Sebastián's culinary landscape, where every dish is a masterpiece and every bite is an adventure. Get ready to discover a world where food isn't just sustenance, it's an expression of passion, creativity, and a deep love for the art of eating.

Atun Ahumado con Tomate Fresco (Smoked Tuna with Fresh Tomato): A simple yet elegant tapa celebrating the Basque region's affinity for high-quality seafood and vibrant, seasonal produce.

Patatas Bravas (Crispy Fried Potatoes): A quintessential Spanish tapas bar staple, these crispy potatoes smothered in spicy tomato sauce and garlicky aioli are a testament to the country's love for bold flavors and simple preparations. Their popularity and satisfying combination of textures make them a showstopper. (Showstopper)

Gambas al Ajillo (Garlic Shrimp): Sizzling with garlic and chili, this classic Spanish dish celebrates the delicate flavors of fresh shrimp, a staple of the country's coastal cuisine. The aroma alone makes it a crowd-pleaser. (Showstopper)

Tortilla Española (Spanish Omelette): A beloved Spanish comfort food, this hearty omelette combines potatoes, onions, and eggs, showcasing the resourcefulness of Spanish home cooking.

Paella Negra (Black Ink Paella): This dramatic and flavorful twist on the iconic Valencian paella incorporates squid ink for a striking presentation and subtly briny flavor, making it a true showstopper. (Showstopper)

Blistered Olives with White Bean & White Anchovy Crema with Toasted Pecorino Crust and Crushed Pistachios: This innovative tapa elevates the humble olive with a creamy white bean and anchovy spread, topped with a crispy pecorino crust and crushed pistachios for a symphony of textures and flavors. Its unexpected combination of ingredients and luxurious presentation make it a showstopper. (Showstopper)

White Bean Nachos with Chorizo, Anchovies & Caramelized Onions: A playful fusion of Spanish and Mexican cuisines, these nachos feature a hearty white bean base, topped with savory chorizo, salty anchovies, and sweet caramelized onions.

Almejas a la Marinera Andaluza con Hinojo y Estragón (Andalusian Clams Marinière with Fennel and Tarragon):: A fragrant and flavorful seafood dish inspired by the coastal regions of Andalusia, this recipe showcases the delicate sweetness of clams with the aromatic notes of fennel and tarragon, creating an elegant and impressive presentation. (Showstopper)

Roasted Butternut Squash with Crispy Prosciutto: A simple yet elegant dish highlighting the natural sweetness of roasted butternut squash, contrasted with the salty crispness of prosciutto.

Pisto Manchego (Spanish Ratatouille): A hearty and colorful vegetable stew bursting with the flavors of summer, this dish showcases the abundance of seasonal produce and the simple yet satisfying cooking techniques of Spanish cuisine. (Showstopper)

Rustic Txakoli & Quince Biscotti with Rosemary, Smoked Paprika, and *Guindilla* Pepper: This innovative biscotti offers a unique blend of sweet, savory, and spicy flavors, incorporating local Basque ingredients like Txakoli wine and *Guindilla* peppers. Its unexpected flavor profile and elegant presentation make it a delightful surprise. (Showstopper)

Piquillo Pepper and Manchego *Gougères*: A savory twist on the classic French gougères, these airy cheese puffs are infused with the smoky sweetness of piquillo peppers and the nutty richness of Manchego cheese, showcasing the fusion of Basque and French culinary influences.

Prep Time: 15 minutes
Cooking Time: 6 minutes total
Servings: 2-3

Atun Ahumado con Tomate Fresco (Smoked Tuna with Fresh Tomato)

The Base:
- 1 crusty baguette, sliced into ½ inch thick rounds (around 10-12 slices)
- 2 tablespoons high-quality olive oil
- 1 large skillet (preferably cast iron)
- Garlic clove, halved
- Sea salt flakes

The Tomato Topping:
- 2 large, vine-ripened tomatoes (peeled, seeded, and diced)
- 1 tablespoon finely chopped shallots (or red onion)
- 1 tablespoon chopped fresh chives
- 1 tablespoon extra virgin olive oil
- 1 tablespoon Sherry vinegar (or to taste)
- Sea salt flakes and freshly cracked black pepper

The Ahi Topping:
- ½ pound high-quality smoked tuna, thinly sliced (around 16-20 slices)
- 1 tablespoon olive oil
- Pinch of smoked paprika

For Garnish (Optional):
- Microgreens (pea shoots, sunflower sprouts)

Heat 1 tablespoon olive oil in a skillet over medium heat. Toast baguette slices in a single layer (2-3 minutes per side) until golden brown and crispy. Watch closely to avoid burning! While warm, rub each toast with halved garlic and sprinkle with salt.

-

Prepare the tomato topping as instructed in steps 2 and 3 of the original recipe (peel, seed, dice tomatoes, combine with shallots, chives, olive oil, vinegar, salt, pepper).

-

Brush smoked tuna slices with olive oil and sprinkle with smoked paprika.

-

Arrange toasted bread slices on a platter. Top each with a generous spoonful of tomato mixture.

-

Drape smoked tuna slices over the tomato layer for a nice presentation.

-

(Optional) Garnish each tapa with microgreens for a pop of color.

-

The Eggplant Option.

- Bread (sliced baguette)
- Garlic (clove, halved)
- Olive Oil
- Tomatoes (diced)
- Shallots (chopped)
- Chives (chopped)
- Sherry Vinegar
- Salt & Pepper
- Eggplant (small, sliced thin)
- Marinade (olive oil, lemon juice, oregano, smoked paprika - optional, salt, pepper, liquid smoke - optional)
- Microgreens (optional garnish)

Steps:

1. Marinate eggplant (30 min): Combine marinade ingredients, toss in eggplant slices.

2. Toast bread (3 min/side): Heat oil, toast bread slices. Rub warm toast with garlic, sprinkle with salt.

3. Tomato topping: Follow original recipe (steps 2 & 3).

4. Grill eggplant (3 min/side): Heat pan, brush eggplant with oil, grill till tender & charred.

5. Assemble: Toasted bread, tomato mix, grilled eggplant, microgreens (optional).

Prep Time: 5 minutes
Cooking Time: 15 minutes
Servings: 2-3

Patatas Bravas (Crispy Fried Potatoes)

- 2 large potatoes, peeled and cubed
- 2 tablespoons olive oil
- 1/2 teaspoon smoked paprika
- 1/4 teaspoon hot paprika (adjust for spice)
- 1 clove garlic, minced
- 1/2 teaspoon dried thyme
- 1 (14.5 oz) can diced tomatoes, undrained
- 1/4 cup chicken broth (optional, for extra richness; optional use reserved double-broth from the Hawaii section of this book)
- Salt and freshly ground black pepper

Flavor Boost: Heat olive oil in a large skillet over medium-high heat. Add the garlic and cook for 30 seconds, until fragrant. Be careful not to burn the garlic.

-

Add the potatoes and cook undisturbed for 5-7 minutes, or until golden brown and crispy on one side.

-

Using a spatula, carefully flip the potatoes and cook for another 3-4 minutes, or until golden brown and crispy all around. Sprinkle generously with smoked paprika and hot paprika while hot.

-

In a separate saucepan, combine diced tomatoes, chicken broth (if using), thyme, salt, and pepper. Bring to a simmer for 5 minutes, allowing the flavors to meld.

-

Arrange the crispy potatoes on a serving platter. Spoon over the warmed tomato sauce. Don't drown them!

Tip: A squeeze of fresh lemon juice adds a zingy touch (optional).

Prep Time: 20-30 minutes
Cooking Time: 15-20 minutes
Servings: 1-2

Gambas al Ajillo (Garlic Shrimp)

- 1 pound large shrimp, peeled and deveined (tails on or off, your choice)
- 4 tablespoons extra virgin olive oil
- 6 cloves garlic, thinly sliced
- 1/2 teaspoon dried red pepper flakes (adjust for heat)
- 1/4 cup white wine (optional, for a touch of acidity)
- 1 tablespoon fresh parsley, chopped (for garnish)
- sea salt and freshly cracked black pepper, to taste

Heat olive oil in a large skillet over medium-high heat. Ensure enough space for the shrimp; cook them in batches if needed.

-

Add shrimp to the hot oil and cook for 1-2 minutes per side, until opaque and pink. Season generously with salt and pepper throughout the cooking process.

-

Once cooked, remove the shrimp and set them aside. Add sliced garlic to the hot oil and cook for 30 seconds, releasing its fragrance. Be mindful not to burn the garlic.

-

(Optional Flavor Boost):
  - Include red pepper flakes, cooking for an additional 10 seconds.
  - If using white wine, deglaze the pan by pouring it in and scraping up any browned bits. Let it simmer for a minute to reduce slightly.

-

Return the cooked shrimp to the pan with the garlic and wine mixture (if used) for 30 seconds to reheat them.

-

Garnish with fresh chopped parsley and serve immediately. Enjoy with crusty bread for dipping in the garlic oil.

Tortilla Español (Spanish Omelette)

Prep Time: 15-20 minutes
Cooking Time: 45-50 minutes
Servings: 4-6

- 2 large russet potatoes (ideally with high starch content for better binding)
- 1 tablespoon extra virgin olive oil
- 1 medium Spanish onion (Vidalia or another sweet onion variety for a touch of sweetness)
- 6 large free-range eggs, preferably at room temperature
- ¼ cup (optional, but highly recommended) freshly grated Manchego cheese (traditional Spanish sheep's milk cheese) or Pecorino Romano for a sharp substitute
- Kosher salt
- Freshly cracked black pepper
- 1 clove garlic, minced (for an extra layer of savory depth)
- 1 bay leaf (adds a subtle herbal aroma)
- 1 sprig fresh thyme (optional, for a touch of floral fragrance)
- Pinch of smoked paprika (for a hint of smokiness)

Prep the Potatoes:
Wash, peel, and thinly slice the potatoes using a mandoline or sharp knife for uniform slices (around 1/8 inch thick). Soak the sliced potatoes in cold water for 30 minutes to remove excess starch, which will help prevent them from sticking together excessively during cooking. Rinse and drain them thoroughly afterwards.

-

Sauté the Aromatics: Heat the olive oil in a 10-inch oven-safe heavy-bottomed skillet (cast iron is ideal) over medium heat. Add the minced garlic and cook for 30 seconds, releasing its fragrance. Add the thinly sliced onions and bay leaf (if using). Cook slowly, stirring occasionally, until softened and translucent, about 15-20 minutes. This low and slow cooking time ensures caramelized onions, adding sweetness and depth of flavor to the tortilla.

-

Season and Dry the Potatoes: While the onions are cooking, pat the drained potato slices dry thoroughly with a clean kitchen towel to remove any remaining moisture. This drying step is crucial for achieving a crispy and well-structured tortilla. Season the potatoes generously with salt and freshly cracked black pepper.

-

Arrange half of the seasoned potato slices in a single layer over the softened onions and aromatics in the skillet. Sprinkle with half of the grated cheese (if using). Top with the remaining potato slices, creating an even layer. Press down gently on the potatoes to form a compact layer.

-

Infuse with Herbs (Optional): If using, add the sprig of fresh thyme on top of the potato layer.

-

In a large bowl, whisk together the eggs until well combined. Season generously with salt, freshly cracked black pepper, and a pinch of smoked paprika.

-

Cook the First Side: Carefully pour the whisked egg mixture over the layered potatoes in the skillet. Tilt the pan to evenly distribute the eggs. Increase the heat to medium-low and cook for 15-20 minutes, or until the bottom of the tortilla is golden brown and set.

-

The Flip: Here comes the impressive part! To achieve a perfectly cooked and restaurant-worthy tortilla, you'll need a large plate that can completely cover the skillet. Carefully place the plate on top of the skillet. Using oven mitts, firmly invert both the pan and plate together in a swift motion. The tortilla should slide out onto the plate, cooked side up.

-

Cook the Second Side: Slide the uncooked side of the tortilla back into the skillet with a drizzle of olive oil. Gently press down on the tortilla with a spatula to ensure even cooking. Cook for another 10-15 minutes, or until golden brown and cooked through.

-

Rest and Serve: Transfer the cooked tortilla to a serving plate and let it rest for at least 10 minutes before slicing. This resting time allows the internal temperature to reach its peak and for the flavors to meld beautifully. Slice into wedges and serve warm or at room temperature.

Prep Time: 15 minutes
Cooking Time: 45-50 minutes
Servings: 4-6

Paella Negra (Black Ink Paella)

The Squid and Ink:
- 1 pound squid, cleaned and chopped (bodies, tentacles)
- 2 tablespoons olive oil
- 1 medium onion, finely chopped
- 2 cloves garlic, minced
- 1 pouch (2 oz) squid ink (available at most specialty grocery stores)

Rice:
- 2 tablespoons olive oil
- 1 medium onion, finely chopped
- 2 bell peppers (red and yellow, diced)
- 1 cup Bomba rice (or short-grain rice)
- 1 teaspoon smoked paprika
- 1/2 teaspoon ground turmeric
- 1/4 teaspoon saffron threads (optional)
- 4 cups fish stock (warmed)
- 1/2 cup dry white wine
- 1 lemon, halved
- Salt and freshly cracked black pepper, to taste

Seafood
- 1 pound mussels, scrubbed and debearded
- 1 pound large shrimp, peeled and deveined (tails on or off)
- 1/2 pound sea scallops, rinsed and patted dry

Sear the Squid:
In a large pot or Dutch oven, heat olive oil over medium heat. Add the chopped squid and cook for 5-7 minutes, or until softened and releasing its juices.

Chef's Note: Avoid overcooking to maintain a tender, not rubbery, texture.

-

Sauté the Aromatics: Introduce the chopped onion and garlic to the pot with the squid. Sauté for an additional 2-3 minutes, or until the vegetables soften and become fragrant.

-

Incorporate the Ink: Once the squid and vegetables are softened, stir in the squid ink.

Chef's Note: Squid ink can stain, so wear gloves if desired. Continue cooking for 1 minute, allowing the ink to infuse the dish with color and flavor.

-

Simmer and Develop Flavor: Pour in 1 cup of warmed fish stock, ensuring all browned bits from the pot's bottom are scraped up to release the full range of flavors from the squid. Bring to a simmer, then reduce heat to low and simmer for 15 minutes, allowing the flavors to meld harmoniously.

-

Prepare the Rice: While the squid simmers, heat an additional 2 tablespoons of olive oil in a large skillet over medium heat. Add the chopped onion and bell peppers, and cook for 5-7 minutes, or until softened.

-

Toast the Rice: Add the Bomba rice to the skillet with the softened vegetables and stir to coat the rice grains evenly. Toast the rice for 1 minute with constant stirring.

-

Sprinkle the rice with smoked paprika and turmeric (and saffron, if using) and cook for an additional 30 seconds, ensuring the rice is evenly coated through continuous stirring.

-

Carefully pour the squid mixture, including all its accumulated juices, into the skillet with the rice and vegetables. Gently stir to create a cohesive mixture.

-

Gradually add the remaining warmed fish stock to the paella, approximately 1 cup at a time. Allow the rice to fully absorb the liquid before adding more stock. This meticulous method ensures each rice grain cooks evenly and becomes infused with the essence of the dish.

-

After adding roughly half of the fish stock, introduce the white wine and stir to incorporate it seamlessly.

-

Squeeze the juice of one lemon half into the paella and add the lemon half itself to the pot. The lemon contributes a touch of acidity, creating a well-balanced flavor profile.

-

Bomba rice is best for paella (high starch, creamy, firm). but is it hard to find? Try:

- Carnaroli (similar texture, pricier)
- Arborio (widely available, softer, adjust liquid)
- Valencia rice (Spanish option, decent sub)

Use less liquid with substitutes, cook time may vary.

Prep Time: 15 minutes
Cooking Time: 10 minutes
Servings: 4-6

Blistered Olives with White Bean & White Anchovy *Crema* with Toasted Pecorino Crust and Crushed Pistachios

Blistered Olive Base:
- 1 cup Kalamata olives (or your preferred olive variety)
- 2 tablespoons good quality olive oil
- 1 sprig fresh rosemary
- Pinch of red pepper flakes

White Bean & Anchovy Smash:
- 1 can (15 oz) cannellini beans, drained and rinsed
- 1/4 cup ricotta cheese
- 2 tablespoons olive oil
- 1 tablespoon lemon juice
- 3 cloves garlic, minced finely
- 5-7 white anchovies, rinsed if salted
- Salt and freshly cracked black pepper, to taste

Toasted Pecorino Crust:
- 4 slices baguette bread
- 2 tablespoons olive oil
- 1/2 cup grated Pecorino Romano cheese

Finishing Touches:
- Sherry vinegar
- Chopped fresh parsley
- 1 tablespoon capers, finely chopped (almost a paste)
- crushed pistachios

Heat olive oil in a skillet over medium-high heat. Add olives, rosemary, and red pepper flakes. Cook 5-7 minutes until blistered, then remove and set aside.

-

Crema: Pulse cannellini beans, ricotta (or yogurt), olive oil, lemon juice, garlic, and anchovies in a food processor until slightly chunky. Season well with salt and pepper.

-

Brush baguette slices with olive oil and toast on a grill pan or grill for 1-2 minutes per side until golden brown.

-

Top toasted bread with Pecorino Romano and broil for 1-2 minutes until cheese melts.

-

Assemble & Garnish: Spread white bean mixture on toasted bread. Top with blistered olives, a drizzle or atomizer spray of sherry vinegar (optional), chopped parsley, capers and crushed pistachios.

Prep Time: 15 minutes
Cooking Time: 22-27 minutes
Servings: 4-6

White Bean Nachos with Chorizo, Anchovies & Caramelized Onions

Nacho Base:
- 1 can (15 oz) cannellini beans, drained and rinsed
- 1 cup grated sharp cheddar cheese
- 1/2 cup grated pepper jack cheese
- 1/4 cup chopped fresh cilantro
- Salt and freshly cracked black pepper, to taste

Chorizo & Anchovy Topping:
- 4 ounces cured chorizo sausage, diced
- 1 tablespoon olive oil
- 2-3 white anchovies (rinsed if salted)

Blistered Red Onions:
- 1 red onion, thinly sliced
- 2 tablespoons olive oil
- Pinch of dried thyme

Finishing Touches:
- Sherry vinegar
- Chopped fresh parsley
- 1 tablespoon capers, finely chopped

Prepare the Nachos Base:
Preheat oven to 400°F (200°C). Combine cannellini beans, grated cheeses, and chopped cilantro in a large bowl. Season generously with salt and pepper.

-

Crispy Chorizo & Anchovies: Heat olive oil in a skillet over medium heat. Add diced chorizo and anchovies. Cook for 5-7 minutes, until chorizo is crisp and anchovies soften. Remove mixture with a slotted spoon and set aside on a paper towel.

-

In the same skillet, heat remaining oil over medium heat. Add red onion and thyme. Cook for 7-10 minutes, stirring occasionally, until onions are softened, caramelized, and slightly blistered.

-

Spread nacho base mixture evenly on a baking sheet. Top with chorizo-anchovy mixture and caramelized onions. Bake for 10-12 minutes, until cheese melts and bubbles.

-

Drizzle with sherry vinegar immediately upon removing from the oven. Garnish with chopped parsley and capers.

-

Chef's Notes:

-For a richer flavor, substitute crumbled queso fresco for some of the grated cheddar cheese.

-Adjust the amount of anchovies based on your desired level of briny flavor.

-Broil the nachos for the last minute of baking if you prefer a more intensely browned cheese topping.

Prep Time: 15 minutes
Cooking Time: 15-20 minutes
Servings: 2-3

Almejas a la Marinera Andaluza con Hinojo y Estragón (Andalusian Clams Marinière with Fennel and Tarragon)

- 1 pound (450g) fresh clams, soaked in cold water for 30 minutes (discard any unopened)
- 1/2 cup dry white wine
- 1 cup fish stock
- 1 tablespoon olive oil
- 1 small fennel bulb, thinly sliced
- 1 garlic clove, roughly chopped
- 1/2 teaspoon smoked paprika
- 1 sprig fresh oregano
- Pinch of red pepper flakes
- 1 tablespoon chopped fresh tarragon
- 1 tablespoon sherry vinegar
- Salt and freshly ground black pepper to taste
- Chopped fresh gremolata (parsley, lemon zest, capers)
- Toasted garlic bread (for serving)

Clean the Clams: Rinse clams thoroughly under cold running water. Discard any clams that are open or cracked. Soak them in cold water for 30 minutes to purge sand.

Heat olive oil in a large pot or Dutch oven over medium heat. Add the sliced fennel and cook for 3-4 minutes, or until softened and translucent.

Add the white wine and fish stock to the pot, scraping up any browned bits from the bottom. Bring to a simmer.

Add the smoked paprika, fresh oregano sprig, and red pepper flakes. Season with salt and pepper.

Steam the Clams: Add the clams and chopped garlic to the pot. Cover tightly and cook for 5-7 minutes, or until the clams have all opened. Discard any unopened clams.

Remove the oregano sprig. Stir in the chopped tarragon and sherry vinegar. Adjust seasoning with salt and pepper.

Serve Immediately: Turn off the heat and let the clams rest in the broth for a minute or two. Ladle the clams and flavorful broth into bowls.

Garnish with chopped fresh gremolata and serve hot with toasted garlic bread for dipping.

Tips:

- Use high-quality, fresh clams for the best results.

- Don't overcook the clams, as they will become tough and rubbery.

- Adjust the amount of red pepper flakes to your desired level of spiciness.

- If the broth seems too thin, you can simmer it uncovered for a few minutes to reduce slightly.

Roasted Butternut Squash with Crispy Prosciutto

Prep Time: 10 minutes
Cook Time: 25-30 minutes
Servings: 4-6 as a side dish

- 1 medium butternut squash (around 3 lbs)
- 2 tablespoons olive oil
- 1/2 teaspoon salt
- 1/4 teaspoon black pepper
- 1/4 teaspoon smoked paprika (a signature San Sebastian spice)
- Pinch of freshly grated nutmeg (optional)
- 4 ounces thinly sliced *Jamón Serrano*
- Fresh rosemary sprigs (for garnish)

Heat oven to 400°F (200°C), line a baking sheet with parchment paper.

Toss squash with olive oil, salt, pepper, paprika, and nutmeg (if using).

Spread squash on the baking sheet and roast 25-30 minutes (tender-crisp & browned).

While squash roasts, heat a large skillet over medium heat.

Cook *Jamón Serrano* slices 1-2 minutes per side (crispy & browned). Drain on paper towels. Once squash is roasted and *Jamón Serrano* is crispy, arrange squash on a platter.

Top with crumbled *Jamón Serrano* and garnish with rosemary (optional).

Serve hot and enjoy!

Pisto Manchego (Spanish Ratatouille)

Prep Time: 5 minutes
Cooking Time: 25-30 minutes
Servings: 4-6 as a side dish

- 2 tablespoons olive oil
- 1/2 onion, chopped
- 1 green bell pepper, chopped
- 1 red bell pepper, chopped
- 1 zucchini, chopped
- 2 ripe tomatoes, chopped
- 2 cloves garlic, minced
- 1/4 teaspoon dried thyme
- Pinch of saffron threads (optional, for extra Spanish flavor)
- 1/4 cup water
- Salt and freshly ground black pepper to taste
- Fresh parsley, chopped (for garnish)

Heat olive oil in a pan over medium heat.

Sauté onion, peppers, and zucchini (5-7 minutes, softened & browned).

Add tomatoes and garlic (cook 5 minutes more, softened tomatoes).

Throw in some water, salt, pepper, and simmer (15-20 minutes, tender veggies & thickened sauce).

Rustic Txakoli & Quince Biscotti with Rosemary, Smoked Paprika, and Guindilla Pepper

Prep Time: 15 minutes
Cook Time: 30-35 minutes
(including both bakes)
Servings: Approximately 24 biscotti

- 1 cup all-purpose flour
- 1/2 cup almond flour
- 1/2 cup granulated sugar
- 1/4 teaspoon baking powder
- 1/2 teaspoon finely chopped fresh rosemary
- 1/4 teaspoon smoked paprika
- 1/4 teaspoon sea salt
- 2 large eggs
- 1/4 cup Txakoli wine
- 1 tablespoon olive oil
- 2 tablespoons quince paste, finely chopped
- 1-2 *Guindilla* peppers (or to taste), finely chopped, or substitute;
- Fresno Chili Peppers: These peppers offer a slightly sweeter heat than jalapeños, with a similar level of spice as *Guindillas*.

Important Note: Regardless of the substitute you choose, be sure to adjust the amount according to your personal taste preference and the spice level of the pepper you're using. Start with a small amount and add more if needed.

Preheat the oven to 350°F (175°C). Line a baking sheet with parchment paper.

In a large bowl, whisk together both flours, sugar, baking powder, rosemary, smoked paprika, and sea salt.

In a separate bowl, whisk together the eggs, Txakoli wine, and olive oil.

Gradually add the wet ingredients to the dry ingredients, stirring until a dough just comes together. Avoid overmixing; the dough should be slightly shaggy and not completely smooth.

Gently fold in the chopped quince paste and Guindilla peppers.

Transfer the dough to the prepared baking sheet and shape it into a rough, rustic log (about 12 inches long and 3 inches wide).

Bake for 20-25 minutes, or until the log is golden brown and firm to the touch.

Let cool slightly (about 10 minutes), then slice the log into 1/2-inch thick slices on a diagonal.

Arrange the slices cut-side down on the baking sheet and bake for an additional 8-10 minutes per side, or until crisp and lightly golden. Watch carefully to avoid over-baking.

Let cool completely on a wire rack before serving.

Piquillo Pepper and Manchego Gougères

Prep Time: 15 minutes
Cooking Time: 20-25 minutes
Servings: Approximately 24 gougères (depends on size)

- 1 cup water
- 1/2 cup unsalted butter
- 1/4 teaspoon salt
- 1 cup all-purpose flour
- 4 large eggs
- 1/2 cup grated Manchego cheese
- 1/2 cup chopped roasted piquillo peppers
- Pinch of cayenne pepper (optional)

Preheat oven to 400°F (200°C). Line a baking sheet with parchment paper.

In a saucepan, combine water, butter, and salt. Bring to a boil, then remove from heat.

Add flour all at once and stir vigorously until dough forms a ball.

Return to low heat and cook for 1 minute, stirring constantly.

Remove from heat and let cool slightly. Beat in eggs one at a time, incorporating fully before adding the next.

Fold in Manchego cheese, piquillo peppers, and cayenne pepper (if using).

Drop rounded tablespoons of dough onto prepared baking sheet.

Bake for 20-25 minutes, or until golden brown and puffed.

Playa del Carmen, Mexico

Playa del Carmen, a vibrant coastal jewel nestled on the Yucatán Peninsula, offers a culinary journey that tantalizes the senses and transports you to the heart of Mexico's rich food heritage. This is a place where ancient Mayan traditions intertwine with modern culinary innovation, resulting in a symphony of flavors that celebrate both the past and the present.

For culinary travelers, Playa del Carmen is a treasure trove of gastronomic delights. The city's bustling streets are lined with taco stands serving up sizzling al pastor, seafood shacks grilling up fresh catches of the day, and vibrant markets overflowing with exotic fruits and vegetables. From casual beachfront eateries to upscale restaurants helmed by renowned chefs, there's something to satisfy every palate and budget.

The allure of Playa del Carmen's food scene lies in its diversity and ingenuity. Chefs here are inspired by the abundance of fresh, local ingredients, from the succulent seafood of the Caribbean to the exotic fruits and vegetables grown in the fertile Yucatecan soil. They also draw inspiration from ancient Mayan cooking techniques, such as slow-roasting meats in underground pits and using indigenous herbs and spices to create complex flavor profiles.

Papadzules (Egg and Pumpkin Seed Envelopes with Tomatillo): A reimagined Yucatán classic, these delicate egg-filled tortillas bathed in a creamy pumpkin seed sauce offer a taste of Mayan culinary history with an elegant twist.

Yucatan-Inspired Tacos with Charred Corn, Queso Fresco, Flank Steak, and Crispy Poblanos: This vibrant taco creation showcases the fiery flavors and fresh ingredients of the Yucatán Peninsula, highlighting the region's unique culinary heritage. (Showstopper)

Pescado Tikin Xic (Grilled Fish with Achiote): Embracing the Mayan tradition of slow-cooking in banana leaves, this dish features achiote-marinated fish infused with smoky flavors and earthy spices, offering a true taste of the Yucatán's ancient culinary heritage.

Fiery Fiesta Dip with Charred Peppers and Pickled Anaheim Chili: This vibrant dip ignites the senses with the smoky heat of charred peppers and the tangy zest of pickled Anaheim chilies, a testament to Mexico's love for bold and complex flavors. (Showstopper)

Meso-American Harvest Salad with Green Mole Drizzle: A celebration of Mexico's rich agricultural heritage, this salad combines fresh seasonal produce with a drizzle of herbaceous green mole, showcasing the versatility of this iconic sauce.

Quick Mini Nopalitos Tamales: A modern take on a traditional Mexican staple, these bite-sized tamales feature the unique texture and flavor of nopalitos (cactus paddles), a symbol of Mexican resilience and resourcefulness. (Showstopper)

Cocoa-Rubbed Roasted Cauliflower with Gouda and Jalapeño Dipping Sauce: This innovative dish blends the rich, earthy flavors of cocoa with the creamy indulgence of gouda cheese and the fiery kick of jalapeño, showcasing the unexpected and playful side of Mexican cuisine. (Showstopper)

Mango Yucatan Spiced Beef Jerky: A delightful fusion of sweet and savory, this jerky combines the tropical sweetness of mango with the complex spices of the Yucatán Peninsula, offering a unique and addictive snack. (Showstopper)

Prep Time: 20 minutes
Cooking Time: 25-30 minutes
Servings: 4

Papadzules (Egg and Pumpkin Seed Envelopes with Tomatillo)

Pumpkin Seed Paste:
- 1 cup raw pumpkin seeds (*pepitas*)
- 2 cloves garlic
- 1/4 white onion, chopped
- 1/2 teaspoon ground cumin
- 1/4 teaspoon ground *achiote* (optional, for a deeper color)
- 1/4 teaspoon dried oregano
- Salt, to taste
- Water, as needed

Tomatillo Sauce:
- 3-4 tomatillos, husked and roasted (or charred over the campfire)
- 1/2 white onion, chopped
- 1 clove garlic, minced
- 1 *ancho* chili, pre-chopped and toasted (optional, adjust for spice preference)
- 1 cup chopped jicama
- 1/2 cup chopped fresh cilantro
- Salt and pepper, to taste
- Water, as needed

Papadzules:
- 4 large eggs
- 8 corn tortillas
- Vegetable oil, for cooking
- Queso fresco, crumbled (optional, for garnish)
- Fresh cilantro, chopped (for garnish)

Make the Pumpkin Seed Paste:
- Heat a dry skillet over medium heat. Toast pumpkin seeds until fragrant and lightly browned, about 3-4 minutes. Keep stirring to prevent burning.

- Transfer toasted seeds to a food processor or blender. Add garlic, onion, spices (cumin, achiote if using, oregano), and salt.

- Pulse until finely ground, adding water gradually for a smooth paste. Set aside.

-

Roast the Tomatillos:
- For campfire char (optional): Char tomatillos over a grill grate or flames for a smoky flavor. Remove skins after charring.

- Oven roasting option: Preheat oven to 400°F (200°C). Place tomatillos on a baking sheet and roast for 10-15 minutes until softened and blistered. Remove skins after roasting.

-

The Tomatillo Sauce:
- In a saucepan, sauté onion, garlic, and jicama in oil over medium heat until onion is translucent.

- Add roasted tomatillos, chopped ancho chili (if using), and cilantro. Season with salt and pepper.

- Blend mixture until smooth. Add water for desired consistency. Set aside.

-

Boil & Peel the Eggs:
- Place eggs in cold water in a pot. Bring to a boil over medium-high heat.

- Once boiling, reduce heat to low and simmer for 9 minutes (soft-boiled) or 12 minutes (hard-boiled).

- Transfer eggs to ice water to cool. Peel and slice lengthwise into quarters. Set aside.

-

Assemble & Cook the Papadzules:
- Heat skillet or griddle over medium heat, lightly oil.

- Warm tortillas for about 30 seconds per side. Spread pumpkin seed paste on each, top with a quarter of a sliced egg. Roll up tortillas, or, fold into long rectangles, for a more elegant look, and place seam-side down in skillet.

- Cook for 1-2 minutes per side until lightly golden brown and heated through.

-

Drizzle Papadzules with tomatillo sauce. Optional: crumble *queso fresco* and sprinkle with fresh herbs before serving. Enjoy warm.

Prep Time: 30 minutes
Cooking Time: 30 minutes
Servings: 4

Yucatan-Inspired Tacos with Charred Corn, Queso Fresco, Flank Steak, and Crispy Poblanos

Charred Corn & *Queso Fresco*:
- 2 ears fresh corn, husked
- 1 tablespoon butter
- 1/2 cup heavy cream
- 1/2 cup crumbled *queso fresco* cheese
- Salt and freshly cracked black pepper, to taste

Marinated Flank Steak:
- 1 pound flank steak, thinly sliced
- 1 tablespoon olive oil
- 1 teaspoon ground cumin
- 1/2 teaspoon chili powder
- Salt and freshly cracked black pepper, to taste

Crispy Poblano Pepper Strips:
- 2 poblano peppers
- 2 egg whites
- 1/4 cup all-purpose flour
- Vegetable oil, for frying

Warming Touches:
- 8 corn tortillas
- Chopped fresh cilantro
- Lime wedges

Charred Corn & Queso Fresco:
- Heat a large skillet over medium-high heat. Add corn kernels and cook for 5-7 minutes until browned.

- Remove corn from the pan. Melt butter in the same pan, add corn back, and cook for 2-3 minutes.

- Pour in heavy cream, simmer for 5 minutes, then stir in crumbled queso fresco. Season with salt and pepper.

—

Marinated Flank Steak:
- Mix olive oil, cumin, chili powder, salt, and pepper in a bowl. Coat sliced flank steak and let it marinate for at least 15 minutes.

- Heat a skillet over medium-high heat. Sear steak for 2-3 minutes per side until desired doneness. Rest for 5 minutes before slicing.

-

Crispy Poblano Pepper Strips:
- Preheat oven to 400°F (200°C) and roast poblano peppers for 15-20 minutes until blackened. Peel, remove seeds, and cut into strips.

- Whisk egg whites until frothy. Dip poblano strips in egg whites, then coat in flour.

- Fry in vegetable oil over medium heat for 1-2 minutes per side until golden and crispy. Drain on paper towels.

Assemble & Serve:
- Warm corn tortillas in a dry skillet. Place a spoonful of charred corn mixture on each tortilla, top with sliced flank steak and crispy poblano strips, and serve warm.

Pescado Tikin Xic (Grilled Fish with Achiote)

Preparing the marinade and marinating the fish: Approximately 15 minutes

Preheating the grill or frying pan: Approximately 5 minutes

Grilling the fish: 5-7 minutes per side

Servings: 2-4

Marinade:
- 1/2 cup achiote paste (available in Latin American markets)
- 1/4 cup freshly squeezed orange juice
- 1/4 cup freshly squeezed lime juice
- 1 tablespoon white vinegar
- 1 clove garlic, minced (about 1 teaspoon)
- 1/2 red onion, finely chopped (about 1/4 cup)
- 1 teaspoon ground cumin
- 1/2 teaspoon dried oregano
- 1/4 teaspoon achiote powder (optional, for extra color)
- Salt and freshly cracked black pepper, to taste

Fish:
- 1 whole white fish (snapper, grouper, or cod), cleaned and scaled (around 1-1.5 lbs)

Cooking:
- Vegetable oil, for brushing
- Banana leaves (optional, for extra smoky flavor) - you can find these at Latin American markets

Prepare the Marinade:
- In a bowl, combine achiote paste, orange juice, lime juice, vinegar, minced garlic, finely chopped red onion, cumin, oregano, achiote powder (if using), salt, and pepper. Whisk until well mixed.

Marinate the Fish:
- Place the whole fish in a shallow dish and pour the marinade over it, ensuring even coating. Cover with plastic wrap and refrigerate for at least 2 hours, preferably overnight.

Preheat and Prep for Cooking:
-Preheat your grill or frying pan first over medium heat. Once it's warmed up, you can then lightly brush the surface of the pan with oil or use a cooking spray before adding the fish. This helps to ensure that the oil evenly coats the surface and creates a non-stick barrier for cooking.

Soak banana leaves in warm water for 30 minutes (if using) and cut into squares large enough to wrap the fish. Lightly brush grill grates with vegetable oil.

Wrap or Direct Grill:
- Banana Leaf Wrap (Optional): Wrap the marinated fish in banana leaf squares, folding edges to secure. Brush the outside with oil.

- Direct Grill (No Banana Leaf): Place the fish directly on preheated grill grates.

Grill fish for 5-7 minutes per side, until flesh flakes easily with a fork and is cooked through. Adjust cooking time based on fish thickness and burner heat.

Serve Warm.

Prep Time: 15 minutes
Cooking Time: 15-20 minutes
Servings: 2-3

Fiery Fiesta Dip with Charred Peppers and Pickled Anaheim Chili

Charred Peppers:
- 1 pasilla pepper
- 1 jalapeño pepper
- 1 serrano pepper
- 1 tablespoon olive oil

To Pickle the Chiles
- Cumin seeds: 1 teaspoon
- Coriander seeds: 1 teaspoon
- Whole black peppercorns: 1/2 teaspoon
- Bay leaves: 2 leaves
- Mexican oregano: 1 teaspoon
- Cloves: 4-6 cloves
- Garlic cloves: 2 cloves
- Black coriander (optional): 1/2 teaspoon
- Allspice (optional): 1/4 teaspoon

Pickled Anaheim Chili:
- 1 chopped pickled Anaheim chili (or another mild pickled pepper)
- 2 tablespoons of the pickling liquid

Dip Base:
- 1/2 cup ricotta cheese
- 1/4 cup crumbled *queso fresco* cheese
- 1/4 cup chopped fresh cilantro
- 1/4 cup chopped fresh parsley
- 1 tablespoon lime juice
- 1 clove garlic, minced
- Salt and freshly cracked black pepper, to taste

Toppings (Optional):
- Chopped fresh avocado
- Diced red onion
- Toasted *pepitas* (pumpkin seeds)
- Tortilla chips, plantain chips, or crudités (cut vegetables) for dipping

Char the Peppers:
- Heat a grill pan or grill over medium-high heat.

- Drizzle pasilla, jalapeño, and serrano peppers with olive oil.

- Grill peppers, turning occasionally, until charred and blistered on all sides, about 5-7 minutes.

- Transfer charred peppers to a paper bag and let them steam for 10 minutes to loosen the skins.

Prep the Peppers:
- Peel charred skin off the peppers once cool enough to handle.

- Seed and roughly chop the peppers.

Prepare the Pickled Anaheim:
- In a small bowl, combine chopped pickled Anaheim chili with 2 tablespoons of its pickling liquid. Set aside.

Create the Creamy Base:
- In a medium bowl, whisk ricotta cheese, crumbled queso fresco, chopped cilantro, chopped parsley, lime juice, and minced garlic.

- Season with salt and freshly cracked black pepper to taste.

Combine and Serve:
- Fold chopped charred peppers and pickled Anaheim chili mixture into the creamy base.

- Adjust seasonings with additional salt, pepper, or lime juice as needed.

Transfer dip to a serving bowl and garnish with favorite toppings like chopped fresh avocado, diced red onion, and toasted pepitas.

Serve with tortilla chips, plantain chips, or crudités for dipping.

How to Pickle the Chiles:

1. Prepare Pickling Liquid: In a saucepan, combine vinegar, water, salt, sugar, and spices (cumin seeds, coriander seeds, black peppercorns, bay leaves, Mexican oregano, cloves, garlic cloves, black coriander, and allspice). Bring to a boil, then simmer for 5 minutes.

2. Pack Chilis: Place chopped Anaheim chilis in a clean jar. Pour hot pickling liquid over the chilis, covering them completely.

3. Cool and Seal: Let the jar cool to room temperature. Seal tightly and refrigerate for at least 24 hours before using.

Meso-American Harvest Salad with Green Mole Drizzle

Prep time: 15 minutes
Cooking time: 15 minutes
Servings: 4-6

- Assorted vegetables (such as bell peppers, onions, and corn)
- Jicama, julienned
- Roasted and shredded game bird (such as pheasant, duck, or quail- optional)

Green Mole Sauce:
- 1 cup fresh cilantro leaves
- 1/2 cup fresh parsley leaves
- 1 jalapeño pepper, deseeded
- 2 cloves garlic
- 1/4 cup pumpkin seeds, toasted
- 1/4 cup almonds, toasted
- 1/4 cup sesame seeds, toasted
- 1 tablespoon ground cumin
- 1 teaspoon ground coriander
- 1 teaspoon dried oregano
- 2 cups chicken or vegetable broth
- Salt and pepper to taste
- Olive oil for grilling

Make the Green Mole Sauce: Blend cilantro, parsley, jalapeño, garlic, toasted seeds, spices, and broth until smooth. Season with salt and pepper.

Char the Vegetables: Grill assorted vegetables until tender and charred, about 5-7 minutes per side.

Assemble the Salad: Arrange charred vegetables and jicama on a serving platter. Top with roasted and shredded game bird.

Serve: Drizzle the green mole sauce over the salad. Garnish with fresh cilantro and a drizzle of olive oil if desired.

Quick Mini Nopalitos Tamales

Prep Time: 20 minutes (including pickling)
Cook Time: 25 minutes
Serving Size: 10-12 mini tamales

For the Tamales:
- 1 cup *masa harina* (corn flour)
- 3/4 cup vegetable broth
- 1/4 cup cooked nopalitos (chopped)
- 1/4 cup shredded Oaxacan cheese
- 2 tablespoons salsa verde
- 2 cloves garlic, minced
- 1/4 cup onion, finely chopped
- 1 Fresno chili, seeded and finely chopped
- Salt to taste

For the Pickled Radish:
- 1/4 cup thinly sliced radishes
- 1/4 cup white vinegar
- 1/2 teaspoon sugar
- Pinch of salt

For the Smoky Cabbage:
- 1/4 cup red cabbage, thinly julienned
- 1 tablespoon olive oil
- Pinch of smoked paprika

Other:
- Corn husks, soaked in warm water for 30 minutes and drained

Pickle radishes (10 min): Thinly slice radishes, mix with vinegar, sugar & salt (all in a bowl). Set aside.

Sauté (5 min): Heat oil, cook chopped nopalitos, onions, chili pepper, cumin & chili powder (to taste).

Mix the Masa (2 min): Combine masa harina & broth (water) for a soft dough.

Add to Masa (2 min): Stir in cooked nopalitos, cheese, salsa, garlic & salt.

Add Crunch (1 min): Drain pickled radishes (save some juice!), add with smoked paprika-sautéed cabbage.

Fill & Steam (25 min): Stuff husks, fold, steam like regular tamales.

Drizzle reserved pickling juice for extra tang.

Cocoa-Rubbed Roasted Cauliflower with Gouda and Jalapeño Dipping Sauce

Prep Time: 5 minutes
Cooking Time: 4 minutes
Servings: 1 Cup

- 1 head cauliflower, cut into florets
- 2 tablespoons cocoa powder
- 1 teaspoon powdered guajillo pepper
- 1 teaspoon powdered pasilla pepper
- 1/2 teaspoon ground cumin
- 1/2 teaspoon garlic powder
- 1/2 teaspoon Mexican oregano
- 1/2 teaspoon black pepper
- 2 tablespoons grapeseed oil or olive oil
- Salt to taste
- Zest of 1 lime
- Splash of white wine vinegar

Preheat the oven to 400°F (200°C).

In a bowl, combine cocoa powder, powdered guajillo pepper, powdered pasilla pepper, ground cumin, garlic powder, Mexican oregano, black pepper, salt, lime zest, and a splash of white wine vinegar.

Toss cauliflower florets with grapeseed oil or olive oil until evenly coated.

Sprinkle the spice mixture over the cauliflower and toss again until well coated.

Spread the cauliflower in a single layer on a baking sheet.

Roast in the preheated oven for 2025 minutes, or until golden and tender.

Serve hot as a unique and flavorful side dish.

Gouda and Jalapeño Dipping Sauce

Ingredients:
- 1 cup shredded Gouda cheese
- 1 jalapeño pepper, seeded and finely chopped
- 1/2 cup sour cream or crème fraîche
- Salt and pepper to taste
- Optional: a splash of lime juice for brightness

1. In a small saucepan, combine the shredded Gouda cheese and chopped jalapeño pepper.
2. Heat the mixture over low heat, stirring constantly, until the cheese is melted and the jalapeño is softened.
3. Once melted, stir in the sour cream or crème fraîche until smooth and creamy.
4. Season the dipping sauce with salt and pepper to taste, adjusting as needed.

Mango Yucatan Spiced Beef Jerky

Prep Time: 15 minutes
Cooking Time: 4-6 hours
Servings: 4

- 1 lb lean beef, thinly sliced against the grain
- 1 ripe mango, peeled and diced
- 1/4 cup soy sauce
- 2 tablespoons lime juice
- 2 tablespoons honey
- 2 cloves garlic, minced
- 1 teaspoon ground cumin
- 1 teaspoon chili powder
- 1/2 teaspoon smoked paprika
- 1/2 teaspoon dried oregano
- 1/4 teaspoon ground cloves
- Salt and pepper to taste

In a blender or food processor, combine the diced mango, soy sauce, lime juice, honey, minced garlic, ground cumin, chili powder, smoked paprika, dried oregano, ground cloves, salt, and pepper. Blend until smooth.
-Place the thinly sliced beef in a resealable plastic bag or shallow dish.

Pour the mango marinade over the beef, making sure it is evenly coated. Seal the bag or cover the dish and marinate in the refrigerator for at least 4 hours, or preferably overnight, to allow the flavors to infuse.

Preheat your oven to 175°F (80°C) or the lowest setting.

Remove the marinated beef from the refrigerator and drain off any excess marinade.

Arrange the beef slices in a single layer on a wire rack set over a baking sheet to catch any drips.

Place the beef in the preheated oven and bake for 4-6 hours, or until the jerky is dried and firm but still slightly pliable.

Allow the jerky to cool completely before storing in an airtight container at room temperature for up to 2 weeks.

Cottesloe Beach, Perth, Australia

Cottesloe Beach, an iconic stretch of coastline in Perth, Western Australia, boasts a food culture that captures the essence of Aussie beach life – relaxed, fresh, and innovative, with a touch of indulgence.

Rooted in a love for the outdoors and a laid-back lifestyle, Cottesloe's culinary scene reflects the abundance of fresh seafood and local produce that flourish in the region's Mediterranean climate. From casual cafes serving up hearty breakfasts and fish and chips to elegant beachfront restaurants offering sophisticated seafood platters and modern Australian cuisine, there's something to satisfy every craving.

Cottesloe's foodways are deeply intertwined with its stunning natural surroundings. Dining alfresco with views of the Indian Ocean is a quintessential Cottesloe experience, whether it's enjoying a leisurely brunch on a sunny terrace or indulging in a seafood feast as the sun sets over the horizon.

In recent years, Cottesloe has emerged as a hub for culinary innovation, with talented chefs pushing boundaries and creating exciting new dishes that showcase the best of local ingredients. The fusion of global flavors and techniques with the freshest seasonal produce results in a unique and constantly evolving dining scene.

But even with all the culinary excitement, Cottesloe remains true to its roots, with a strong emphasis on quality, simplicity, and a deep appreciation for the natural beauty that surrounds it. Whether you're indulging in a classic Aussie burger or savoring a plate of locally caught seafood, the flavors of Cottesloe are sure to leave a lasting impression.

Aussie Fusion Cornbread with Vegemite, Macadamia, & Feta: A savory twist on a classic American staple, this cornbread incorporates the iconic Aussie spread, Vegemite, and crunchy macadamia nuts for a unique flavor experience. (Showstopper)

Pan-Seared Beef and Prawn Patties on Toasted Buns: This Aussie Fusion Burger is a culinary masterpiece that celebrates the best of Australian surf and turf, combining a succulent beef patty with a spicy chili prawn sausage. Grilled pineapple adds a touch of tropical sweetness, while the homemade Aussie Fire Hot Sauce delivers a fiery kick, making it a true showstopper. It's a symphony of textures and flavors that reflects Australia's vibrant food culture and love for culinary innovation. (Showstopper)

Our A+ Smoked Paprika and Olive Damper: A showstopper campfire bread, this elevated damper is infused with the smoky warmth of paprika and the briny essence of olives, creating a rustic yet refined taste of the Australian bush. (Showstopper)

One-Pan Thyme and Zest Flatfish with Plum Sauce and Hazelnut Crumble: A delicate and flavorful seafood dish showcasing the freshness of Australian flatfish, enhanced with aromatic thyme, zesty lemon, and a sweet and tangy plum sauce.

Our A+ Lamington: An Aussie Classic Elevated: A decadent twist on the beloved Australian Lamington, this dessert elevates the classic sponge cake with layers of rich chocolate ganache and a generous coating of shredded coconut. (Showstopper)

Roasted Sweet Potato and Wattleseed Salad with Bush Tomato Vinaigrette: This vibrant salad celebrates the unique flavors of the Australian bush, combining roasted sweet potatoes with earthy wattleseed and a tangy bush tomato vinaigrette.

Grilled Pineapple with Chili Lime & Mango Salsa: This tropical delight features grilled pineapple infused with the sweet heat of chili and lime, topped with a refreshing mango salsa for a burst of summer flavors.

Prep Time: 15 minutes
Cooking Time: 25-30 minutes
Servings: 9 squares

Aussie Fusion Cornbread with Vegemite, Macadamia, & Feta

- 1 1/4 cups stone-ground cornmeal
- 3/4 cup all-purpose flour
- 1 tablespoon black treacle (or dark brown sugar)
- 1 teaspoon baking powder
- 1/2 teaspoon baking soda
- 1/2 teaspoon salt
- 1 cup milk (or buttermilk)
- 1/4 cup macadamia oil
- 2 large eggs
- 1/4 cup crumbled feta cheese
- 1/4 cup chopped roasted macadamia nuts
- 2 tablespoons Vegemite
- 1/2 teaspoon ground ginger
- 1/2 teaspoon ground coriander
- 1/4 cup fresh basil, chopped

Honey-Chili Glaze:

- 1/4 cup honey
- 1 tablespoon chili flakes
- 1 tablespoon lime juice
- 1/4 teaspoon ground cumin (optional)

Preheat oven to 400°F (200°C). Grease an 8x8 inch baking pan.

-

In a large bowl, whisk together cornmeal, flour, treacle, baking powder, baking soda, salt, ginger, and coriander.

-

In a separate bowl, whisk together milk, oil, eggs, and feta.

-

Pour wet ingredients into dry ingredients and stir until just combined. Fold in macadamia nuts and basil.

-

Pour half the batter into the prepared pan. Dollop spoonfuls of Vegemite over the batter. Swirl gently with a knife. Top with the remaining batter.

-

Bake for 20-25 minutes, or until a toothpick inserted into the center comes out clean.

-

While cornbread bakes, whisk together honey, chili flakes, lime juice, and optional cumin for the glaze.

-

Once cornbread is done, drizzle with glaze and let cool slightly before cutting.

Pan-Seared Beef and Prawn Patties on Toasted Buns

Prep Time: 15 minutes
Cooking Time: 10-12 minutes
Servings: 2 burgers

For the Seasoned Beef Patty:

- 1 pound high-quality ground beef (preferably grass-fed for extra flavor)
- 1 tablespoon Worcestershire sauce
- 1/2 teaspoon ground coriander
- 1 teaspoon smoked paprika
- 1/4 teaspoon ground white pepper
- 1/4 teaspoon ground mace
- Pinch of cayenne pepper
- Salt and freshly cracked black pepper, to taste

For the Homemade Chili Prawn Sausage:

- 1/2 pound ground pork
- 1/2 pound fresh, raw prawns, peeled, deveined, and roughly chopped
- 1 tablespoon finely chopped shallots
- 1 clove garlic, minced
- 1 tablespoon finely chopped fresh coriander (cilantro)
- 1 teaspoon finely chopped fresh lemon myrtle (or 1/2 teaspoon dried)
- 1/2 teaspoon fennel seed
- Pinch of cayenne pepper
- Salt and freshly cracked black pepper, to taste
- 1 tablespoon olive oil

For the Aussie Fire Hot Sauce:

- 2 ripe red chilies (such as Fresno or Jalapeño)
- 1 tablespoon mixed peppercorns (green and pink)
- 1 tablespoon pitted Medjool dates
- 1 tablespoon lime juice
- 1 tablespoon olive oil
- 1/4 cup white vinegar

For the Burger Assembly:

- Toasted hamburger buns
- Slices of grilled pineapple (optional)
- Lettuce leaves
- Tomato slices
- Red onion slices
- Avocado slices (optional)
- Aioli (optional)

Mix beef patty ingredients, shape into 2 patties.

-

Sauté shallots & garlic. Mix pork, prawns, spices, and sautéed ingredients. Shape into 2 sausages.

-

Heat a pan, sear beef patties 3-4 minutes per side.

-

Sear prawn sausages 2-3 minutes per side. (Optional: Smoke with smoker gun or liquid smoke)

-

Toast buns, spread aioli (optional).

-

Assemble: Beef patty, prawn sausage, pineapple (optional), lettuce, tomato, onion, avocado (optional).

-

Drizzle with hot sauce, top with bun.

A+ Smoked Paprika and Olive Damper

Prep Time: 15 minutes
Cooking Time: 20-25 minutes
Servings: 6-8 squares

- 2 cups high-protein bread flour (strong flour)
- 1 tablespoon active dry yeast
- 1 teaspoon caster sugar
- 1 teaspoon smoked paprika
- 1/2 teaspoon sea salt flakes
- 1 tablespoon olive oil, plus extra for brushing
- 1 cup buttermilk, chilled
- 1/4 cup mixed finely chopped Manzanillo and Kalamata olives

Activate the yeast: Combine yeast, sugar, and warm water in a bowl. Let it sit for 5 minutes until foamy.

Mix dry ingredients: In a separate bowl, whisk together flour, paprika, and salt.

Combine wet & dry: Make a well in the dry ingredients. Pour in activated yeast mixture, olive oil, and buttermilk. Mix until a shaggy dough forms.

Knead the dough: Turn the dough onto a floured surface and knead for 10 minutes.

First rise: Place dough in an oiled bowl, cover, and let it rise in a warm spot for 1 hour (doubled in size).

Shape & second rise: Fold in olives, shape into a round loaf, place on a baking sheet with parchment paper. Brush with olive oil, sprinkle with salt flakes, cover loosely, and let rise for 30 minutes.

Bake: Preheat oven to 430°F (220°C). Bake the damper for 25-30 minutes, or until golden brown and crusty.

Cool & enjoy: Let the damper cool slightly on a wire rack before serving.

Prep Time: 10 minutes
Cooking Time: 15-20 minutes
Servings: 2-3

One-Pan Thyme and Zest Flatfish with Plum Sauce and Hazelnut Crumble

- 2 flatfish fillets (such as flounder, sole, or halibut)
- Olive oil
- Salt and freshly cracked black pepper
- 1 tablespoon unsalted butter
- 1 shallot, finely chopped
- 1 garlic clove, minced
- 1/2 cup dry white wine
- 1 cup fresh or frozen plums, pitted and chopped (or 1/2 cup tart plum jam)
- 1/4 cup chicken broth
- 1 tablespoon honey
- 1 tablespoon lemon juice
- 1 sprig fresh thyme
- 1/2 cup hazelnuts, toasted and roughly chopped

For the Citrus Zest:

- Zest of 1 lemon
- Zest of 1 orange

Pat fish dry, season with salt & pepper.

-

Mix lemon & orange zest in a bowl.

-

Pulse hazelnuts in a food processor for a coarse crumble.

-

Heat olive oil & butter in a pan. Sauté shallot & garlic (2 minutes).

-

Add white wine, scrape browned bits (simmer 2-3 minutes). Add plums (or jam), broth, honey, & lemon juice. Simmer 5-7 minutes (thicken sauce). Add thyme sprig (optional), simmer 1 minute, then remove.

-

Gently place fish fillets in the pan, top with sauce. Cook 3-4 minutes per side (opaque & flakes easily).

-

Serve fish & sauce on a plate. Top with zest & hazelnut crumble.

Prep Time: 15 minutes
Cooking Time: 30-35 minutes
Servings: 12-16 squares

A+ Lamington: An Aussie Classic Elevated

For the Vanilla Bean Sponge:

- 1 1/2 cups (195g) all-purpose flour
- 1 teaspoon baking powder
- 1/4 teaspoon salt
- 1/2 cup (113g) unsalted butter, softened
- 1 cup (200g) granulated sugar
- 3 large eggs
- 1 teaspoon vanilla bean paste
- 1/2 cup (120ml) milk

For the Dark Chocolate Ganache:

- 1 cup (240ml) heavy cream
- 8 ounces (225g) high-quality dark chocolate (60% cacao or higher), chopped

For the Toasted Coconut Crumble:

- 2 cups (100g) unsweetened shredded coconut
- 2 tablespoons granulated sugar
- 1/2 teaspoon ground cinnamon

Preheat oven to 350°F (180°C), grease & line an 8x8 inch pan. Whisk flour, baking powder, and salt (set aside).

-

Cream butter & sugar, beat in eggs, stir in vanilla paste. Alternate dry ingredients and milk with wet ingredients (mix just until combined).

-

Bake batter in pan for 25-30 minutes (cool completely). Make ganache by heating cream, pouring over chocolate, and whisking until smooth.

-

Toast coconut with sugar and cinnamon (2-3 minutes, watch to avoid burning).

-

Cut cooled cake into squares. Dip squares in ganache, letting excess drip off.

-

Roll dipped squares in toasted coconut.

-

Place Lamingtons on a wire rack to set. Serve.

Roasted Sweet Potato and Wattleseed Salad with Bush Tomato Vinaigrette

Prep Time: 15 minutes
Cook Time: 20-25 minutes
Serving Size: 2-4 servings

- 2 medium sweet potatoes, peeled and cut into 1-inch cubes
- 1 tablespoon olive oil
- 1/2 teaspoon ground coriander
- Salt and freshly cracked black pepper (to taste)
- 1/4 cup toasted wattleseed (optional, substitute with chopped walnuts)

Vinaigrette:
- 2 tablespoons olive oil
- 1 tablespoon fresh lemon juice (or lime juice)
- 1 tablespoon bush tomato paste (or substitute with balsamic vinegar)
- 1 teaspoon honey
- Salt and freshly cracked black pepper (to taste)
- Fresh herbs (optional): Chopped parsley, thyme, or mint

Preheat oven to 400°F (200°C). Line a baking sheet with parchment paper.

Toss sweet potato cubes with olive oil, coriander, salt, and pepper. Spread on the baking sheet and roast for 20-25 minutes (tender & browned).

Toast wattleseed in a dry pan (a few minutes, fragrant & browned). Skip if not using.

Mix olive oil, lemon juice, bush tomato paste (or vinegar), honey, salt, and pepper for a dressing. Add herbs (optional).

Toss roasted sweet potato, wattleseed (if using), and dressing together.

Serve at room temperature

Grilled Pineapple with Chilli Lime & Mango Salsa

Prep Time: 15 minutes
Cooking Time: 10-20 minutes
Servings: 4-6

For the Grilled Pineapple:
- 1 ripe pineapple
- Skewers (optional)
- Olive oil

For the Chilli Lime Glaze:
- 1/4 cup brown sugar
- 2 tablespoons lime juice
- 1 tablespoon soy sauce
- 1 tablespoon water
- 1/2 teaspoon grated ginger
- 1 clove garlic, minced
- Pinch of cayenne pepper (optional)

For the Mango Salsa:
- 1 ripe mango, peeled and diced
- 1/4 red onion, finely chopped
- 1 jalapeno pepper, seeded and finely chopped (adjust amount for desired heat)
- 1 tablespoon chopped fresh cilantro
- 1 tablespoon fresh lime juice
- Salt and freshly cracked black pepper (to taste)

Prep the Pineapple: Cut the pineapple top off and remove the core. Cut the pineapple into rings or wedges, depending on your preference. If using skewers, thread the pineapple pieces onto them.

Make the Mango Salsa: In a medium bowl, combine diced mango, red onion, jalapeno pepper (adjust amount for spice preference), cilantro, lime juice, salt, and pepper. Toss to combine and set aside.

Make the Glaze: Combine all glaze ingredients (brown sugar, lime juice, soy sauce, water, ginger, garlic, and cayenne pepper) in a small saucepan over medium heat. Bring to a simmer and cook for 5-7 minutes, or until slightly thickened.

Preheat & Grease: Preheat your grill to medium-high heat. Lightly brush or spray the grill grates with oil to prevent sticking.

Grill the Pineapple: Place the pineapple slices or skewers on the preheated grill. Grill for 2-3 minutes per side, or until lightly charred and warmed through.
-Glaze it Up: Brush the grilled pineapple generously with the prepared chilli lime glaze while still hot on the grill. You can baste it a couple of times for extra flavor.

Serve: Serve the warm grilled pineapple drizzled with any remaining glaze and a dollop of the homemade mango salsa. Enjoy the sweet, spicy, and refreshing flavors!

Bali, Indonesia

Bali, an island paradise renowned for its vibrant culture and breathtaking landscapes, is also a treasure trove of culinary delights. Rooted in ancient traditions and influenced by a rich tapestry of cultures, Balinese cuisine is a symphony of flavors, aromas, and textures that awaken the senses.

In this chapter, we invite you to savor a curated selection of dishes that capture the essence of Bali's culinary heritage. Each recipe has been carefully chosen to reflect the island's unique blend of indigenous ingredients, aromatic spices, and time-honored cooking techniques. From delicate steamed dishes to fiery curries, each recipe tells a story of Bali's rich culinary traditions and its openness to culinary innovation.

Inspired by the fragrant spice markets, the vibrant street food stalls, and the elegant restaurants that dot the island, we've crafted a collection that pays homage to the classics while embracing the modern culinary landscape. Get ready to discover a world of flavors that will transport you to the heart of Bali's vibrant food culture.

Spicy Duck & Rye Bread Open-Faced Sandwiches with Poached Egg: A delightful fusion of East and West, this dish marries the rich flavors of Balinese spice-rubbed duck with the hearty comfort of European rye bread and a perfectly poached egg, showcasing Bali's openness to culinary innovation. (Showstopper)

Pepes Ikan **in Banana Leaves (Steamed Marinated Fish):** Steeped in ancient Balinese culinary tradition, this dish features fragrantly spiced fish steamed in banana leaves, a time-honored technique that imparts delicate flavors and aromas.

Balinese *Lawar* with Minced Chicken: A vibrant and texturally complex salad, this dish is a testament to Bali's rich culinary heritage, showcasing the intricate balance of flavors and the use of fresh, local ingredients.

Mie Goreng **(Indonesian Fried Noodles):** A staple of Indonesian street food, this flavorful noodle dish, infused with sweet soy sauce and aromatic spices, reflects Bali's diverse culinary influences.

Nasi Goreng **(Indonesian Stir-Fried Rice):** A beloved comfort food across Indonesia, this aromatic fried rice dish is a testament to the resourcefulness of Balinese cooking, where leftover rice is transformed into a satisfying and flavorful meal.

Gado-Gado **Salad with Peanut Sauce:** A celebration of fresh vegetables and vibrant flavors, this salad, served with a rich and creamy peanut sauce, showcases the Indonesian love for bold, contrasting tastes and textures.

Coconut Curry Glass Noodles: This innovative dish takes the familiar flavors of Balinese curry and elevates them with the delicate texture of glass noodles and the richness of coconut milk, resulting in a unique and unforgettable culinary experience. (Showstopper)

Prep Time: 15 minutes
Cooking Time: 15-20 minutes
Servings: 2-4

Spicy Duck & Rye Bread Open-Faced Sandwiches with Poached Egg

Spicy Sambal:
- Dried chilies
- Shallots
- Garlic
- Ginger
- Lemongrass
- Lime juice
- Fish sauce
- Palm sugar (or brown sugar)
- Salt

Rye Bread:
- Rye bread slices
- Butter

Toppings:
- Smoked duck breast (or ham)
- Raclette cheese (or Comte cheese)
- Eggs
- Fresh cilantro
- Fresh mint
- Olive oil

Make the Sambal: Dry roast chilies in a pan until blistered. Pulse with shallots, garlic, ginger, and lemongrass in a food processor.

Sauté the Sambal: Heat oil, add sambal mixture, and cook for a few minutes. Stir in lime juice, fish sauce, palm sugar, and salt. Simmer for 5 minutes and set aside.

Toast the Rye Bread: Toast rye bread slices until golden brown. Assemble the Sandwiches: Layer rye bread with duck (or ham), then cheese.

Poach the Eggs: Poach eggs in simmering water for 3-4 minutes (runny yolks).

Melt the Cheese: Melt butter in a pan and cook sandwiches for 2-3 minutes per side (melted cheese).

Make the Herb Salad: Combine chopped cilantro, mint, olive oil, lime juice, and salt.

Serve: Place each open-faced sandwich on a plate. Top with a poached egg, sambal, pepper, and a dollop of herb salad.

Prep Time: 15-20 minutes
Cooking Time: 35-40 minutes
Servings: 2-3

Pepes Ikan in Banana Leaves (Steamed Marinaded Fish)

Spice Paste:
- Shallots (chopped)
- Ginger (chopped)
- Garlic (chopped)
- Lemongrass (chopped)
- Turmeric powder
- Coriander powder
- Chili flakes

Marinade:
- Coconut milk
- Salt
- Lime juice
- Fish fillets (cleaned)

Optional Vegetables:
- Bell peppers (sliced)
- Zucchini (sliced)
- Banana Leaves: (large & softened)
- Kaffir Lime Leaves

Make Spice Paste: Sauté chopped shallots, ginger, garlic, and lemongrass. Let cool slightly. Grind with turmeric, coriander, and chili flakes (mortar & pestle or food processor).

Marinate Fish: Mix spice paste, coconut milk, salt, and lime juice. Marinate fish for at least 30 minutes.

Prep Banana Leaves: Oil the shiny side of a softened banana leaf.

Assemble *Pepes*: Place fish on the leaf, top with kaffir lime leaves and vegetables (optional).

Fold & Seal: Fold the banana leaf like a package, securing it tightly. Repeat with remaining fish and leaves.

Steam the Fish: Steam packets in a pot with simmering water for 20-25 minutes (cooked through).

Optional Crisp: Heat oil in a pan. Carefully open a packet and cook fish skin-side down for a crispy finish (optional).

Balinese Lawar with Minced Chicken

Prep Time: 10-15 minutes
Cooking Time: 15-20 minutes
Servings: 2-4

- Cooked and shredded chicken breast
- Green beans, trimmed and chopped
- Long beans, trimmed and chopped
- Sprouted mung beans
- Kaffir lime leaves, thinly sliced
- Coconut, grated (both fresh and toasted)
- Shallot, thinly sliced
- Ginger, thinly sliced
- Balinese spice paste (available online or substitute with a combination of turmeric powder, coriander powder, cumin, and chilies)
- Coconut milk
- Shrimp paste (optional)
- Lime juice
- Salt
- Vegetable oil

Vegetable Prep: Boil water in a pot. Blanch green beans and long beans until tender-crisp. Drain and cool under cold water. If using, blanch sprouted mung beans for a minute or two.

Spice Paste: Heat oil in a pan. Sauté shallots and ginger until fragrant. Add Balinese spice paste (or substitute) and cook for another minute to release aromas.

Flavor Building: Add grated coconut (both fresh and toasted) to the pan. Cook for a couple of minutes to enhance flavors.

Prep Time: 15-20 minutes
Cooking Time: 35-40 minutes
Servings: 2-3

Mie Goreng (Indonesian Fried Noodles)

- 150g (5 oz) fresh yellow egg noodles or dried Hakka noodles
- 100g (3.5 oz) protein of choice: chicken, shrimp, or tofu
- 1 tablespoon vegetable oil
- 1 small shallot, thinly sliced
- 1 clove garlic, minced
- 1 red chili pepper, thinly sliced (seeds removed for less heat)
- 1 small red bell pepper, thinly sliced
- 100g (3.5 oz) sugar snap peas or broccolini florets
- 50g (1.7 oz) snow peas
- 1 handful baby corn, halved
- 1 stalk lemongrass, white part only, thinly sliced
- 1 kaffir lime leaf, torn
- 1/2 teaspoon ground turmeric
- 1/2 teaspoon ground coriander
- 1/4 teaspoon smoked paprika (optional)
- 1 tablespoon kecap manis (sweet soy sauce)
- 1 tablespoon oyster sauce
- 1 tablespoon soy sauce
- 1/2 lime, juiced
- Salt and freshly cracked black pepper to taste
- Optional garnishes: fried shallots, chopped fresh cilantro, lime wedges

Cook protein and noodles according to package instructions. Set aside.

Heat vegetable oil in a pan over medium-high heat. Add shallot, garlic, and chili pepper. Sauté for 30 seconds.

Add bell pepper, sugar snap peas, snow peas, and baby corn. Stir-fry for 2-3 minutes until crisp-tender.

Add lemongrass, kaffir lime leaf, turmeric, coriander, and smoked paprika. Stir-fry for 1 minute.

Pour in kecap manis, oyster sauce, soy sauce, and lime juice. Simmer for 1 minute.

Add cooked noodles and protein to the pan. Toss until well combined and heated through. Season with salt and pepper to taste.

Serve hot, garnished with fried shallots, cilantro, and lime wedges if desired.

Nasi Goreng (Indonesian Stir-Fried Rice)

Prep Time: 15-20 minutes
Cooking Time: 15-20 minutes
Servings: 4

Base Gede:
- 5 shallots, roughly chopped
- 3 cloves garlic, peeled and roughly chopped
- 2-3 red chilies (depending on spice preference), seeded and roughly chopped
- 1 inch ginger, peeled and roughly chopped
- 1 lemongrass stalk, white part only, roughly chopped (lightly charred for smokiness)
- 1/2 teaspoon turmeric powder
- 1/4 teaspoon coriander powder
- 1 teaspoon terasi shrimp paste
- Pinch of salt

Nasi Goreng:
- 2 tablespoons vegetable oil
- 2 eggs
- 1 cup cooked cold rice (preferably day-old jasmine rice)
- 1/2 cup chopped shrimp (optional)
- 1/4 cup shredded chicken or tempeh (optional)
- 1/4 cup chopped green beans
- 1/4 cup shredded carrots
- 1 stalk green onion, sliced
- 1 tablespoon kecap manis (sweet soy sauce)
- 1 tablespoon soy sauce
- Salt and freshly ground black pepper to taste
- Fried shallots, for garnish (optional)

Blend: In a food processor, mix shallots, garlic, chilies, ginger, lemongrass, turmeric, coriander, shrimp paste, and salt until coarse.

Heat Oil: Heat vegetable oil in a wok until very hot.

Cook Aromatics: Add blended paste to hot oil, cook for 2-3 mins until fragrant and oil separates.

Make Omelet: Push paste aside, pour whisked eggs in the center, cook slightly, then fold for a fluffy omelet.

Add Protein (Optional): If using shrimp or other protein, add now and cook until done.

Stir-Fry Veggies: Add green beans and carrots, stir-fry until blistered and tender-crisp.

Add Rice: Mix cold cooked rice with paste, omelet, and veggies in the pan.

Season: Pour in kecap manis and soy sauce, stir-fry for 1 min, season with salt and pepper.

Garnish: Transfer to a plate, top with sliced green onions and fried shallots (optional).

Gado-Gado Salad with Peanut Sauce

Prep Time: 30-40 minutes
Cook Time: 7-10 minutes
Serving Size: 4-6 servings

For the Salad:
- 1 bunch green beans, trimmed and blanched
- 1 head broccolini, cut into florets and blanched
- 1/2 head cauliflower, cut into florets and blanched
- 1 red bell pepper, thinly sliced
- 1 yellow bell pepper, thinly sliced
- 1 cucumber, thinly sliced
- 1 cup cherry tomatoes, halved
- 1 package firm tofu, cubed and pan-fried until golden brown (optional)
- 1 package tempeh, cubed and pan-fried until golden brown (optional)
- 2 hard-boiled eggs, quartered (optional)

For the Creamy Peanut Sauce:
- 1 cup creamy peanut butter (unsweetened)
- 1/2 cup coconut milk
- 2 tablespoons soy sauce
- 1 tablespoon lime juice
- 1 tablespoon brown sugar
- 1 tablespoon tamarind paste (or substitute with an additional tablespoon of lime juice)
- 1 red chili pepper, seeded and finely chopped (adjust for spice preference)
- 1 clove garlic, minced
- 1 inch ginger, grated
- 1/4 cup water (optional, for thinning)

For Garnish (Optional):
- Fried shallots (store-bought or homemade)
- Crispy wonton strips
- Fresh cilantro leaves

Prepare the Vegetables: Blanch the green beans, broccolini, and cauliflower florets in boiling water for 2-3 minutes, or until tender-crisp. Drain and refresh under cold water. Slice the bell peppers and cucumber.

Pan-Fry the Protein (Optional): If using tofu or tempeh, heat oil in a pan and fry the cubed tofu or tempeh until golden brown on all sides. Set aside.

Make the Creamy Peanut Sauce: In a blender or food processor, combine peanut butter, coconut milk, soy sauce, lime juice, brown sugar, tamarind paste, chili pepper, garlic, and ginger. Blend until smooth and creamy. If the sauce is too thick, add a little water to thin it out.

Assemble the Salad: Arrange the blanched vegetables, sliced bell peppers, cucumber, cherry tomatoes, and pan-fried protein (if using) on a platter or individual plates.

Pour the Creamy Peanut Sauce: Drizzle the creamy peanut sauce generously over the salad ingredients.

Garnish and Serve: Top the salad with your chosen garnish options, such as fried shallots, crispy wonton strips, and fresh cilantro leaves.

Tips:

For a richer flavor, toast the peanut butter in a dry pan for a few minutes before adding it to the blender.

Coconut Curry Glass Noodles

Prep Time: 5 minutes
Cooking Time: 10-12 minutes
Servings: 2-3

- 8 oz Glass noodles
- 1 can (13.5 oz) Coconut milk
- 2 tbsp Balinese Curry Paste - *Find the real deal online or specialty stores.*
- 1 tbsp *Kecap Manis*
- 1-2 tbsp Palm sugar
- ½ cup Napa Cabbage
- ½ cup Bok Choy
- 1 tbsp Vegetable oil
- Salt
- Fresh Kaffir lime leaves
- Fresh cilantro

Boil the noodles: Follow package instructions (usually 3-5 minutes). Rinse with cold water.

Spice it up: Heat oil, cook Balinese curry paste for 1 minute.

Add coconut milk, kecap manis, palm sugar. Simmer 2-3 minutes.

Toss in shredded cabbage and bok choy, cook for 1-2 minutes (crunchy, not mushy!).

Add cooked noodles, toss to coat. Season with salt.

Garnish with cilantro (optional), and serve.

*Kecap manis is a sweet soy sauce from Indonesia, adds a rich, molasses-like depth to both savory and sweet dishes. Substitute Hoisin Sauce and Honey/Maple Syrup at a 3:1 ratio for a **Kecap manis** substitute, i.e, 3 parts Hoisin to 1 part honey or maple syrup.*

Phuket, Thailand

Phuket, a tropical paradise in the Andaman Sea, is a haven for both sun-seekers and food enthusiasts. The island's culinary scene is a vibrant tapestry woven from ancient Thai traditions, Chinese influences brought by early settlers, and the creative flair of modern chefs.

Historically, Phuket's cuisine relied heavily on the bounty of the sea, with fresh seafood forming the backbone of many dishes. Spicy curries, aromatic soups, and stir-fries infused with local herbs and spices like lemongrass, galangal, and chili peppers became the cornerstones of Phuket's culinary identity.

Today, the island's food scene is a captivating blend of tradition and innovation. Luxury resorts offer exquisite fine dining experiences, showcasing the best of Thai cuisine with modern techniques and global influences. Meanwhile, street food vendors continue to tantalize taste buds with their authentic flavors and time-honored recipes.

Here, we invite you on a culinary journey through Phuket, exploring the vibrant flavors, unique ingredients, and diverse culinary traditions that define this tropical paradise. From the bustling night markets to the elegant beachfront restaurants, you'll discover a world of culinary delights that will transport you to the heart of Thai culture.

Simple Green Curry: This approachable recipe demystifies the fragrant and flavorful world of Thai green curry, perfect for a quick and satisfying weeknight meal.

Pad See Ew: A beloved Thai street food staple, this stir-fried noodle dish boasts a harmonious blend of sweet, salty, and savory flavors, showcasing the versatility of wide rice noodles.

Tom Yum Goong (Thai Hot & Sour Soup): A symphony of bold flavors, this iconic soup tantalizes the taste buds with its vibrant broth infused with lemongrass, galangal, lime leaves, and chili peppers.

Phuket-Style *Yum Pla Duk Foo*: This regional specialty showcases the coastal bounty of Phuket, featuring crispy catfish tossed in a tangy and spicy salad with a medley of fresh herbs.

Phuket-Style *Rad Na* **with** *Mussaman* **Curry Beef:** This dish elevates the classic Rad Na with a luxurious twist, featuring tender beef slow-cooked in a fragrant Massaman curry, served over a bed of silky rice noodles. Its complexity of flavors and textures makes it a standout dish that showcases Phuket's culinary prowess. (Showstopper)

Khao Pad Krapow (Thai Basil Fried Rice): A simple yet satisfying one-pan dish, this flavorful fried rice highlights the aromatic holy basil and packs a punch of spice, a testament to Thai street food ingenuity.

Gang Khua Gai (Thai Coconut Curry Vegetables): This vegetarian-friendly curry celebrates the vibrant colors and flavors of fresh vegetables, simmered in a creamy coconut milk broth infused with fragrant Thai spices.

Khao Pad Sapparot (Pineapple Fried Rice with Cashew Nuts): A sweet and savory delight, this fried rice dish showcases the tropical flavors of pineapple and cashews, a perfect balance of textures and tastes.

Tom Yum Soup with Shrimp: A lighter, seafood-centric variation on the classic tom yum soup, this dish features succulent shrimp in a fragrant broth bursting with herbs and spices.

Yum Nua Sai (Spicy Minced Pork Salad): A refreshing and fiery salad, this dish balances the richness of minced pork with the bright acidity of lime juice and the heat of Thai chilies.

Khanom Jeen Sot Curry Variante: This innovative take on a traditional Thai noodle dish features crispy fried rice vermicelli noodles served alongside a rich and flavorful curry dip, creating a unique and unforgettable culinary experience. (Showstopper)

Prep Time: 10-15 minutes
Cooking Time: 15-20 minutes
Servings: 2-4

Simple Green Curry

- Cooked and shredded chicken breast
- Green beans, trimmed and chopped
- Long beans, trimmed and chopped
- Sprouted mung beans
- Kaffir lime leaves, thinly sliced
- Coconut, grated (both fresh and toasted)
- Shallot, thinly sliced
- Ginger, thinly sliced
- Balinese spice paste (available online or substitute with a combination of turmeric powder, coriander powder, cumin, and chilies)
- Coconut milk
- Shrimp paste (optional)
- Lime juice
- Salt
- Vegetable oil

Vegetable Prep: Boil water in a pot. Blanch green beans and long beans until tender-crisp. Drain and cool under cold water. If using, blanch sprouted mung beans for a minute or two.

Spice Paste: Heat oil in a pan. Sauté shallots and ginger until fragrant. Add Balinese spice paste (or substitute) and cook for another minute to release aromas.

Flavor Building: Add grated coconut (both fresh and toasted) to the pan. Cook for a couple of minutes to enhance flavors.

Prep Time: 15-20 minutes
Cooking Time: 35-40 minutes
Servings: 2-3

Pad See Ew

- 150g (5 oz) fresh yellow egg noodles or dried Hakka noodles
- 100g (3.5 oz) protein of choice: chicken, shrimp, or tofu
- 1 tablespoon vegetable oil
- 1 small shallot, thinly sliced
- 1 clove garlic, minced
- 1 red chili pepper, thinly sliced (seeds removed for less heat)
- 1 small red bell pepper, thinly sliced
- 100g (3.5 oz) sugar snap peas or broccolini florets
- 50g (1.7 oz) snow peas
- 1 handful baby corn, halved
- 1 stalk lemongrass, white part only, thinly sliced
- 1 kaffir lime leaf, torn
- 1/2 teaspoon ground turmeric
- 1/2 teaspoon ground coriander
- 1/4 teaspoon smoked paprika (optional)
- 1 tablespoon kecap manis (sweet soy sauce)
- 1 tablespoon oyster sauce
- 1 tablespoon soy sauce
- 1/2 lime, juiced
- Salt and freshly cracked black pepper to taste
- Optional garnishes: fried shallots, chopped fresh cilantro, lime wedges

Cook protein and noodles according to package instructions. Set aside.

Heat vegetable oil in a pan over medium-high heat. Add shallot, garlic, and chili pepper. Sauté for 30 seconds.

Add bell pepper, sugar snap peas, snow peas, and baby corn. Stir-fry for 2-3 minutes until crisp-tender.

Add lemongrass, kaffir lime leaf, turmeric, coriander, and smoked paprika. Stir-fry for 1 minute.

Pour in kecap manis, oyster sauce, soy sauce, and lime juice. Simmer for 1 minute.

Add cooked noodles and protein to the pan. Toss until well combined and heated through. Season with salt and pepper to taste.

Serve hot, garnished with fried shallots, cilantro, and lime wedges if desired.

Prep Time: 10-15 minutes
Cooking Time: 15-20 minutes
Servings: 2-4

Tom Yum Goong (Thai Hot & Sour Soup)

- Cooked and shredded chicken breast
- Green beans, trimmed and chopped
- Long beans, trimmed and chopped
- Sprouted mung beans
- Kaffir lime leaves, thinly sliced
- Coconut, grated (both fresh and toasted)
- Shallot, thinly sliced
- Ginger, thinly sliced
- Balinese spice paste (available online or substitute with a combination of turmeric powder, coriander powder, cumin, and chilies)
- Coconut milk
- Shrimp paste (optional)
- Lime juice
- Salt
- Vegetable oil

Vegetable Prep: Boil water in a pot. Blanch green beans and long beans until tender-crisp. Drain and cool under cold water. If using, blanch sprouted mung beans for a minute or two.

Spice Paste: Heat oil in a pan. Sauté shallots and ginger until fragrant. Add Balinese spice paste (or substitute) and cook for another minute to release aromas.

Flavor Building: Add grated coconut (both fresh and toasted) to the pan. Cook for a couple of minutes to enhance flavors.

Prep Time: 10 minutes
Cooking Time: 15 minutes
Servings: 2-3

Phuket-Style Yum Pla Duk Foo

- 1 pound white fish (snapper, grouper, cobia) - cleaned and gutted
- Water (enough to cover the fish)
- 2-3 tbsp lime juice
- 1 tbsp fish sauce
- 1 tbsp palm sugar
- Splash of soy sauce
- A few ginger slices
- Lettuce or greens (salad base)
- Vegetable oil
- Shallots (thinly sliced)
- Diced fresh pineapple
- Cashews (roughly chopped)
- Fresh herbs (cilantro, mint) - for garnish
- Optional (use sparingly): Dried shrimp (chopped) or a touch of shrimp paste

Dressing:
- Lime juice (to taste)
- Fish sauce (to taste)
- Palm sugar (to taste)
- Red chilies (thinly sliced, adjust for spice)
- Minced shallot
- Minced garlic cloves
- Splash of water
- Optional (Phuket twist): A touch of tamarind paste

Poach the fish: In a pot, simmer water with lime juice, fish sauce, palm sugar, soy sauce, and ginger. Gently add fish and cook for 5-7 minutes (until cooked through). Flake the fish.

-

Optional - Crispy shallots: Heat oil in a pan (separate burner) and fry shallots until golden brown. Set aside.

-

Optional - Flash fry fish: Heat oil in a pan and fry the flaked fish in batches for 1-2 minutes (warm and slightly crisp).

-

Assemble the salad: Arrange lettuce/greens on a plate. Top with flaked fish.

-

Make the dressing: Combine lime juice, fish sauce, palm sugar, chilies, shallot, garlic, and water in a bowl. Add tamarind paste (optional) for a tangy twist.

-

Garnish and serve: Drizzle the dressing over the salad. Top with fried shallots (optional), pineapple, cashews, dried shrimp/shrimp paste (optional), and fresh herbs.

Prep Time: 15 minutes
Cooking Time: 20 minutes
Servings: 2-3

Phuket-Style Rad Na with Mussaman Curry Beef

- Beef (flank steak or sirloin): Thinly sliced
- Marinade: Soy sauce, oyster sauce (optional), fish sauce, pepper
- Rice noodles (Sen yai)
- Vegetable oil
- Shallots (thinly sliced)
- Garlic (minced)
- Red chili (thinly sliced, adjust for spice)
- Palm sugar (or brown sugar)
- Tamarind paste
- Ground spices: coriander, cumin, cinnamon, cloves (optional)
- Coconut milk
- Fish sauce
- Lime juice
- Broth (optional)
- Fried shallots or crispy onions (garnish)
- Cilantro (chopped, garnish)
- Roasted peanuts (optional, garnish)
- Lime wedges (optional)

Marinate the beef: Mix soy sauce, oyster sauce (optional), fish sauce, and pepper. Toss sliced beef in the marinade. Let it sit for at least 30 minutes (or overnight for more flavor).

Cook the noodles: Bring water or broth to a simmer. Add rice noodles and cook for 3-4 minutes (until tender-chewy). Drain.

Sear the beef: Heat oil in a pan. Sear the marinated beef for 30-45 seconds per side (browned outside, pink inside). Set aside.

Make the sauce: In the same pan, saute shallots, garlic, and chili. Add palm sugar, tamarind paste, and spices. Cook for a minute.

Simmer and season: Pour in coconut milk and fish sauce. Simmer, scraping browned bits. Add lime juice and broth (if needed) for desired consistency.

Assemble: Divide noodles on plates. Top with beef and sauce. Garnish (optional): Add fried shallots, cilantro, peanuts, and lime wedges.

Khao Pad Krapow (Thai Basil Fried Rice)

Prep Time: 5 minutes
Cook Time: 15-20 minutes
Serving Size: 2-3

- 2 cups cooked jasmine rice (preferably day-old, slightly dried out)
- 1 tbsp vegetable oil
- 1 clove garlic, minced
- 1-2 Thai chilies, thinly sliced (adjust for spice preference)
- ½ pound ground meat (chicken, pork, or tofu - cubed)
- 1-2 tbsp soy sauce
- 1 tbsp oyster sauce (optional)
- ½ cup holy basil leaves
- Salt (to taste)
- Fried egg (optional, for garnish)

Heat oil: In a wok or large pan, heat oil over medium-high heat.

Stir-fry aromatics: Add garlic and chilies, stir-frying for 30 seconds until fragrant.

Cook the protein: Add the ground meat and cook until browned and cooked through.

Season and add rice: Pour in the soy sauce and oyster sauce (if using). Then, add the cooked rice and stir-fry for a few minutes to heat through.

Basil time: Stir in the holy basil leaves until just wilted (30 seconds or so).

Serve and enjoy! Season with salt to taste. Serve hot, with a fried egg on top.

Gang Khua Gai (Thai Coconut Curry Vegetables)

Prep Time: 5 minutes
Cook Time: 15-20 minutes
Serving Size: 4-6, as a side dish

- 1 pound fresh green beans, trimmed
- 1 tablespoon olive oil
- 1/2 teaspoon garlic powder
- 1/4 teaspoon smoked paprika (optional, for a smoky twist)
- 1/4 teaspoon kosher salt
- 1/4 teaspoon black pepper
- 1/4 cup grated Parmesan cheese
- 1/4 cup chopped macadamia nuts, toasted (optional, for added crunch)

Heat oven to 425°F (220°C), line a baking sheet with parchment paper.

Toss green beans with olive oil, garlic powder, salt & pepper. Spread beans on the baking sheet and roast 15-20 minutes (tender-crisp & browned).

Remove from oven (optional): sprinkle with Parmesan cheese & macadamia nuts.

Broil 2-3 minutes (optional): melt cheese & get a little nutty crunch.

Serve hot.

Khao Pad Sapparot (Pineapple Fried Rice with Cashew Nuts)

Prep Time: 5 minutes
Cook Time: 15-20 minutes
Serving Size: 2-3 servings

- 2 cups cooked jasmine rice (preferably day-old, slightly dried out)
- 1 tbsp vegetable oil
- 1 egg, beaten
- 1/2 cup chopped fresh pineapple
- 1/4 cup roasted cashews
- 1/4 cup diced red onion
- 1-2 cloves garlic, minced
- 1 tbsp soy sauce
- 1 tbsp fish sauce (optional)
- 1 tbsp palm sugar (or brown sugar)
- Pinch of white pepper
- Chopped green onions (for garnish)

Heat oil: In a wok or large pan, heat oil over medium-high heat.

Scramble the egg: Push the oil to the side of the pan and pour in the beaten egg. Scramble the egg until cooked through, then set aside on a plate.

Stir-fry aromatics: Add the garlic and diced red onion to the pan, stir-frying for 30 seconds until fragrant.

Add rice and sauce: Push the aromatics to the side and add the cooked rice. Pour in the soy sauce, fish sauce (optional), palm sugar, and white pepper. Stir-fry for a few minutes, breaking up any clumps of rice.

Incorporate pineapple and cashews: Stir in the chopped pineapple and roasted cashews. Cook for another minute or two, until heated through.

Finishing touches: Fold in the scrambled egg back into the rice mixture. Season with additional soy sauce or fish sauce to taste (optional).

Garnish with chopped green onions before serving.

Tom Yum Soup with Shrimp

Prep Time: 5 minutes
Cooking Time: 15 minutes
Servings: 2

- 1 tbsp vegetable oil
- 2 stalks lemongrass, bruised
- 2 kaffir lime leaves
- 2-3 slices galangal (or substitute with ginger)
- 1-2 Thai chilies, thinly sliced (adjust for spice preference)
- 4 cups chicken broth
- 1 can (13.5 oz) coconut milk (full fat, unsweetened)
- 2 tbsp lime juice
- 2 tbsp fish sauce
- 1 tbsp palm sugar
- (½ pound shrimp, peeled and deveined
- Fresh cilantro leaves (for garnish)
- Optional (for garnish): Lime wedges, sliced red chili

Heat oil: In a large pot or Dutch oven, heat vegetable oil over medium heat.

Release the aromatics: Add lemongrass, kaffir lime leaves, and galangal (or ginger). Sauté for 30 seconds, releasing their fragrant oils.

Add the chilies and cook for another 30 seconds.

Pour in the chicken broth and bring to a simmer.

Add the coconut milk, lime juice, fish sauce, and palm sugar. Simmer for 2-3 minutes, letting the flavors meld.

Yum Nua Sai (Spicy Minced Pork Salad)

Prep Time: 5 minutes
Cook Time: 5-7 minutes
Chilling Time: 30 minutes (not included in cook time)
Servings: 2-3

- ½ pound ground pork
- 1 red onion, thinly sliced
- 2-3 Thai chilies, thinly sliced (adjust for spice preference)
- ½ cup chopped fresh mint leaves
- ¼ cup chopped fresh cilantro leaves
- 2 tbsp lime juice
- 1 tbsp fish sauce
- 1 tbsp palm sugar (or brown sugar)
- Pinch of white pepper
- Roasted peanuts, roughly chopped (for garnish)
- Optional (for a smoky flavor): ½ tsp toasted shrimp paste

Cook the pork: Heat a pan or wok over medium heat. Add the ground pork and cook until browned and cooked through, breaking it up with a spoon.

Combine and chill: In a large bowl, combine cooked pork, red onion, chilies, mint leaves, and cilantro.

Make the dressing: In a separate bowl, whisk together lime juice, fish sauce, palm sugar, and white pepper. Pour the dressing over the salad ingredients and toss to coat.

Chill and garnish: Refrigerate the salad for at least 30 minutes for the flavors to meld. Before serving, garnish with chopped roasted peanuts and (optional) a sprinkle of toasted shrimp paste for a smoky depth of flavor.

Khanom Jeen Sot Curry Variante

Prep Time: 5 minutes
Cooking Time: 15 minutes
Servings: 2

For the Noodles:
- 1 package rice vermicelli noodles
- Vegetable oil for frying

For the Curry Dip: (Adjust according to your favorite Thai curry recipe)
- 1 cup vegetable broth
- 1 can (13.5 oz) coconut milk (full fat, unsweetened)
- 2 tbsp yellow curry paste (or green curry paste for a different flavor)
- 1 tbsp fish sauce
- 1 tbsp palm sugar
- Pinch of turmeric powder

Make the Curry Dip: (Optional - Skip if you already have a favorite Thai curry dip)

In a saucepan, heat the vegetable broth.

In a separate pot, combine coconut milk, curry paste, fish sauce, palm sugar, and turmeric powder. Bring to a simmer and cook for 5-7 minutes, stirring occasionally, until slightly thickened. Keep warm.

Fry the Noodles:

Heat enough oil in a large pot or wok (use a thermometer!) to medium-high heat.
Separate the rice vermicelli noodles.

Working in batches, carefully add noodles to the hot oil and fry for 1-2 minutes, or until golden brown and crispy.

Drain on paper towels to remove excess oil.

Serve and enjoy: Arrange the fried rice vermicelli noodles on a serving dish. Place the warm curry dip alongside the noodles.

Bonus: Garnish with chopped fresh herbs and a lime wedge for a restaurant touch.

SKY

Our journey through the world's most vibrant flavors now takes flight. Ascending from the bustling streets and sun-kissed shores, we reach for the boundless expanse of the sky, a metaphor for the limitless potential of culinary inspiration. This final chapter explores three extraordinary destinations, each offering a unique perspective on the intersection of tradition, innovation, and playful experimentation.

Chettinad, a hidden gem in Southern India, reveals a treasure trove of aromatic spices, fiery curries, and vegetarian delights. We honor this region's rich culinary heritage with a curated selection of traditional recipes, showcasing the complexity and depth of Chettinad cuisine.

Montreal, a cultural crossroads in Canada, boasts a culinary scene that effortlessly blends French, English, and Indigenous influences. Here, we embrace the city's diverse foodways, re-working classic dishes with a playful twist and showcasing the creativity of its talented chefs.

Alberta, a vast province in Western Canada, is a land of rugged beauty and hearty flavors. We delve into the heart of Alberta's culinary traditions, transforming familiar dishes with a touch of whimsy and a focus on locally sourced ingredients.

Finally, New Orleans, a city steeped in history and a melting pot of cultures, is a culinary playground where Creole and Cajun flavors reign supreme. We pay homage to this city's rich culinary legacy with a selection of classic dishes, while also embracing its penchant for playful experimentation with a trio of show-stopping creations that will leave your taste buds tingling.

In this final chapter, we invite you to soar above the ordinary and explore the boundless possibilities of culinary creativity. Let your imagination take flight as you savor the flavors of Chettinad, Montreal, Alberta, and New Orleans. This is a journey of discovery, a celebration of culinary artistry, and a testament to the power of food to transport us to new heights.

Chettinad, India

Chettinad, a region steeped in the rich history and vibrant culture of Tamil Nadu, India, is a culinary haven waiting to be discovered. Home to the Chettiars, a renowned trading community with a penchant for global spices and flavors, the cuisine of Chettinad is a symphony of bold aromas, fiery chilies, and complex spice blends that dance on the palate.

From sun-dried meats and salted vegetables to freshly ground masalas and aromatic curries, Chettinad's culinary traditions are a testament to the region's resourcefulness and ingenuity. Its signature dishes, like the fiery Chicken Chettinad or the flavorful Meen Kuzhambu, are just a glimpse into a world of culinary possibilities waiting to be explored.

This chapter offers a tantalizing *amuse-bouche*, a mere taste of the vibrant flavors and rich culinary heritage that define Chettinad cuisine. Think of it as a culinary invitation, a whisper of the aromatic spices and bold flavors that await you on a journey to this extraordinary region. Let these recipes ignite your curiosity and inspire you to delve deeper into the world of Chettinad cooking, where every bite tells a story of history, culture, and a passion for food that spans centuries.

Spicy Yogurt Marinated Fried Chicken: A vibrant dish showcasing the bold flavors of Chettinad, this chicken is marinated in a fiery yogurt sauce and fried to crispy perfection.

Hetty Chicken 65: A fiery and flavorful chicken dish bursting with the aromatic spices of Chettinad, this innovative recipe elevates the classic Chicken 65 with a unique blend of flavors and a touch of heat. (Showstopper)

Spicy Chettinad Shrimp Skewers: Succulent shrimp are marinated in a fiery Chettinad spice blend and grilled to perfection, offering a tantalizing taste of Southern Indian flavors.

Chettinad Eggplant Roast: This hearty vegetarian dish showcases the bold flavors of Chettinad cuisine, featuring roasted eggplant infused with a rich and aromatic spice blend.

Our A+ *Meen Kuzhambu* (Tangy Fish Curry): A symphony of flavors, this tangy fish curry captures the essence of Chettinad cuisine with its complex blend of spices, tamarind, and coconut milk, creating a truly unforgettable culinary experience. (Showstopper)

Our A+ *Appalam* (Crispy Lentil Crackers): These delicate, crispy lentil crackers are an unexpected delight, transforming a humble ingredient into a playful and flavorful snack. Their interactive preparation and versatile nature make them a culinary highlight for any occasion. (Showstopper)

Our A+ Coconut Rice Crackers: These crispy and flavorful crackers, made with leftover rice, grated coconut, and a medley of aromatic spices, offer a unique twist on a traditional ingredient, showcasing the resourcefulness and creativity of Chettinad cuisine. Their versatility as both a standalone snack and a textural element in various dishes makes them a standout addition to any table. (Showstopper)

Chettinad Cauliflower Popcorn: A playful and innovative twist on a classic snack, these cauliflower florets are coated in a flavorful Chettinad spice blend and roasted to crispy perfection, creating a unique and addictive appetizer or side dish. (Showstopper)

Chettinad Pineapple Raita: A refreshing and cooling yogurt-based condiment, this raita features the sweetness of pineapple and the spice of Chettinad flavors, offering a harmonious balance to rich and flavorful dishes.

Spicy Yogurt Marinated Fried Chicken

Prep Time: 15-20 minutes
Cooking Time: 15-20 minutes
Servings: 2-4

- ½ cup plain yogurt
- 2 tbsp lemon juice
- 1 tbsp grated ginger (fresh or ground)
- 2 cloves garlic, minced
- Spices: 1 tsp paprika, ½ tsp ground coriander, ¼ tsp each of turmeric and cumin, pinch of cinnamon (optional), pinch of cayenne pepper (optional)
- ½ tsp *garam masala*
- Salt to taste

Coating:
- ⅓ cup buttermilk (or DIY by adding 1 tbsp vinegar/lemon juice to ⅓ cup milk, letting it sit for 5 minutes)
- ½ cup gram flour (chickpea flour)

Frying:
- Vegetable oil for frying (see notes)

Marinate: In a bowl, mix yogurt, lemon juice, ginger, garlic, spices, and salt. Add chicken, coat well, and marinate (30 minutes to overnight) in the fridge.

Heat oil: Heat enough oil (halfway up your pot) over medium heat.

Double-coat the chicken: Prepare two bowls - one with thinned buttermilk and another with gram flour. Dip marinated chicken in buttermilk, then dredge in gram flour, coating well.

Fry and drain: Fry chicken pieces in batches for 3-4 minutes per side until golden brown and cooked through (oil temperature around 350°F). Drain on paper towels.

Serve: Enjoy hot, garnished with optional curry leaves and cilantro.

Notes on Oils:

Both peanut oil and a peanut and mustard oil mix can be used for cooking, but they have different properties and are suited for different purposes:

Peanut Oil:
- Neutral Flavor: Peanut oil has a very mild, slightly nutty flavor that won't overpower other ingredients. This makes it a versatile choice for a variety of dishes.
- High Smoke Point: Peanut oil has a high smoke point (around 437°F), making it ideal for high-heat cooking methods like stir-frying, deep-frying, and searing.

Peanut and Mustard Oil Mix:

- Stronger Flavor: This combination adds a more pronounced peanut and mustard flavor to your dish. It's particularly well-suited for Asian-inspired dishes where these flavors are prominent.
- Lower Smoke Point: Mustard oil typically has a lower smoke point (around 400°F) than peanut oil. While the mix might have a slightly higher smoke point depending on the ratio, it's generally not recommended for extremely high-heat cooking.

Here's a quick recommendation for choosing between them:

- Use peanut oil: If you prioritize a neutral flavor and high smoke point for high-heat cooking, peanut oil is the better choice.
- Use peanut and mustard oil mix: If you want to add a specific peanut and mustard flavor profile to your dish, and the cooking method uses medium or lower heat, this mix can be a good option.

Additional factors to consider:

- Personal preference: If you enjoy a more robust flavor, the peanut and mustard oil mix might be more appealing.
- Availability: Peanut oil is generally easier to find in most grocery stores.

Ultimately, the best choice depends on your specific recipe and desired flavor profile.

Hetty Chicken 65

Prep Time: 15-20 minutes (excluding marinading time)
Cooking Time: 10-15 minutes
Servings: 2-3

Chicken:
- 1 lb boneless, skinless chicken thighs (cut into bite-sized pieces)

Spicy Marinade:
- ½ cup plain yogurt
- 2 tbsp lemon juice
- 1 tbsp grated ginger (fresh or ground)
- 2 cloves garlic, minced
- 1 tbsp red chili powder (adjust for heat)
- 1 tsp ground cumin
- ½ tsp ground coriander
- Pinch of *garam masala*
- Pinch of *asafoetida* (*hing*)
- 1 tsp mango powder
- Salt to taste

Crispy Coating:
- ¾ cup cornstarch
- ¼ cup rice flour
- Pinch of cayenne pepper (optional, for extra spice)

Frying:
- Vegetable oil for frying

Marinate for Maximum Flavor: Combine yogurt, lemon juice, ginger, garlic, red chili powder, cumin, coriander, garam masala, asafoetida, mango powder, and salt in a bowl. Add the chicken pieces and toss to coat them evenly. Marinate for at least 30 minutes, or up to overnight for deeper flavor.

Prepare the Crispy Coating: In a separate bowl, whisk together the cornstarch, rice flour, and optional cayenne pepper.

Heat the Oil: Heat enough vegetable oil (to come halfway up your pot) over medium heat.

Coat & Fry to Perfection: Dip the marinated chicken pieces into the coating mixture, ensuring full coverage. Carefully lower them into the hot oil and fry for 3-4 minutes per side, or until golden brown and cooked through.

Drain & Enjoy: Transfer the cooked chicken bites to a paper towel-lined plate to drain excess oil. Serve hot with your favorite dipping sauce.

Tips:

Cutting chicken into bite-sized pieces guarantees even cooking. Adjust the spice level in the marinade and coating according to your preference.

Maintain a steady oil temperature for consistent cooking.

Start with a small amount of asafoetida: As it has a strong flavor, a pinch is enough. You can always add more to taste later.

Prep Time: 15-20 minutes
Cooking Time: 5-10 minutes
Servings: 2-3

Spicy Chettinad Shrimp Skewers

Shrimp:
- 1 lb medium shrimp (peeled and deveined)

Chettinad Marinade:
- ½ cup Chettinad masala powder (store-bought or homemade - see recipe below)
- ¼ cup thick coconut yogurt
- 1 tbsp tamarind paste (or 1 tsp lime juice)
- 1 tbsp vegetable oil
- Pinch of jaggery (or brown sugar)

Homemade Chettinad Masala Powder (Optional):
- 2 tbsp coriander seeds
- 1 tbsp fennel seeds
- 1 tsp cumin seeds
- 1 tsp dried red chilies (adjust for spice)
- ½ tsp black peppercorns
- 1 tsp turmeric powder
- ½ tsp fenugreek seeds (optional)
- Pinch of cloves

Marinate your shrimp for big flavor: In a bowl, combine *Chettinad masala* powder (store-bought or see recipe), coconut yogurt, tamarind paste (or lime juice), oil, and jaggery (or brown sugar).

-

Toss peeled, deveined shrimp in the marinade. Let them soak up the goodness for at least 30 minutes, or up to overnight in the fridge.

-

Skewer and sear for smoky goodness:

Thread the marinated shrimp onto skewers and heat a grill pan or cast iron skillet over medium heat. Add a thin layer of oil to prevent sticking.

-

Sear the shrimp skewers for 2-3 minutes per side, until cooked through and slightly charred.

Prep Time: 20-25 minutes
Cooking Time: 30-35 minutes
Servings: 4-5

Chettinad Eggplant Roast

Eggplant:
- 2 large eggplants (peeled and cubed)

Spice Mix (Homemade)
- 2 tbsp coriander seeds
- 1 tbsp fennel seeds
- 1 tsp cumin seeds
- 1 tsp dried red chilies (adjust for spice)
- ½ tsp black peppercorns
- 1 tsp turmeric powder
- ½ tsp fenugreek seeds (optional)
- Pinch of cloves
- 1 small cinnamon stick
- 2 black cardamoms

Marinade:
- ½ cup thick coconut yogurt
- 1 tbsp tamarind paste (or 1 tsp lime juice)
- 1 tbsp vegetable oil
- Salt to taste

Other Ingredients:
- 2 tbsp curry leaves
- 1 tbsp chopped ginger
- 2 cloves garlic, minced
- 1 medium onion, thinly sliced
- 1 medium tomato, chopped
- 1 sprig curry leaves
- 2 tbsp chopped fresh coriander leaves (for garnish)
- 2 tbsp vegetable oil (for cooking)

Marinate: Combine yogurt, tamarind paste (or lime juice), oil, and salt in a bowl. Toss the cubed eggplant in the marinade and let it sit for at least 15 minutes.

-

Sauté the Aromatics: Heat oil in a large pan or Dutch oven. Add curry leaves, ginger, and garlic. Sauté for 30 seconds until fragrant.

-

Caramelize the Onions: Add the sliced onions and cook until softened and translucent, about 5-7 minutes.

-

Add the *Chettinad masala* powder and cook for another minute, stirring constantly to release the aroma.

-

Simmer & Blend: Pour in the chopped tomatoes and simmer for 5 minutes, letting the flavors combine.

-

Add the marinated eggplant along with any leftover marinade. Stir gently to combine everything.

-

Cover the pan and simmer for 20-25 minutes, or until the eggplant is tender. Stir occasionally to prevent sticking.

-

Garnish with fresh coriander leaves and serve hot with rice or flatbreads.

Prep Time: 15 minutes
Cooking Time: 20-25 minutes
Servings: 2-3

A+ Meen Kuzhambu (Tangy Fish Curry)

Spicy Paste:
- 4-5 Dry Red Chillies (adjust for spice preference)
- 1 tsp each: Coriander Seeds, Cumin Seeds, Fennel Seeds
- 1 tsp Black Peppercorns
- 1 tsp Cloves
- 1-inch Cinnamon Stick
- 1 tbsp Coconut (grated)
- 1 small Onion (chopped)

Fish Curry:
- 1 tbsp Coconut Oil
- 1 medium Tomato (chopped)
- 1 tsp Tamarind Paste
- 1.5 tsp Palm Sugar (or brown sugar)
- 1/2 tsp Turmeric Powder
- Salt to taste
- 1 (1-pound) Fish Fillet (thick cut, white fish recommended)
- Fresh Cilantro (chopped, for garnish)
- Lime Wedges (for serving)

In a pan, dry roast the chillies, coriander seeds, etc. for a few minutes until fragrant. Grind with coconut and onion into a paste (mortar and pestle or food processor work!).

-

Heat oil in a pot. Add the spice paste and cook, stirring, for 2-3 minutes.

-

Add the chopped tomato and cook for another 2-3 minutes.

-

Stir in tamarind paste, sugar, turmeric, and salt. Add a little water if needed.

-

Simmer for 5 minutes. Adjust seasonings to taste.

-

Gently add the fish and simmer for 8-10 minutes, or until cooked through.

-

Garnish with cilantro and a squeeze of lime before serving.

A+ Appalam (Crispy Lentil Crackers)

Prep Time: 10 minutes, plus drying time (overnight)
Cooking Time: 2-3 minutes per appalam
Servings: 20-25 small appalams

- 1 cup whole *urad dal* (black gram lentils)
- 1/4 tsp salt
- Water

Wash & Soak: Rinse the urad dal in water for 4-5 hours, or overnight.

Grind to Paste: Drain the lentils and grind them into a fine paste using a grinder or food processor. Add a little water as needed to achieve a smooth consistency.

Season & Spread: Add the salt to the lentil paste and mix well. Spread a thin layer of the batter onto a clean, dry plate or plastic sheet. You can use a spoon or your fingers to spread it evenly.

Drying Time: Leave the spread batter to dry overnight in a well-ventilated area. Aim for the appalams to be completely dry and firm to the touch.

Sun or Oven (Optional): If drying overnight seems slow, you can speed up the process by drying the appalams in direct sunlight for a few hours. Alternatively, preheat your oven to the lowest setting (around 150°F) and dry the appalams on a baking sheet for 1-2 hours, or until completely dry.

Hot & Crispy: Heat a deep frying pan or wok with enough oil for shallow frying. Once hot (around 350°F), carefully slide a single appalam into the oil. It should sizzle and puff up quickly.

Fry & Flip: Fry the appalam for 2-3 seconds per side, or until golden brown and crispy. Use a slotted spoon to remove and drain on paper towels. Repeat with remaining appalams.

Let the appalams cool slightly before serving. Enjoy them as a snack on their own, or pair them with chutneys or dips for added flavor.

Tips:

To adjust the texture, you can grind the lentils a little coarser for a slightly thicker appalam.

Be careful not to overcrowd the pan while frying, as this can lower the oil temperature and prevent the appalams from crisping properly. Appalams can be stored in an airtight container at room temperature for up to a week.

Prep Time: 15 minutes
Cooking Time: 10-12 minutes
Servings: 20-25 small crackers

A+ Coconut Rice Crackers

- 1 cup cooked, leftover white rice (cooled)
- ½ cup grated coconut (fresh or desiccated)
- 1 tbsp chopped curry leaves
- 1 green chili pepper, finely chopped (adjust for spice)
- 1 tsp red chili powder
- ½ tsp ground cumin
- ¼ tsp turmeric powder
- Salt to taste
- Vegetable oil for frying

In a large bowl, combine the cooled cooked rice, grated coconut, curry leaves, green chili pepper, red chili powder, cumin, turmeric powder, and salt. Mix well to distribute the spices evenly.

-

Form the Crackers: Using your hands, shape the rice mixture into small, flat patties. Aim for a thickness of about ¼ inch.

-

Heat the Oil: Heat enough oil in a frying pan or skillet over medium heat (around 350°F). You want the oil to be shallow but hot enough for frying.

-

Carefully add a few rice patties to the hot oil at a time. Don't overcrowd the pan. Fry for 2-3 minutes per side, or until golden brown and crispy.

-

Use a slotted spoon to remove the fried rice crackers from the oil and drain them on paper towels to absorb excess oil.

-

Repeat & Serve: Repeat steps 3-5 with the remaining rice mixture, frying in batches. Serve the Chettinad Coconut Rice Crackers hot or at room temperature, as a delicious accompaniment to your meal or as a satisfying snack

Prep Time: 15 minutes
Cook Time: 20-25 minutes
Serving Size: 4-6 servings

Chettinad Cauliflower Popcorn

- 1 head cauliflower, cut into florets
- 1/4 cup *besan flour* (gram flour)
- 1/2 tsp turmeric powder
- 1 tsp red chili powder (adjust for spice)
- 1/2 tsp coriander powder
- 1/4 tsp cumin powder
- Salt to taste
- Vegetable oil for frying

Marinate the Florets: In a bowl, toss the cauliflower florets with besan flour, turmeric powder, red chili powder, coriander powder, cumin powder, and salt. Let them marinate for 15 minutes.

Heat the Oil: Heat enough oil in a large pot or Dutch oven for deep frying. Aim for a medium-high heat (around 375°F).

Carefully add the marinated cauliflower florets to the hot oil in small batches. They will sizzle and puff up like popcorn. Fry for 2-3 minutes per batch, or until golden brown and crispy.

Drain the fried cauliflower on paper towels to remove excess oil. Serve hot as a side dish alongside your Chettinad menu.

Prep Time: 10 minutes
Cooking Time: n/a
Servings: 4-6

Chettinad Pineapple Raita

- 1 cup chopped fresh pineapple
- 1/2 cup plain yogurt
- 1/4 cup chopped cucumber
- 1/4 cup chopped red onion
- 1 tbsp chopped fresh cilantro
- 1 tsp lime juice
- 1/4 tsp ground cumin
- Pinch of salt (or to taste)

Combine & Chill: In a bowl, combine the chopped pineapple, yogurt, cucumber, red onion, cilantro, lime juice, ground cumin, and salt. Stir gently to combine.

For an extra flavor kick, you can add a chopped green chili pepper or a pinch of red chili powder.

Serve Chilled: Taste and adjust seasonings as needed. Cover and refrigerate the raita for at least 30 minutes to allow the flavors to meld. Serve chilled as a refreshing side dish on your Chettinad buffet.

Montreal, Canada

Montreal, a city where culinary traditions run deep, yet the spirit of innovation is always simmering just beneath the surface. A place where French, English, and Indigenous influences converge, creating a culinary landscape as diverse as its people. Here, smoked meats meet maple syrup, bagels transform into unexpected delights, and the bounty of Quebec's *terroir* inspires chefs to push the boundaries of flavor and creativity.

In this chapter, we delve into the heart of Montreal's culinary evolution, where classic techniques and local ingredients are turned in a symphony of modern flavors. Inspired by the city's vibrant food scene and its rich culinary heritage, we've crafted a collection of dishes that defy expectations and celebrate the unexpected.

From the delicate sweetness of maple syrup to the smoky depths of grilled meats, the recipes in this chapter showcase the diverse flavors that define Montreal cuisine. We've taken inspiration from the city's love for hearty, comforting dishes, coaxing them into greatness with a touch of elegance and sophistication. You'll find nods to traditional ingredients like wild blueberries, Quebec cheeses, and local game, all elevated with innovative techniques and unexpected flavor pairings.

This is a culinary journey that transcends the familiar, inviting you to experience Montreal's food culture through a new lens. It's a celebration of the city's culinary evolution, where tradition and innovation collide to create a truly unforgettable dining experience.

Lobster Blinis with Maple Drizzle: This luxurious appetizer elevates a classic Russian dish with the quintessentially Canadian flavor of maple syrup, creating a unique and unforgettable combination of sweet and savory. (Showstopper)

Blueberry Maple Flank Steak with Pine Nut Crunch: This dish celebrates the bounty of Quebec's wild blueberries and the region's love for maple syrup, elevating a simple steak to a gourmet experience with its unexpected yet harmonious flavor combination and crunchy texture. (Showstopper)

Montreal Portobello Steak with Fig-Infused Red Wine Vinaigrette and Black Pepper Roasted Walnut: This vegetarian masterpiece elevates the humble portobello mushroom to a main-course star, thanks to the rich, complex flavors of the fig-infused red wine vinaigrette and the added texture of the roasted walnuts. (Showstopper)

Spicy Montreal Bagel Panzanella Salad: A playful twist on a classic Italian bread salad, this dish incorporates the iconic Montreal bagel, adding a chewy texture and subtle sweetness to the mix of fresh vegetables and herbs. (Innovative Fusion)

Elevated Tourtière with Pork & Wild Mushroom Ragout and Oka Mash: This elevated take on a beloved Quebecois classic features a hearty ragout of pork and wild mushrooms, enrobed in a creamy Oka mash and encased in a flaky, buttery crust. The addition of caramelized onions and a hint of maple syrup elevates this rustic dish to gourmet status, making it a true showstopper. (Showstopper)

Montreal Hazelnut Tartlets with Genmaicha Custard: These delicate tartlets showcase the city's European influences, combining a buttery hazelnut crust with a creamy genmaicha custard for a unique and sophisticated dessert experience. (Showstopper)

Lobster Blinis with Maple Drizzle

Prep Time: 30 minutes
Cooking Time: 20 minutes
Servings: 4-6

Blinis:
- 1 cup warm milk
- 1 tbsp yeast
- 1 tbsp sugar
- 1 ½ cups flour
- 1 egg yolk
- ¼ tsp salt
- 2 tbsp melted butter

Lobster Topping:
- 1 pound cooked lobster meat, chopped
- ¼ cup thinly sliced red radishes
- Chopped fresh chives (for garnish)

Maple Dijon Aioli:
- ¼ cup mayonnaise
- 2 tbsp Dijon mustard
- 1 tbsp pure maple syrup
- 1 tbsp lemon juice
- Pinch of salt
- Black pepper (to taste)

Finishing Touch:
- High-quality maple syrup (for drizzling)

Blinis: Combine warm milk, yeast, and sugar in a bowl. Let it sit for 5 minutes until foamy. In another bowl, whisk flour, egg yolk, and salt. Gradually whisk in the yeast mixture until a smooth batter forms. Cover and let rise for 1 hour. Gently fold in melted butter.

Cook Blinis: Heat a griddle or pan over medium heat. Use a measuring cup to portion batter onto the griddle. Cook for 2-3 minutes per side, until golden brown and puffed. Don't overcrowd the pan.

Aioli: Whisk together mayonnaise, Dijon mustard, maple syrup, lemon juice, salt, and pepper in a bowl.

Assemble: Arrange blinis on a platter. Top each with aioli, lobster, radish slice, and chives.

Serve: Drizzle with maple syrup for a touch of sweetness.

Blueberry Maple Flank Steak with Pine Nut Crunch

Prep Time: 15 minutes
Cooking Time: 20 minutes
Servings: 4

- Flank steak (1.25-1.5 lbs), trimmed
- Olive oil
- Montreal steak spice
- Black pepper
- Worcestershire sauce
- Fresh blueberries
- Fresh thyme
- White wine
- Maple syrup
- Pine nuts
- Lemon zest
- Parsley
- Garlic

Marinate: Combine olive oil, steak spice, pepper, and Worcestershire sauce. Marinate steak for at least 4 hours or overnight.

Glaze: Sauté blueberries and thyme in a pan. Add wine and simmer for 5 minutes. Add maple syrup and simmer for 10-12 minutes, then strain.

Cook Steak: Grill or pan-sear steak to desired doneness (2-3 minutes per side for medium-rare). Let it rest for 10 minutes.

Gremolata: Toast pine nuts until golden brown. Chop pine nuts, lemon zest, parsley, and garlic.

Assemble: Slice steak and arrange on a plate. Drizzle with glaze, then sprinkle with gremolata.

Prep Time: 30 minutes
Cooking Time: 20 minutes
Servings: 2

Montreal Portobello Steak with Fig-Infused Red Wine Vinaigrette and Black Pepper Roasted Walnuts

Portobello Steaks:
- 2 large portobello mushrooms (6-8 oz each)
- 2 tbsp olive oil
- 1 tbsp Montreal steak spice
- ½ tsp Worcestershire sauce
- Salt and pepper

Fig Vinaigrette:
- ½ cup red wine vinegar
- ¼ cup chopped fresh figs
- 1 tbsp olive oil
- Pinch of salt

Walnut Crunch:
- ½ cup walnut halves
- 1 tbsp olive oil
- 1 tsp black pepper
- Pinch of salt

Marinate: Clean portobellos, scrape gills. In a dish, combine olive oil, steak spice, Worcestershire sauce. Brush on portobellos, cover, and refrigerate at least 30 minutes.

Vinaigrette: In a saucepan, simmer red wine vinegar, figs, for 15-20 minutes, or until figs soften and vinegar reduces by half. Let steep for 30 minutes. Strain, discard solids, whisk in olive oil, and salt.

Walnuts: Preheat oven to 375°F. Toss walnuts with olive oil, pepper, and salt. Spread on a baking sheet and roast for 8-10 minutes, or until golden brown, stirring occasionally.

Cook Portobellos: Heat a grill pan or skillet over medium-high heat. Season portobellos with salt and pepper. Grill for 4-5 minutes per side, or until tender and juicy.

Assemble: Plate portobellos, drizzle with vinaigrette, and top with roasted walnuts.

Prep Time: 15 minutes
Cooking Time: 12 minutes
Servings: 4-6

Spicy Montreal Bagel Panzanella Salad

Salad:
- 2 Montreal bagels, cubed
- 2 tbsp olive oil
- Salt and pepper
- 2 cups mixed greens
- 2 cups cherry tomatoes, halved
- ½ cucumber, diced
- ½ fennel bulb, thinly sliced
- ¼ cup crumbled goat cheese
- ¼ cup toasted pecans, chopped
- 2 tbsp chopped fresh dill
- 1 tbsp chopped fresh chives

Dressing:
- 2 tbsp olive oil
- 1 tbsp lemon juice
- 1 tbsp maple syrup
- 1 tsp brown mustard
- 1 clove garlic, minced
- ¼ tsp dried thyme
- Pinch of cayenne pepper (optional)
- Salt and pepper

Toast Bagels: Preheat oven to 375°F (190°C). Toss bagel cubes with olive oil, salt, and pepper. Spread on a baking sheet and bake for 10-12 minutes, or until golden brown and crispy. Let cool.

Combine Salad: In a bowl, mix greens, tomatoes, cucumber, fennel, goat cheese, pecans, dill, and chives.

Whisk Dressing: Combine olive oil, lemon juice, maple syrup, mustard, garlic, thyme, cayenne pepper (if using), salt, and pepper in a small bowl.

Assemble: Toss cooled bagel cubes with salad ingredients. Drizzle with dressing and gently mix.

Prep Time: 45 minutes
Cooking Time: 75 minutes
Servings: 8-10

Elevated Tourtière with Pork & Wild Mushroom Ragout and Oka Mash

Pâte Brisée (Flaky Pastry Dough):
- 1 ¼ cups all-purpose flour
- 1/2 tsp salt
- 1 stick (½ cup) cold unsalted butter, cut into cubes
- 1/4 cup ice water

Savory Ground Pork & Wild Mushroom Ragout:
- 1 tbsp olive oil
- 1 shallot, finely diced
- 2 cloves garlic, minced
- 1 lb ground pork
- 8 oz mixed wild mushrooms (such as chanterelles, cremini, or shiitake), chopped
- 1/2 tsp fresh thyme leaves
- 1/4 tsp fresh sage leaves (or 1/8 tsp dried)
- 1/4 tsp dried marjoram
- 1/4 tsp freshly ground black pepper
- 1 cup beef broth
- 1/2 cup dry white wine
- 1 tbsp tomato paste
- Salt and pepper to taste

Creamy Yukon Gold Mash with Oka:
- 4 Yukon Gold potatoes, peeled and cut into similar-sized pieces
- 1/4 cup heavy cream
- 2 tbsp unsalted butter
- 1/2 cup grated Oka cheese
- Pinch of freshly grated nutmeg
- 1 tbsp maple syrup
- Salt and freshly ground white pepper

Caramelized Onions:
- 1 large onion, thinly sliced
- 1 tbsp butter
- Salt and pepper to taste

Make the *Pâte Brisée*: Combine flour and salt. Cut in butter until mixture resembles coarse crumbs. Gradually add ice water until a dough forms. Wrap and refrigerate for at least 30 minutes.

-

Sauté the Filling: Heat olive oil in a large skillet over medium-high heat. Sauté shallot until translucent. Add garlic and cook for 1 minute.

-

Add ground pork and cook until browned, breaking up any lumps. Add mushrooms and cook until softened.

-

Deglaze with wine, reduce by half. Add tomato paste, broth, herbs, and pepper. Simmer for 20-25 minutes until thickened. Season with salt.

-

Boil and Mash Potatoes: Boil potatoes until tender. Drain and mash with cream, butter, Oka cheese, nutmeg, maple syrup, salt, and pepper.

-

Caramelize Onions: Melt butter in a skillet over medium heat. Add onions and cook until softened and golden brown.

-

Assemble and Bake: Roll out chilled dough and fit into a pie dish. Blind bake for 10 minutes at 400°F.

-

Fill the pie crust with the ragout, top with mashed potatoes, then caramelized onions.

-

Bake at 400°F for 20-25 minutes, or until golden brown and bubbly.

-

Let cool slightly before serving.

Chef Tips:

Pâte Brisée: Fear Not, It's Easier Than You Think!

This flaky pastry might sound fancy, but don't be intimidated. It's all about keeping things cold and working quickly:

1. Chill Out: Make sure your butter is COLD – straight from the fridge. Cold butter creates those lovely flaky layers we want.

2. Pulse It: Instead of using your fingertips, try a food processor. Pulse the flour and salt with the butter until it looks like coarse crumbs (think the size of peas).

3. Ice Water Trick: Use ice water, not just cold water. This keeps the butter chilled and prevents the dough from getting tough.

4. Don't Overwork: Mix the dough until it just comes together. We want it shaggy, not smooth. Overmixing develops gluten, which makes it tough.

5. Rest Easy: Chill the dough for at least 30 minutes. This relaxes the gluten and makes it easier to roll out.

-

Oka Cheese: Substitutes

Oka is a semi-soft, washed-rind cheese from Quebec. If you can't find it, don't panic! Here are some tasty alternatives:

1. Fontina: This Italian cheese has a similar creamy texture and nutty flavor, melting beautifully into the mashed potatoes.

2. Gruyère: A classic Swiss cheese with a slightly sharper flavor, Gruyère adds complexity and melts well.

3. Raclette: This Swiss cheese is known for its meltability, making it a great choice for topping the tourtière.

4. Sharp Cheddar: For a more accessible option, a good quality sharp cheddar will provide the cheesy richness we're looking for.

Montreal Hazelnut Tartlets with Genmaicha Custard

Prep Time: 1 hour 15 minutes (includes chilling dough)
Cooking Time: 45 minutes
Servings: 6-8 tartlets

Pastry Shells:
- 1 1/4 cups flour
- 1/2 tsp salt
- 1/2 cup cold butter, cubed
- 1/4 cup ice water (plus extra if needed)
- 1 large egg yolk

Genmaicha Custard:
- 2 cups whole milk
- 1/4 cup loose-leaf *genmaicha* tea
- 3 large egg yolks
- 1/2 cup sugar
- 1/4 cup brown sugar
- 2 tbsp cornstarch
- 1/4 tsp salt
- 1/2 cup toasted hazelnuts, chopped

Finishing Touches:
- Maple syrup, for drizzling (optional)
- Whipped cream, for serving (optional)

Make Pastry Shells:

- In a bowl, whisk flour and salt. Cut in cold butter with a pastry cutter or your fingertips until crumbly.

- In a separate bowl, whisk egg yolk with a splash of ice water. Gradually add to dry ingredients, mixing with a fork until just combined. Add more ice water, 1 tbsp at a time, only if needed to form a dough.

- Wrap dough in plastic wrap and chill for at least 30 minutes. On a floured surface, roll out dough to 1/8-inch thickness.

- Cut circles and press into tartlet molds. Prick bottoms with a fork. Pre-bake at 375°F (190°C) for 10-12 minutes, or until lightly golden brown. Let cool completely.

Make Genmaicha Custard:

- Heat milk with genmaicha tea in a saucepan over medium heat. Steep for 5 minutes, then strain, discarding tea leaves.
- In a large bowl, whisk together egg yolks, sugars, cornstarch, and salt. Slowly whisk in warm milk until fully combined.
- Return mixture to the saucepan and cook over medium heat, stirring constantly, until thick and bubbly.
- Remove from heat and stir in hazelnuts. Let cool slightly.

Assemble and Bake:

- Preheat oven to 350°F (175°C). Divide custard evenly among pre-baked tartlet shells.
- Bake for 20-25 minutes, or until edges are set and centers are slightly jiggly.
- Let cool slightly on a wire rack.

Serve:
- Drizzle with maple syrup and dollop with whipped cream.

Tips:
- Use high-quality ingredients for best results.
- Don't overwork the pastry dough for a flakier crust.
- Let custard cool before filling to prevent a soggy bottom.

Alberta, Canada

Alberta, a land of sprawling prairies, rugged mountains, and vibrant cities, boasts a culinary scene that is as diverse and dynamic as its landscape. Rooted in hearty pioneer fare and influenced by the indigenous traditions of the First Nations people, Alberta's cuisine has evolved into a unique blend of flavors, textures, and ingredients.

Historically, Alberta's foodways were shaped by the harsh climate and the resourceful spirit of its early settlers. Game meats like bison and elk, wild berries, and foraged roots were staples of the diet, cooked over open fires and preserved for the long winter months. The arrival of European settlers introduced new ingredients and cooking techniques, resulting in a fusion of flavors that reflected the region's diverse cultural influences.

Today, Alberta's culinary scene is thriving, with a new generation of chefs embracing local ingredients and innovative techniques to create dishes that are both familiar and surprising. While traditional favorites like steak and potatoes still hold a special place in the hearts of Albertans, the province's food culture is constantly evolving, embracing global flavors and culinary trends.

Here, we've taken inspiration from the province's rich culinary heritage, reworking classic dishes with a playful twist and a focus on locally sourced ingredients. You'll find innovative takes on familiar favorites, showcasing the versatility of Alberta's bounty and the ingenuity of its chefs.

Alberta Rib-Eye Chili: A hearty and robust chili showcasing Alberta's renowned beef, this dish elevates the classic chili with tender ribeye steak, a rich tomato-based broth, and a fiery kick of spices. The unexpected addition of ribeye steak, along with the depth of flavor from slow-cooked beef and aromatic spices, elevates this classic comfort food to gourmet status. (Showstopper)

Alberta Sizzlin' Hash: This vibrant vegetarian hash celebrates the bounty of Alberta's farm-fresh produce, featuring a medley of colorful vegetables like rapini, zucchini, and cauliflower, tossed with crispy fingerling potatoes and a sweet chili glaze. The unique combination of roasted vegetables, the crispy texture of fingerling potatoes, and the sweet and spicy glaze create a visually stunning and flavorful dish that celebrates Alberta's fresh ingredients. (Showstopper)

Alberta Wild Mushroom Tartlets with Goat Cheese: A delicate and savory appetizer showcasing the earthy flavors of Alberta's wild mushrooms, these elegant tartlets are filled with a creamy goat cheese mixture and a hint of thyme, offering a sophisticated take on local ingredients. (Showstopper)

Spiced Peach and Apricot Cobbler: This warm and comforting cobbler celebrates the sweetness of Alberta's summer fruits, combining peaches and apricots with warm spices like cinnamon and nutmeg, topped with a buttery, flaky biscuit crust. The combination of flavors and textures makes it a delightful dessert that showcases the region's seasonal bounty. (Showstopper)

Prep Time: 50-75 minutes
Cooking Time: 6-8+ hours
Servings: 8-10

Alberta Rib-Eye Chili

Chili:
- Olive oil
- Diced onion, garlic, poblano pepper, jalapeños
- Spices: cumin, paprika, ancho chili powder, cayenne pepper
- Crushed tomatoes, fire-roasted tomatoes, beef broth
- Cubed ribeye steak (seared), shredded pork shoulder, pinto beans
- Fresh or frozen corn (browned), salt, pepper
- 2 Cups of dry Pinto Beans
- Beef Broth

Roasted Corn Salsa:
- Corn kernels, bell pepper, red onion, jalapeño, Roma tomato
- Cilantro, lime juice, cumin, salt, pepper

Roasted Corn Salsa:
Preheat oven to 400°F (200°C). Toss corn kernels, bell pepper, red onion, jalapeño, and Roma tomato with 1 tablespoon olive oil. Season with salt and pepper. Spread on a baking sheet and roast for 15-20 minutes, or until vegetables are slightly softened and charred. Remove from heat and let cool slightly. Stir in cilantro, lime juice, and cumin. Set aside.
-

Roast the Pinto Beans:
- Soak the dried pinto beans: Soak the dried pinto beans in a large bowl with plenty of cold water for at least 8 hours, or overnight. Drain the soaking water and rinse the beans.
-Cook the beans: In a separate pot, cover the beans with fresh water and bring to a boil. Reduce heat, simmer for 1-2 hours, or until tender. Drain the cooked beans.
-Roast the beans: Preheat oven to 400°F (200°C). Toss the cooked pinto beans with 1 tablespoon olive oil and a sprinkle of salt and pepper. Spread them on a baking sheet in a single layer and roast for 15-20 minutes, or until slightly browned and crispy around the edges.
-

Homemade Beef Broth

- Olive oil
- 1 lb beef bones (marrow or mixed)
- 1/2 onion, chopped
- 1 carrot, chopped
- 1 celery stalk, chopped
- 1 sprig thyme
- 1 bay leaf
- Water

- 1. Roast the Bones (400°F, 30 min): Preheat your oven to 400°F (200°C). Toss the bones with 1 tablespoon of olive oil to coat them lightly. Spread the bones on a baking sheet in a single layer and roast for 30 minutes. This step adds depth of flavor to the broth.

Homemade Beef Broth (cont)
Steps:

- 2. Sauté the Veggies (Same Pan!): While the bones are roasting, heat another tablespoon of olive oil in a large pot or Dutch oven over medium heat on the stovetop. You can use the same baking sheet the bones were on, but make sure to remove any excess drippings or grease first. Add the chopped onion, carrot, and celery to the pot and sauté for about 5 minutes, or until softened.

- 3. Combine all ingredients, simmer 4+ hrs (covered, skim foam).

- 4. Strain, season.
-

Cook the Pork Shoulder:
- Season the pork shoulder with salt and pepper. Sear in a Dutch oven over medium heat. Add enough liquid (beef broth, water, or a combination) to come halfway up the pork. Bring to a simmer, cover, and braise in a preheated oven at 325°F (163°C) for 2-3 hours, or until very tender. Shred with two forks.
-

Heat oil, sear ribeye (batches) in hot pan.
-

Sauté onion, garlic, peppers.
-

Add spices. Let the spices toast for 30 seconds to release their aromas. Deglaze with tomatoes. Pour in the 1 cup of low-sodium beef broth and bring to a simmer. Season with salt and pepper to taste. Add pinto beans.
-

Simmer broth for 15 minutes, add ribeye, cooked pork, beans, roasted corn (reserve some salsa).
-

Simmer 30-45 minutes for thickened chili.
-

Serve: Chili with salsa, cilantro (optional), lime wedge.

Prep Time: 15-20 minutes
Cooking Time: 20-25 minutes
Servings: 4-6

Alberta Sizzlin' Hash

Hash:
- Olive oil
- Rapini (chopped, stems removed)
- Zucchini (batons)
- Cauliflower (chopped)
- Sugar snap peas (trimmed, halved)
- Fingerling potatoes (halved or quartered)
- Shallots (thinly sliced)
- Pepitas (pumpkin seeds)

Sweet Chili Glaze:
- Sweet onion (chopped)
- Garlic (minced)
- Diced tomatoes (undrained)
- Brown sugar (or jaggery, see note)
- Champagne vinegar
- Chipotle chili powder
- Cilantro (chopped)

Garnish:
- Radish (sliced)

Boil Potatoes: Cook fingerling potatoes in boiling salted water for 5-7 minutes (tender-crisp). Drain and set aside.

-

Sauté Vegetables: Heat olive oil in a large pan. Add rapini stems, zucchini, and cauliflower. Season with salt and pepper. Cook for 5-7 minutes (slightly softened with char).

-

Finish Vegetables: Add peas, cook 2 minutes. Push veggies aside, add more oil, and fry shallots until golden. Remove shallots and set aside.

-

Glaze: Sauté onion and garlic in the same pan. Add brown sugar (or jaggery), tomatoes, vinegar, and chili powder. Simmer 5-7 minutes (thicken). Season with salt and pepper. (For jaggery, use slightly less than brown sugar and adjust to taste).

-

Combine and Serve: Add potatoes, cooked vegetables, and most shallots back to the pan with the glaze. Toss to coat, heat 2-3 minutes.

-

Garnish: Sprinkle with remaining shallots, cilantro, and radish.

Chef Notes:
Jaggery is a natural sweetener traditionally made from concentrated sugarcane juice or palm sap. Here's why it works in this recipe:

- Rich, Caramelized Flavor: Jaggery has a deeper, more complex flavor than brown sugar due to the minimal processing it undergoes. This richer taste complements the savory elements in the hash (vegetables, potatoes) and adds a subtle caramel note that pairs well with the sweet chili glaze.

- Mineral Content: Jaggery retains some minerals and nutrients from the sugarcane juice during processing, unlike refined sugars. While the amount isn't significant, it can contribute a slightly different taste profile compared to brown sugar.

- Texture: Jaggery can have a slightly grainy texture depending on how it's processed. This can add a touch of textural interest to the glaze, contrasting with the smooth sauce consistency.

-

Why it's a good option in this recipe:

- Experimentation: The recipe positions jaggery as an alternative to brown sugar, encouraging you to try both versions and see which you prefer. Since jaggery has a deeper flavor, it might be a good choice for those who enjoy a more complex sweetness in savory dishes.

- Balanced Sweetness: The recipe suggests using slightly less jaggery than brown sugar due to its richer taste. This helps ensure the glaze doesn't become overly sweet while still providing a satisfying sweetness level.

- Overall, jaggery offers a unique and potentially more flavorful alternative to brown sugar in the Sweet Chili Glaze. The final choice depends on your personal preference and what you have available.

Alberta Wild Mushroom Tartlets with Goat Cheese

Prep Time: Around 30 minutes (not including chilling dough)

Cook Time: 40-50 minutes (including blind baking - optional)

Serving Size: 12 tartlets (appetizer size)

For the Tart Dough:
- 1 1/2 cups all-purpose flour
- 1/2 teaspoon salt
- 1/2 cup cold unsalted butter, cubed
- 2-3 tablespoons ice water

For the Filling:
- 1 tablespoon olive oil
- 1 shallot, finely minced
- 1 clove garlic, minced
- 12 oz mixed wild mushrooms (cremini, chanterelles, etc.), cleaned and sliced
- 1/4 cup dry white wine (optional)
- 1/2 cup heavy cream
- 4 oz goat cheese, crumbled
- 1 tablespoon chopped fresh thyme
- Salt and freshly cracked black pepper, to taste

For the Egg Wash (optional):
- 1 egg yolk
- 1 tablespoon milk

Prep the Dough:

1. In a bowl, whisk flour and salt.
2. Using a pastry cutter or your fingers, cut cold butter into the dry ingredients until crumbly.
3. Slowly add ice water (1 tbsp at a time) using a fork until the dough just comes together. Avoid overworking it.
4. Form dough into a disc, wrap in plastic, and refrigerate at least 30 minutes (or overnight).

Preheat and Prep the Tin:

1. Preheat oven to 400°F (200°C). Lightly grease a 12-cup muffin tin.

Roll & Shape the Dough:

1. On a floured surface, roll out chilled dough to 1/8-inch thickness.
2. Cut dough circles slightly larger than muffin cups using a cookie cutter (or drinking glass).
3. Gently press dough circles into greased cups, letting excess hang over the edges.

Optional Blind Bake:

1. For a flakier crust, line each dough cup with parchment paper and fill with pie weights or dried beans.
2. Bake for 10-12 minutes, then remove weights and paper and bake for an additional 5 minutes, or until edges are golden brown. Let cool slightly.

Sauté the Mushrooms:

1. Heat olive oil in a skillet over medium heat. Add shallot and garlic, cook until softened (about 3 minutes).
2. Add sliced wild mushrooms and cook for 5-7 minutes, or until golden brown and releasing juices.

Deglaze (Optional) & Add Cream & Cheese:

1. (Optional) Pour in white wine (if using) and scrape browned bits from the bottom of the pan. Let simmer for a minute or two.
2. Stir in heavy cream and bring to a simmer. Reduce heat and simmer for 5 minutes, or until the sauce thickens slightly.
3. Remove from heat and stir in crumbled goat cheese and chopped thyme. Season with salt and pepper.

Assemble & Bake:

1. Fill pre-baked tart shells with the mushroom mixture.
2. If not blind baking, brush the dough edges with egg wash (optional) for a golden brown crust.
3. Bake for 15-20 minutes, or until the filling is bubbly and the crust is golden brown.

Serve Warm:

1. Let the tartlets cool slightly before serving warm.
2. Garnish with a sprig of fresh thyme or a drizzle of balsamic reduction (optional).

Spiced Peach and Apricot Cobbler

Prep Time: 15-20 minutes
Cooking Time: 20-25 minutes
Servings: 4-6

For the Fruit:
- 4 large ripe peaches, peeled, pitted, and cut into wedges
- 2 large ripe apricots, halved and pitted
- 1/2 cup water
- 1/2 cup granulated sugar
- 1/4 cup packed light brown sugar
- 1 vanilla bean, split lengthwise, seeds scraped
- 1 cinnamon stick
- 3 cloves
- 1/4 teaspoon freshly grated nutmeg
- 1/8 teaspoon ground cardamom
- Pinch of freshly grated ginger (optional, but recommended)
- 1 star anise (optional, but recommended)

For the Biscuit Dough:
- 1 1/2 cups all-purpose flour
- 2 teaspoons baking powder
- 1/4 teaspoon salt
- 1/2 cup cold unsalted butter, cubed
- 1/2 cup buttermilk (or milk with 1 tablespoon lemon juice added)
- 2 tablespoons granulated sugar, for sprinkling

In a large pot, combine the peach wedges, apricot halves, water, granulated sugar, brown sugar, vanilla bean pod and seeds, cinnamon stick, cloves, nutmeg, cardamom, ginger (if using), and star anise (if using).

-

Bring the mixture to a simmer over medium heat. Cook for 10-12 minutes, or until the fruit is softened and the juices have thickened slightly. Trust your instincts - you want the fruit tender but not mushy! Remove from heat and discard the cinnamon stick, cloves, vanilla bean pod, and star anise.

-

The Flaky Biscuit Dough: While the fruit simmers, preheat your oven to 400°F (200°C). In a large bowl, whisk together flour, baking powder, and salt. Using a pastry cutter or your fingertips, smash that cold butter into the dry ingredients until it resembles coarse crumbs. Remember, don't overmix! Lumps are your friends here, they create those fluffy pockets of air. Gently stir in the buttermilk just until combined - a shaggy dough is what you're aiming for.

-

Assemble and Bake:
Transfer the simmered fruit and its juices to a shallow baking dish or oven-safe skillet. Now, comes the fun part! Dollop spoonfuls of the biscuit dough evenly over the top of the fruit, leaving space between each for spreading. Sprinkle the tops generously with the remaining 2 tablespoons of granulated sugar for a delightful crunch.

-

Bake the cobbler for 20-25 minutes, or until the biscuit dough is golden brown and cooked through. A toothpick inserted into the center of a dough piece should come out clean. No peeking! A seasoned chef can tell by looking for that beautiful golden hue.

-

Let the cobbler cool slightly before serving warm. But wait, there's more. Don't settle for just ice cream. Get creative. A dollop of crème fraîche or a drizzle of a homemade fruit reduction will add a touch of acidity that'll take this dessert to the next level.

New Orleans, Louisiana

New Orleans, a city steeped in a rich tapestry of history, culture, and culinary traditions, is a place where Creole and Cajun flavors reign supreme. The intoxicating aromas of simmering gumbo, the fiery spice of jambalaya, and the buttery goodness of beignets are all part of the city's vibrant culinary identity. These dishes, passed down through generations, have become ingrained in the very fabric of New Orleans life, a source of comfort, community, and celebration.

Creole cuisine, born from the fusion of French, Spanish, African, and Caribbean influences, is characterized by its elegant sauces, complex flavors, and use of fresh, local ingredients. Cajun cuisine, on the other hand, reflects the resourceful cooking of Acadian settlers, featuring hearty one-pot dishes, smoky flavors, and a focus on locally sourced seafood and game.

These two culinary traditions, while distinct, have become intertwined over time, influencing and enriching each other. They are the foundation upon which New Orleans' modern food scene is built, providing a wealth of inspiration for chefs and home cooks alike.

So, let's explore the endless possibilities of Creole and Cajun cuisine. Rather than retreading familiar territory, let's dive into the heart of these culinary traditions, seeking out new permutations and nuances that will surprise and delight even the most seasoned palates. Our recipes, a blend of the unexpected and the familiar, showcase the versatility of these iconic flavors and the creativity that thrives in New Orleans kitchens.

Smoked Ricotta & Cajun Deviled Eggs on Pecan Parmesan Crisps: A playful twist on a Southern classic, these deviled eggs are elevated with smoked ricotta, a touch of Cajun spice, and a crispy Parmesan pecan base, showcasing the vibrant flavors and unexpected combinations of New Orleans cuisine. (Showstopper)

Cherrystone Clam Seafood Gumbo: A symphony of the sea, this gumbo showcases the bounty of Louisiana's waters with a trio of succulent seafood - plump cherrystone clams, delicate white fish, and sweet shrimp. The addition of collard greens and filé powder adds a unique depth and earthiness, creating a truly memorable and flavorful dish that embodies the heart of Creole cuisine. (Showstopper)

Sweet Corn Pudding with Peas & Pecans: A unique and surprising take on classic corn pudding, this dish incorporates sweet peas and crunchy pecans, creating a delightful medley of flavors and textures that elevate a familiar comfort food to new heights. (Showstopper)

Dirty Rice: This dish, a staple of Creole cuisine, is enlivened with a Michelin-worthy twist, a medley of aromatic vegetables, and the rich flavor of chicken livers (or a vegetarian option with cremini mushrooms), offering a culinary adventure for the discerning palate. (Showstopper)

Sweet or Savory Vanilla Shrimp Croquettes: A delightful and unexpected twist on traditional croquettes, these bite-sized treats offer a choice between a sweet vanilla-infused filling and a savory parmesan and herb mixture, both showcasing the versatility of shrimp in Creole cuisine and the city's penchant for playful experimentation. (Showstopper)

Smoked Ricotta & Cajun Deviled Eggs on Pecan Parmesan Crisps

Prep Time: 20-25 minutes (not including boiling eggs)

Cook Time: Deviled Eggs: 10-12 minutes (hard boiling); Pecan Parmesan Crisps (Optional): 30 minutes chilling dough + 10-12 minutes baking

Serving Size: 4-6

Smoked Ricotta:
- Ricotta cheese
- Olive oil
- Salt & pepper
- Smoked paprika
- Lemon zest

Cajun Deviled Eggs:
- Hard-boiled eggs (separate yolks & whites)
- Mayonnaise
- Cayenne pepper
- Smoked paprika
- Lemon zest

Assembly:
- Creole crackers (or your preferred cracker)
- Shredded endive
- White wine vinegar (spray bottle)
- Fresh chives (optional garnish)

Pecan Parmesan Crisps:
- Flour
- Grated Parmesan cheese
- Chopped pecans
- Dried thyme
- Salt
- Cold butter

Smoked Ricotta: Mix ricotta, olive oil, spices, and zest in a bowl. Set aside.

-

Deviled Eggs: Mash yolks with mayo, spices, and zest in a separate bowl.

-

Assemble: Spread ricotta on crackers, top with deviled egg mixture.

-

Finishing Touches: Garnish with endive and a light spray of vinegar. Add chives for extra flair (optional).

-

Pecan Parmesan Crisps:

1. Mix dry ingredients (flour, cheese, pecans, spices).

2. Cut in cold butter until crumbly.

3. Add water to form dough. Chill.

4. Roll out dough, cut shapes, and bake until golden brown and crisp.

Prep Time: 15-20 minutes
Cooking Time: 20-25 minutes
Servings: 3-4

Cherrystone Clam Seafood Gumbo

Fat:
- 1/4 cup butter
- 1/4 cup bacon drippings (or rendered bacon fat)

Roux:
- 1/2 cup all-purpose flour

- Veggies (chopped):
- 1 large onion
- 1 green bell pepper
- 2 stalks celery
- 3-4 cloves garlic

Other:
- 1 (28oz) can diced tomatoes, undrained
- 4 cups chicken broth
- 4 cups seafood broth (clam juice or fish stock)
- 1 teaspoon dried thyme
- 1 teaspoon smoked paprika
- 1 bay leaf
- 1/4-1/2 teaspoon cayenne pepper (adjust to taste)
- Salt and black pepper to taste
- 1 pound large shrimp, peeled and deveined
- 1 pound white fish fillets, cut into bite-sized pieces
- 2 dozen cherrystone clams, scrubbed
- 1 tablespoon filé powder
- 1 cup chopped collard greens
- Chopped fresh parsley (for garnish)
- Optional: 1/2 cup dry white wine

Note: These are estimated amounts and can be adjusted based on personal preference.

Roux: Melt fat in a large pot. Whisk in flour and cook until deep brown (15-20 minutes). Be patient and don't burn.

-

Holy Trinity: Add chopped veggies and cook until softened (5-7 minutes). Season with salt and pepper.

-

Stock & Simmer: Stir in tomatoes, broths, collards, seasonings, and bay leaf. Simmer 30 minutes to meld flavors.

-

Spice & Seafood: Add cayenne pepper, adjust salt and pepper. Add shrimp and fish, cook 5-7 minutes (until pink & cooked through). Remove and set aside.

-

Clams: Add clams and wine (optional) with 7-8 minutes cook time remaining. Cover, simmer 5-7 minutes more (discard unopened clams).

-

Filé Finesse: Turn off heat, whisk in filé powder (start with a teaspoon, taste and add more if needed).

-

Reunite & Serve: Return seafood to pot with clams and gumbo. Heat for a minute or two.

-

Garnish & Enjoy: Ladle gumbo into bowls, garnish with parsley. Serve with crusty bread for dipping!

Sweet Corn Pudding with Peas & Pecans

Prep Time: 10-15 minutes
Cook Time: 20-25 minutes
Serving Size: 4-6

- 2 cups corn (fresh or thawed frozen)
- 2 tablespoons butter
- 1 cup milk
- 1 tablespoon bourbon (optional)
- 1 tablespoon cornstarch
- 2 large eggs
- 2 tablespoons sugar
- 1/2 teaspoon vanilla extract
- 1/4 teaspoon nutmeg
- 1/4 teaspoon salt
- 1/2 cup peas (fresh or thawed frozen)
- 1/4 cup chopped and toasted pecans
- Bourbon drizzle (optional, for garnish)
- Mint sprigs (optional, for garnish)

Brown the Corn: In a skillet, melt butter over medium heat. Add corn and cook 5 minutes, stirring occasionally, until slightly browned.

-

Warm the Milk: In a saucepan, warm milk with bourbon (optional) for a few minutes.

-

Mix the Eggs: In a bowl, whisk eggs, sugar, vanilla, nutmeg, and salt.

-

Temper the Eggs: Slowly whisk the warm milk mixture into the egg mixture (prevents scrambling).

-

Thicken Up: Pour the egg mixture back into the pan with corn. Add cornstarch slurry (cornstarch mixed with a little milk) and cook on low heat, stirring constantly, until thick like custard.

-

Once thickened, gently fold in the peas. Don't overmix.

-

Spoon warm pudding into bowls. Top with toasted pecans for a delightful crunch. Drizzle with bourbon and garnish with mint (optional).

Dirty Rice

Prep Time: 15-20 minutes
Cook Time: 30-35 minutes
Serving Size: 4-6 servings

The Base:
- 2 tablespoons olive oil
- 1 medium onion, finely chopped
- 1 green bell pepper, finely chopped
- 2 celery stalks, finely chopped
- 2 cloves garlic, minced
- 1 pound ground chicken or turkey
- 1 bay leaf
- 1 teaspoon dried thyme
- 1/2 teaspoon dried oregano
- Pinch of cayenne pepper (adjust for heat)
- 1 cup cooked long-grain white rice
- 1 (14.5 oz) can diced tomatoes, undrained

The Dirty Bits:
- 1/2 cup chopped cooked chicken livers (OR (Michelin Option 2 - Vegetarian Twist: Replace chicken livers with 1/2 cup chopped cremini mushrooms)
- 1/4 cup chopped fresh parsley
- Kosher salt and freshly cracked black pepper, to taste

Sauté the Aromatics: Heat olive oil in a large skillet or Dutch oven over medium heat. Add the onion, bell pepper, and celery and cook, stirring occasionally, until softened and translucent (about 5 minutes).

Add the garlic, bay leaf, thyme, oregano, and cayenne pepper. Cook for an additional minute, allowing the spices to release their fragrance.

Increase the heat to medium-high and add the ground chicken or turkey. Cook, breaking it up with a spoon, until browned all over.

Stir in the cooked rice and diced tomatoes (with their juices). Season with salt and pepper to taste. Bring to a simmer, then reduce heat to low, cover, and cook for 15 minutes, or until the rice is heated through and the liquid has been absorbed.

Dirty Decisions: (Choose one option)

Option 1 (Classic Dirty): If using chicken livers, in a separate pan, sauté them in a little oil until cooked through (about 5 minutes). Add them to the rice mixture along with the chopped parsley. Stir gently to combine.

Option 2 (Vegetarian Twist): If using mushrooms, sauté them in a separate pan with a little oil until golden brown (about 5 minutes). Add them to the rice mixture along with the chopped parsley. Stir gently to combine.

Taste and adjust seasonings with salt and pepper as needed. Garnish with a sprinkle of fresh parsley (optional) and serve immediately.

Sweet or Savoury Vanilla Shrimp Croquettes

Prep Time: 15 minutes (not including chilling time)
Cooking Time: 10-15 minutes
Servings: 10-12 croquettes

- 1 cup flour (plus extra for dusting)
- 1/2 cup cold butter, cubed
- 1/2 cup milk
- 2 egg yolks

Sweet Filling (choose one):
- 1/2 cup cooked, chopped shrimp
- 1/4 cup powdered sugar
- 1 tsp vanilla extract

or

Savory Filling (choose one):
- 1/2 cup cooked, chopped shrimp
- 1/4 cup grated Parmesan
- 1 tbsp chopped chives
- 1/4 tsp dried dill

- 1 cup panko breadcrumbs
- 2 eggs, beaten
- Vegetable oil for frying

Whisk flour in a bowl. Cut in cold butter with a pastry cutter or your fingers until crumbly. Mix in milk and egg yolks just until a dough forms. Don't overmix!

Pick your flavor! Gently fold in your chosen filling (sweet or savory).

Chill the dough for at least 30 minutes (makes shaping easier). Roll and flatten dough balls into patties.

Set up a 3-bowl assembly line: flour (optional dusting), beaten eggs, panko crumbs.

Coat the croquettes: Dip each patty in flour (optional), then egg, then panko crumbs.

Heat oil to 350°F in a large skillet or Dutch oven.

Fry croquettes in batches for 2-3 minutes per side, until golden brown. Drain on paper towels.

Optional Finish: Drizzle sweet croquettes with vanilla glaze (powdered sugar mixed with a touch of milk or water) or sprinkle with powdered sugar. Dust savory croquettes with Parmesan cheese or fresh herbs.

STREET, BEACH & SKY

THE EXTRAS

Beyond the Recipe: A Culinary Remix Around the World

Have you outgrown the limitations of basic cookbooks and predictable flavors? Do you crave a deeper exploration of global cuisines, a chance to challenge your skills and tantalize your palate with the unexpected? This e-book preview is your invitation to a world of culinary adventure.

Move Past the Familiar, Embrace the Bold:

We take iconic dishes from vibrant food cultures and use them as springboards for exciting innovation. Our focus isn't on replicating the ordinary, but on elevating familiar formats with unexpected twists and multi-layered flavor profiles.

This is a journey for the adventurous gourmand, a chance to expand your repertoire with dishes that are both sophisticated and audacious.

Master New Techniques, Explore Unfamiliar Ingredients:

While some recipes may offer a deeper exploration of flavor due to their intricate nature, our clear and concise instructions ensure success regardless of your experience level. We ditch the overly complicated jargon and focus on practical techniques, empowering you to recreate these dishes with confidence.

Embark on a Global Culinary Tour:

New Delhi: Delve into India's rich vegetarian heritage with creamy *Dahi Bhalla* and fragrant Vegetable Biryani, a symphony of spices that will transport you to bustling street markets.

Taipei: Master the art of the comforting *Gua Bao* bun and the Oyster Omelette (Taiwanese style), a delightful example of Taiwanese street food bursting with fresh oysters and a sweet-and-savory sauce.

Seoul: Unleash your inner gourmand with *Kimchi Jeon*, a fiery savory pancake, and Korean Fried Dumplings, staples in Korea's innovative cuisine built on the art of fermentation.

Rio de Janeiro: Celebrate Brazil's sun-kissed approach to fresh flavors with crispy *Coxinha de Frango* and sunshine-infused *Pão de Queijo* with *achiote*, perfect for a festive gathering filled with exotic tastes.

Become a Global Culinary Explorer:

This e-book is your guide, offering step-by-step instructions and helpful tips for success. Ditch the bland, embrace the bold – let's explore a world of culinary possibilities, one extraordinary dish at a time!

Our Kitchen Challenge: Mastering Global Flavors with Minimal Tools

Craving global flavors but stuck in a kitchen with limited firepower? This recipe preview is your passport to a world of street food sensations, all achievable with a minimalist approach! We ditched the fancy restaurant kitchens and embraced the spirit of resourceful cooking, using just a butane campstove.

Think gourmet requires a battalion of gadgets? Think again! These recipes, designed for any home kitchen, focus on clever techniques and the freshest ingredients to elevate everyday meals. While our test kitchen embraced the minimalist luxury of DeBuyer cookware and a professional Iwatani butane stovetop for this preview, don't worry – the vast majority of dishes can be recreated using the basic tools you already have on hand. There might be a slow cooker or Dutch oven needed for a few slow-cooked recipes like our melt-in-your-mouth chicken, but that's the exception, not the rule!

So, ditch the intimidation factor and get ready to embark on a delicious journey! This preview offers a taste of what's to come in the full book, where you'll find a treasure trove of street, beach and destination food recipes designed for the home cook who craves challenge, seeks adventure and delights in bold, unforgettable flavor!

Tools of the Trade for this e-Book

To ensure success in your culinary adventures, we've streamlined these recipes to require minimal kitchen equipment and techniques. While some dishes boast complex flavors, we've focused on achievable methods that can be mastered in any home kitchen.

Here's a breakdown of the cookware you'll need for each region's recipes:

India:

Dahi Bhalla: This dish involves soaking and frying lentils. You'll need a pot for soaking and a frying pan for cooking. A grinder or mortar and pestle (if making the lentil paste from scratch) is helpful.

Vegetable *Biryani*: This rice dish requires simmering vegetables and rice. You'll need a pot with a lid for cooking.

Taiwan:

Oyster Omelette: This recipe involves frying an egg mixture with oysters. A frying pan or skillet is all you need.

Gua Bao: These steamed buns require steaming and assembling. A steamer basket placed over a pot of boiling water will work. You'll also need a bowl for mixing and assembling.

Korea:

Kimchi Jeon: This savory pancake involves mixing and pan-frying kimchi with other ingredients. A frying pan or skillet is all you need.

Korean Fried Dumplings: While making dumpling wrappers from scratch requires a rolling pin and additional workspace, pre-made wrappers are readily available, and frying only requires a pot or deep fryer (depending on the recipe).

Brazil:

Brazilian Chicken Croquettes: These fried snacks involve making a dough, shaping it, and frying. A pot for boiling and a frying pan or deep fryer will be used. A slow cooker or Dutch Oven is also required.

Sun-Kissed *Pão de Queijo*: These cheese puffs are fried in a deep frying pan or pot. A thermometer is helpful to monitor the oil temperature for accurate frying.

Enjoy your global culinary journey!

Dahi Bhalla with Sprouted Moong Dal, Pickled Mango & Bold Filling

Prep Time: 2 hours (includes soaking time for dal)
Cook Time: 30 minutes
Serving Size: 4-6

For the *Vadas*:
- 1 cup *urad dal* (whole black gram)
- 1/2 cup sprouted *moong dal* (split green gram)
- 1 tsp ginger, grated
- 1 red chili, finely chopped (adjust for heat preference)
- 1/4 tsp mustard seeds
- Salt to taste
- Oil for frying

For the Filling:
- 1/4 cup chopped fresh spinach
- 1/2 cup chopped pickled mango (increase for more tang)
- 1 tbsp chopped red onion
- 1 tbsp chopped fresh coriander leaves
- 1 tsp *garam masala*
- 1 tbsp cashew butter
- 1 tbsp lime juice
- Salt to taste

For the Dahi (Yogurt):
- 2 cups plain yogurt, whisked
- 1/2 cup water
- Salt to taste

For the Garnishes:
- 1 tbsp chopped fresh coriander leaves
- 1 tbsp green chutney (mint or coriander)
- 1 tbsp tamarind chutney
- *Sev* (fried gram noodles) (optional)

Soak *urad dal* for 4-6 hours, then grind into a fine paste with minimal water. Soak sprouted *moong dal* for 30 minutes, then grind into a coarse paste. Combine both pastes with ginger, red chili, mustard seeds, and salt.

-

In a separate bowl, mix chopped spinach, pickled mango, red onion, coriander leaves, *garam masala*, cashew butter, and lime juice. Season with salt.

-

Heat oil in a pan. Take small portions of the *vada* batter and flatten them slightly. Add a spoonful of filling, then fold the batter around it to form a ball.

-

Fry the *vadas* until golden brown and crisp. Drain on paper towels.

-

Whisk yogurt and water in a bowl. Add salt to taste. Soak the *vadas* in the yogurt mixture for at least 30 minutes.

-

Arrange the soaked *vadas* on a plate. Drizzle with chutneys, sprinkle with coriander leaves, and add *sev* (optional). Serve chilled.

What to Expect:
Dahi Bhalla looks like a colorful and refreshing appetizer or light meal. Imagine crispy golden balls (*vadas*) made from lentils, served in a pool of creamy white yogurt (*dahi*).

The *vadas* might be topped with vibrant green and red chutneys (sauces), and maybe some crunchy fried noodles (*sev*) for added texture.

This recipe takes it up a notch with a surprise filling hidden inside the *vadas*! It's a burst of flavors and textures - crispy on the outside, creamy and tangy in the middle.

Homemade Pickled Mango

- 1 ripe mango, chopped
- 1/2 cup white vinegar
- 1/4 cup sugar
- 1 teaspoon salt
- 1-2 teaspoons red chili flakes (adjust for spice preference)
- 3 cloves
- 5 black peppercorns
- 1 cinnamon stick (optional)
- 1/2 bay leaf (optional)

Instructions

Peel and chop the ripe mango into bite-sized pieces.

In a saucepan, combine vinegar, sugar, salt, red chili flakes (start with 1 teaspoon), cloves, peppercorns, cinnamon stick (if using), and bay leaf (if using). Bring the mixture to a simmer over low heat.

Add the chopped mango to the simmering pickling liquid and stir gently to coat. Reduce heat and simmer for 20-25 minutes, or until the mango softens slightly but retains some texture.

Remove the pan from heat and let the pickle cool completely. Transfer the pickled mango and its liquid to an airtight container. Store in the refrigerator for at least a few hours, or ideally overnight, for the flavors to develop further. The pickle will keep for several weeks in the refrigerator.

Vegetable Biryani with Crispy Green Beans & Marinated Cauliflower

Prep Time: 20 minutes (including chopping vegetables and marinating cauliflower)

Cook Time: 1 hour (including simmering vegetables, cooking rice, and steaming)

Serving Size: 4-6 people

Rice:
- 2 cups basmati rice, rinsed and soaked for 30 minutes
- 2 tablespoons *ghee* (clarified butter) or vegetable oil
- 1 tsp cumin seeds
- 1 bay leaf
- 1 cinnamon stick (2-inch)
- 3 cloves
- 2 black cardamom pods
- 1 green cardamom pod (optional)
- Salt to taste
- 4 cups water (or vegetable broth)

Vegetables:
- 1 medium onion, thinly sliced
- 1 green bell pepper, diced
- 1 carrot, diced
- 1 cup frozen peas
- 1/2 cup chopped cauliflower florets (marinated, see below)
- 1/4 cup chopped green beans (fried, see below)
- 10-12 okra pods, trimmed and cut into ½ inch pieces
- 1/2 tsp turmeric powder
- 1 tsp coriander powder
- 1/2 tsp *garam masala*
- 1/4 tsp red chili powder (adjust for spice preference)
- 1/4 cup chopped fresh cilantro

Marinated Cauliflower (prepare overnight):
- 1/2 cup chopped cauliflower florets
- 1/4 cup plain yogurt
- 1 tbsp chopped fresh coriander leaves
- 1/2 tsp ginger-garlic paste
- Pinch of turmeric powder
- Salt to taste

Combine chopped cauliflower, yogurt, coriander leaves, ginger-garlic paste, turmeric powder, and salt in a bowl. Mix well, cover, and refrigerate for at least 8 hours or overnight.

-

After marinating the cauliflower, take the bowl and hold it over a sink or a large container.

Gently lift the cauliflower florets with a slotted spoon or a fork, letting any excess marinade drip back into the bowl.

You don't need to remove all the yogurt, just enough to prevent a thick yogurt coating on the florets. While yogurt adds a nice tanginess, too much can overpower other flavors in the dish. Shaking off some yogurt ensures a balanced overall flavor profile.

-

Heat oil in a pan. Fry green beans for 3-4 minutes until crisp-tender. Drain on paper towels.

-

Rinse and soak basmati rice for 30 minutes. Drain well.

-

In a large pot or Dutch oven, heat ghee (or oil) over medium heat. Add cumin seeds, bay leaf, cinnamon stick, cloves, and cardamom pods. Let them splutter for a few seconds.

-

Add the sliced onion and cook until golden brown, about 7-8 minutes.

-

Stir in turmeric powder, coriander powder, *garam masala*, and red chili powder. Cook for a minute.

-

Add the diced bell pepper, carrot, peas, marinated cauliflower, and okra. Cook for 5-7 minutes, stirring occasionally, until the vegetables are slightly softened.

-

Add the drained rice to the pot and spread it evenly over the vegetables. Season with salt. Pour in the water (or vegetable broth).

-

Bring to a boil, then reduce heat to low, cover the pot tightly with a lid, and simmer for 18-20 minutes, or until the rice is cooked and fluffy.

-

Once cooked, turn off the heat and let the biryani steam for an additional 5 minutes. Fluff the rice gently with a fork.

-

Once the rice is cooked and fluffed with a fork, gently fold in the fried green beans.

-

For extra smokiness you can:
1. Heat a small skillet over medium heat. Add a drizzle of oil or ghee and carefully transfer a portion of the biryani (rice and vegetables with some green beans) to the skillet.
2. Spread the biryani mixture in a thin layer and toast for a minute or two, until slightly browned and fragrant.
3. This adds a smoky flavor and a bit of a crisp texture to some of the green beans.
4. Repeat for 1/2 or all of the rice mixture, to taste. As this technique adds a smoky flavour profile, you might not wish to impart it throughout the dish.

-

Garnish with chopped fresh cilantro and serve hot.

Gua Bao: Taiwanese Steamed Pork Belly Buns with Marinated Daikon, Greens & Green Beans

Prep Time: 30 minutes

Cook Time: 2-2 1/2 hours (including simmering the pork belly and steaming the buns)

Serving Size: 8-10 buns

For the Pork Belly:
- 1 pound (450g) skin-on pork belly
- 1 tablespoon vegetable oil
- 2 cloves garlic, smashed
- 1 green onion, chopped
- 2 dried chili peppers (optional)
- 3 tablespoons soy sauce (light and dark)
- 2 tablespoons *Shaoxing* wine (or dry sherry)
- 1 tablespoon brown sugar
- 1/2 teaspoon white peppercorns
- 3 cups chicken broth

For the Buns:
- 2 cups all-purpose flour
- 1 teaspoon active dry yeast
- 1 tablespoon sugar
- 1/2 teaspoon salt
- 3/4 cup warm milk (105°F/40°C)
- 1 tablespoon vegetable oil

For the Marinated Daikon:
- 1/2 cup daikon radish, cut into *brunoise* (tiny cubes)
- 1 tablespoon rice vinegar
- 1/2 teaspoon sugar
- Pinch of salt

For the Vegetables:
- 1 cup chopped radish greens, washed and trimmed
- 1/2 cup chopped green beans, trimmed and cut into bite-sized pieces

For Assembly:
- Pickled mustard greens (store-bought)
- Chopped fresh cilantro (optional)
- Toasted peanuts (optional)
- Sesame seeds (optional)

Heat oil in a large pot or Dutch oven over high heat. Season the pork belly generously with salt and pepper. Sear the pork belly on all sides until deeply golden brown and caramelized. Don't be afraid of a good sear - that's what creates incredible flavor!

-

Add garlic and green onion to the pot and sauté for a minute until fragrant.

-

Pour in soy sauce, *Shaoxing* wine, brown sugar, white peppercorns, and chicken broth. Bring to a boil, then reduce heat to low, cover, and simmer for 1-1/2 to 2 hours, or until the pork belly is very tender.

-

Once cooked, remove the pork belly from the pot and let it cool slightly. Shred the pork belly with two forks, discarding the fat and bones. Set aside.

-

Strain the remaining braising liquid into a bowl, discarding the solids. You can skim off some fat if desired. Reserve 1/4 cup of the braising liquid for later.

-

Combine the *brunoise* daikon, rice vinegar, sugar, and salt in a small bowl. Mix well and let it marinate for at least 15 minutes, or until slightly softened.

-

Wash and trim the radish greens, then chop them into bite-sized pieces. Trim and cut the green beans into bite-sized pieces as well.

-

Heat a separate wok or frying pan with a drizzle of oil over medium-high heat. Stir-fry the green beans for 2-3 minutes until tender-crisp, then transfer them to a plate. In the same pan, add another drizzle of oil and stir-fry the radish greens for a minute or two until slightly softened but still vibrant green. Combine them with the green beans.

In a large bowl, combine warm milk, sugar, and yeast. Let it sit for 5-10 minutes, or until the yeast becomes foamy. Add flour and salt to the yeast mixture and stir until a shaggy dough forms. Add vegetable oil and knead for 10 minutes on a lightly floured surface until smooth and elastic. Place the dough in a greased bowl, cover with plastic wrap, and let it rise in a warm place for 1-2 hours, or until doubled in size.

-

Punch down the dough, divide it into 8-10 equal pieces, and roll each piece into a smooth ball. Use a rolling pin to roll out each ball into a slightly oval shape, about 3-4 inches wide. Place the buns on a lightly floured baking sheet, leaving space between them. Cover loosely with plastic wrap and let them rise for another 30 minutes.

-

Prepare a steamer basket over a pot of boiling water. Gently transfer the buns to the steamer basket and steam for 10-12 minutes, or until cooked through and fluffy.

-

Reheat the shredded pork belly in the reserved 1/4 cup of braising liquid over medium heat until warmed through.

-

To assemble the *Gua Bao*, slice the steamed buns open. Arrange the components for maximum visual appeal: first a layer of pickled mustard greens on the bottom, then the shredded pork belly, followed by the marinated daikon, and finally the stir-fried green beans and radish greens.

-

(Optional) Drizzle with a touch of the reserved braising liquid for extra flavor. Garnish with chopped fresh cilantro (optional), toasted peanuts (optional), and sesame seeds (optional). Enjoy immediately!

Oyster Omelette (Taiwanese style)

Prep Time: 10-15 minutes (including shucking and cleaning oysters)

Cook Time: 5-7 minutes

Serving Size: 2-3 people (as an appetizer or light meal)

- 10-12 medium fresh oysters, shucked and patted dry
- ⅓ cup sweet potato starch (or tapioca flour)
- 2 large eggs
- ¼ cup cold water
- ¼ cup chopped garlic chives
- 3 tablespoons high-oleic sunflower oil
- 1 tablespoon oyster sauce
- Kosher salt and freshly ground white pepper to taste
- *Har Har Hot Bean Sauce* (for serving)

Prep the Oysters: Carefully shuck the oysters, discarding the shells. Rinse them thoroughly under cold running water and pat them dry with paper towels. Excess moisture will prevent the omelette from crisping properly.

-

Coat the Oysters: In a bowl, toss the oysters with the sweet potato starch (or tapioca flour) to coat them lightly. This coating helps create a crisp texture.

-

Make the Egg Mixture: In a separate bowl, whisk together the eggs, cold water, and oyster sauce. Season with a pinch of salt and white pepper.

-

Heat the Oil: Heat the high-oleic sunflower oil in a large non-stick skillet or frying pan over medium-high heat. A hot pan is crucial for a crispy omelette.

-

Cook the Egg Base: Pour the egg mixture into the hot oil. Swirl the pan to evenly coat the bottom.

-

Add Flavorings: Once the egg starts to set around the edges, sprinkle the chopped garlic chives over the omelette.

-

Arrange the Oysters: Carefully arrange the dry oysters on top of the partially cooked egg mixture.

-

Embrace the Flip: Taiwanese Oyster Omelettes are typically cooked using a flipping method. This is a simpler approach for home cooks.

Option 1: Allow the omelette to cook until mostly set on the bottom and the edges start to solidify. Carefully flip the entire omelette using a wide spatula. You can do this in sections if needed.

Option 2: If you're feeling even more comfortable, try a two-flip method. Once the bottom is set and the edges are starting to brown, use a spatula to fold the omelette in half. Then, carefully flip the folded omelette to cook the other side.

Cook to Perfection: Continue cooking for another minute or two, or until the omelette is cooked through and beautifully golden brown on both sides. The oysters should be cooked through and slightly firm to the bite.

-

Serve and Enjoy: Slide the omelette onto a plate and serve immediately. Enjoy hot alongside *Har Har Hot Bean Sauce* for those who like a touch of spice.

Chef's Tips:

- Fresh oysters are essential for the best flavor.
- Use a hot pan to ensure a crispy omelette.
  Don't overcrowd the pan with too many oysters.
- Practice your flipping skills for a more confident presentation.
- You can substitute sweet potato starch with tapioca flour for a similar texture.

Embrace the Taiwanese Twist:

The addition of garlic chives and oyster sauce in this recipe elevates the flavor profile beyond a standard oyster omelette. Oyster sauce adds a subtle depth of umami flavor that complements the oysters perfectly, while garlic chives provide a welcome touch of oniony and garlicky notes.

Spice it Up (Optional):

Har Har Hot Bean Sauce adds a fiery kick to this dish. However, it's offered as a condiment on the side, allowing diners to adjust the heat level to their preference. *Har Har Hot Bean Sauce* can be found at most specialty Asian markets and online retailers.

SEOUL, SOUTH KOREA MAIN DISHES- STREET

Kimchi Jeon with Shrimp and Radicchio

Prep Time: 15 minutes
Cook Time: 10-15 minutes
Servings: 2-3

- 1 cup chopped kimchi (well-fermented napa cabbage kimchi is preferred)
- ½ cup all-purpose flour
- ½ cup kimchi brine (from the kimchi jar)
- 1 egg
- 1 tablespoon vegetable oil
- ¼ cup chopped scallions (optional)
- ½ cup cooked and chopped shrimp
- 1 cup thinly shredded radicchio
- ¼ cup pomegranate seeds
- Salt and black pepper to taste

For the Dipping Sauce (optional):
- 3 tablespoons soy sauce
- 1 tablespoon rice vinegar
- 1 tablespoon *gochujang* (Korean chili paste)
- 1 teaspoon sesame oil
- 1 clove garlic, minced

If your kimchi is very wet, squeeze out some of the excess moisture. Roughly chop the kimchi into bite-sized pieces.

In a large bowl, whisk together the flour, kimchi brine, and egg until smooth. Season with salt and pepper to taste.

Fold the chopped kimchi, scallions (if using), cooked shrimp, and shredded radicchio into the batter. Ensure everything is evenly distributed.

Heat the vegetable oil in a large non-stick pan or griddle over medium heat. Once hot, pour about ¼ cup of batter per pancake into the pan. Spread the batter slightly to form a thin circle.

Cook the *kimchi jeon* for 3-4 minutes per side, or until golden brown and crispy. You can gently press down on the pancake with a spatula to ensure even cooking.

Transfer the cooked *kimchi jeon* to a plate lined with paper towels to drain any excess oil. Sprinkle with pomegranate seeds and serve hot with your desired dipping sauce on the side.

What to Expect:
This recipe creates savory Korean pancakes called Kimchi Jeon. Imagine a crispy, golden brown flatbread packed with the tangy, spicy kick of kimchi (fermented cabbage).

These pancakes are studded with juicy chopped shrimp and vibrant red pomegranate seeds for a burst of sweetness. Thinly shredded radicchio, a slightly bitter and crunchy Italian lettuce, adds a surprising pop of color and texture.

It's a flavor explosion in every bite, perfect as an appetizer or light meal. The recipe is easy to follow and uses common ingredients, but the combination creates a unique and exciting dish that will impress anyone who tries it!

Korean Fried Dumplings with Diced Ribeye and Jicama

Prep Time: 30 minutes
Cook Time: 15-20 minutes
Servings: 40-50 dumplings (depending on size)

For the Filling:
- ½ pound ground pork
- ½ pound diced ribeye steak (finely chopped)
- ½ cup chopped kimchi (well-fermented napa cabbage kimchi preferred)
- ¼ cup chopped scallions
- 1 tablespoon grated ginger
- 1 tablespoon minced garlic
- 1 tablespoon soy sauce
- 1 tablespoon sesame oil
- ½ teaspoon black pepper
- ¼ cup finely chopped jicama
- 2 tablespoons chopped pickled garlic

For the Dumplings:
- 1 package (40-50 wrappers) *gyoza* wrappers (or store-bought *mandu* wrappers)
- Water for sealing

Chef Notes:

These Korean Fried Dumplings are bursting with flavor and texture! The combination of ground pork and diced ribeye creates a rich and decadent filling, while the jicama offers a delightful textural contrast. Kimchi and pickled garlic add a surprising tang, and pre-made wrappers make them easy to assemble at home. The pan-frying technique ensures crispy perfection.

Make the Filling: In a large bowl, combine ground pork and diced ribeye. Heat a separate pan with a drizzle of oil and brown the ribeye for a few minutes. Add the browned ribeye to the bowl with the pork.

-

Add kimchi, scallions, ginger, garlic, soy sauce, sesame oil, black pepper, jicama, and pickled garlic to the meat mixture. Mix well and set aside.

-

Place a wrapper on a flat surface. Moisten the edges with a little water. Spoon a small amount of filling (about 1 tablespoon) in the center of the wrapper.

-

Folding Technique: There are various folding methods for *mandu*. Here's a simple one: Fold the wrapper in half over the filling, forming a crescent shape. Pinch the edges together to seal, creating pleats along the seam. Repeat with remaining wrappers and filling.

-

Heat a large skillet or pan with enough vegetable oil to coat the bottom. Once hot, arrange the dumplings in a single layer, leaving some space between them.

-

Fry the dumplings for 3-4 minutes per side, or until golden brown and crispy. Add a splash of water to the pan, cover it, and steam for a few minutes to cook the filling through. Alternatively, for a healthier option, steam the dumplings for 10-12 minutes in a steamer basket over boiling water.

-

Serve and Enjoy: Serve the cooked *mandu* hot with your favorite dipping sauce, such as soy sauce with a touch of vinegar and sesame oil, or a spicy *gochujang* sauce.

Quick Pickled Garlic for Dumplings -

- 1 head garlic, separate cloves and peel
- 1 cup white vinegar (5% acidity)
- 1 cup water
- 1 tablespoon whole white peppercorns
- 1 teaspoon whole black peppercorns 1/2 teaspoon red pepper flakes
- 1 tablespoon sea salt
- 1 thin slice Korean pear (for a touch of sweetness)

Instructions:

1. Clean Jar: Wash a small jar (around 250ml/8oz) with hot soapy water. Rinse well.

2. Pack Jar: Put garlic cloves and the Korean pear slice in the jar.

3. Make Brine: In a saucepan, heat vinegar, water, peppercorns, red pepper flakes, and salt. Don't boil, just dissolve salt.

4. Pour Brine: Carefully pour hot brine over garlic and pear slice in jar, submerge everything.

5. Cool & Pickle: Let jar cool, then refrigerate for at least 24 hours (ideally 3-4 days) for pickling.

Brazilian Chicken Croquettes (Coxinha de Frango)

Prep Time: 30 minutes
Cook Time: 5-6 hours (slow cooker) + 10 minutes (frying)
Serving Size: Approximately 20-24 Coxinhas (depending on size)

For the Filling:
- 4 bone-in, skin-on chicken thighs
- 2 tbsp olive oil
- 1 medium onion, chopped
- Generous amount of garlic cloves, minced
- 2 dried guajillo peppers, seeded and chopped
- 1 (4-oz) can diced fire-roasted tomatoes (undrained)
- 1/2 cup chicken broth
- 1/4 cup chopped fresh cilantro
- 1 tbsp soy sauce
- 1 tsp dried oregano
- 1/2 tsp ground nutmeg
- Plenty of black pepper
- 1/4 tsp salt
- 6-8 Biquinho peppers (or 1-2 cherry peppers, seeded and chopped)
- Hot sausage links (enough for desired filling)

For the Dough:
- 2 cups shredded cooked chicken breast (reserve some for shaping later)
- 3 cups all-purpose flour (adjust as needed)
- 1 1/2 cups chicken broth (warmed)
- 1 tbsp vegetable oil

For Coating:
- 2 large eggs, beaten
- 2-3 cups breadcrumbs

Slow Cook the Chicken: Heat olive oil and sear chicken thighs until golden. Sauté onion and garlic. Blend chopped guajillo peppers with some chicken broth. Add blended sauce, diced tomatoes, remaining broth, cilantro, soy sauce, spices, and salt to the pan. Simmer. Transfer everything to a slow cooker with chicken and biquinho peppers. Cook on low for 3-4 hours, or until chicken shreds easily.

-

Or, Dutch Oven Method:
Time: 1-1.5 hours
Temperature: Simmer on low heat (around 200°F)

-

Cook sausage links in a separate pan until browned. Chop into bite-sized pieces.

-

Shred Chicken and Sauté Filling: Shred cooked chicken, discarding skin and bones. In the same pan (add more oil if needed), sauté additional garlic. Combine shredded chicken, vegetables, spices, and cooked sausage (if using). Let cool slightly.

-

Make the Dough: Combine shredded chicken breast and flour in a bowl. Gradually add warmed broth to form a soft, pliable dough (not sticky). Knead in vegetable oil for smoothness.

-

Assemble and Fry: Pinch off dough, flatten slightly. Add filling, dust hands with reserved chicken to prevent sticking, and fold dough over filling, sealing edges into a teardrop shape. Repeat. Dip assembled coxinhas in beaten egg, then roll in breadcrumbs. Fry in hot oil (350°F) for 3-4 minutes per side, or until golden brown and crispy. Drain and serve hot.

What to Expect:
Imagine crispy golden brown teardrop-shaped pastries filled with a flavorful shredded chicken mixture. The filling is seasoned with a touch of smokiness and warmth, thanks to the guajillo peppers and black pepper, and a hint of Brazilian flair from oregano and nutmeg. The sausage is there for a spicy kick.

Don't worry if this is your first time, the instructions are clear and will help you achieve restaurant-worthy results at home.

-

Tips:

-Season the slow-cooked chicken for added flavor.

-Adjust dough consistency by adding more flour if too sticky.

-Don't overcrowd the pan while frying to maintain crispness.

-

Important note:
It's important to monitor the internal temperature of the chicken in both methods using a meat thermometer. Regardless of the cooking time, the chicken is considered safe for consumption once it reaches an internal temperature of 165°F.

Remember: Cook times based on the recipe and desired outcome. The actual cooking time can vary depending on the size and thickness of your chicken thighs. It's always best to check the internal temperature for safe consumption.

Sun-Kissed Pão de Queijo with Achiote

Prep Time: 15 minutes
Cook Time: 10-15 minutes
Serving Size: Approximately 15-20 *Pão de Queijo* (depending on size)

- 1 cup tapioca flour
- ⅔ cup grated Parmesan cheese (reserve some for topping)
- ⅓ cup finely chopped sun-dried tomatoes (oil-packed, well-drained)
- 1 teaspoon *achiote* powder
- 1/2 teaspoon salt
- 1/2 cup milk (warmed)
- 1 large egg
- Vegetable oil for frying

Prepare the Dough: In a large bowl, combine tapioca flour, grated Parmesan cheese, chopped sun-dried tomatoes, *achiote* powder, and salt. Make a well in the center and add the warmed milk and egg. Mix well with a spoon or spatula until a soft dough forms. It should be slightly sticky but manageable. If the dough feels too wet, add a little more tapioca flour, one tablespoon at a time, until it becomes less sticky.

-

Heat the Oil: Pour enough vegetable oil into a large skillet to reach a depth of about 1/4 to 1/2 inch. Heat the oil over medium heat. You can test the oil temperature by dropping a small piece of dough – if it sizzles and floats to the surface, the oil is hot enough. Alternately- check the temp with a kitchen or frying thermometer. The correct temp should be 350°F.

-

Form and Fry: With wet or oiled hands, pinch off small pieces of dough and roll them into balls. Gently place them into the hot oil, ensuring there's enough space between each for them to cook without crowding.

-

Achieve Golden Perfection: Fry the *Pão de Queijo* for 4-5 minutes per side, or until they turn golden brown. Be attentive and adjust the heat slightly if they brown too quickly.

-

Drain and Serve: Use a slotted spoon to transfer the fried *Pão de Queijo* to a plate lined with paper towels to absorb excess oil. Sprinkle with some reserved grated Parmesan cheese for an extra cheesy touch (optional). Let them cool slightly before serving. Enjoy these warm, crispy cheese puffs with a fiery twist!

Tips:

In this recipe we are ditching the ordinary and embracing a flavor adventure! This recipe takes the beloved *Pão de Queijo* on a delicious detour, infusing it with tangy sun-dried tomatoes and earthy *achiote* powder. The result? Crispy, cheesy puffs with a delightful surprise in every bite. Be warned, the *achiote* powder adds a subtle kick – perfect for those who enjoy a touch of heat.

-

Sun-dried Tomato Options: If the sun-dried tomatoes seem too wet, you can chop them even finer or pat them with paper towels to remove additional moisture.

Achiote Powder Strength: *Achiote* powder can vary in strength. Start with 1 teaspoon and adjust to your taste preference.

Don't Overcrowd the Pan: This is especially important for these *Pão de Queijo* with the filling, as they might be slightly more delicate than the plain version.

This recipe is sure to tantalize your taste buds with its unique flavor combination. Remember, if you find the *achiote* powder a bit too much, you can always start with less and adjust to your spice preference.

www.ingramcontent.com/pod-product-compliance
Lightning Source LLC
Chambersburg PA
CBHW081146060526
44107CB00135B/694